Whittaker

Charles E. Whittaker. From the archives of *The Kansas City Star.* Used by permission.

Whittaker

Struggles of a Supreme Court Justice

Richard Lawrence Miller

Contributions in Legal Studies, Number 102

GREENWOOD PRESS
Westport, Connecticut • London

Library of Congress Cataloging-in-Publication Data

Miller, Richard Lawrence.
Whittaker : struggles of a Supreme Court justice / by Richard Lawrence Miller.
p. cm.—(Contributions in legal studies, ISSN 0147–1074 ; no. 102)
Includes bibliographical references and index.
ISBN 0–313–31250–8 (alk. paper)
1. Whittaker, Charles Evans, 1901–1973. 2. Judges—United States—Biography.
3. United States. Supreme Court—Biography. I. Title. II. Series.
KF8745.W53 M55 2002
347.73'2634—dc21 2001023334
[B]

British Library Cataloguing in Publication Data is available.

Library of Congress Catalog Card Number: 2001023334
ISBN: 0–313–31250–8
ISSN: 0147–1074

First published in 2002

Greenwood Press, 88 Post Road West, Westport, CT 06881
An imprint of Greenwood Publishing Group, Inc.
www.greenwood.com

Printed in the United States of America

The paper used in this book complies with the Permanent Paper Standard issued by the National Information Standards Organization (Z39.48–1984).

10 9 8 7 6 5 4 3 2 1

Copyright Acknowledgments

The author and publisher gratefully acknowledge permission for use of the following material:

Extracts from Jesse Childers. Interview with Cynthia Dodge. May 14, 1998. Used by permission of Jeffrey Thomas.

Extracts from Bob Donnellan. Interview with Cynthia Dodge. April 20, 1998. Used by permission of Jeffrey Thomas.

Extracts from Kent Whittaker. Interview with Cynthia Dodge. May 13 and 18, 1998. Used by permission of Jeffrey Thomas.

Extracts from "Charles E. Whittaker," *Missouri Bar Journal* (Jan.–Feb. 1974): 61–62.

Extracts from "Charles Evans Whittaker: The Supreme Court Years," *Texas Law Review* 40 (1962): 744–50.

Extracts from "Advocacy—Advance or Adieu?" *Kansas Law Review* 13 (1964): 233–45.

Extracts from Charles Evans Whittaker, "Law and Order." Reprinted with permission from the: *New York State Bar Journal*, October 1965, Vol. 37, No. 5, published by the New York State Bar Association, One Elk Street, Albany, New York, 12207.

Extracts from Charles Evans Whittaker, "Lawyers, Laymen & Traffic Courts: Concerted Effort Needed for Improvement," *American Bar Association Journal* 49 (1963): 333–36. Copyright © 1963 by the AMERICAN BAR ASSOCIATION. Reprinted by permission of the **ABA Journal**.

Extracts from Charles Evans Whittaker, "Reflections on Mr. Justice Brandeis," *Saint Louis University Law Journal* 11 (1996): 6–8.

Extracts from Charles Evans Whittaker, "A Tribute to Judge John B. Sanborn, *Minnesota Law Review* 44 (1959): 197–99.

Extracts from Charles Evans Whittaker, "The Causes, and the Effects upon Public Order, of Planned, Mass Violations of the Law" in Charles Evans Whittaker and William Sloane Coffin, Jr., *Law, Order and Civil Disobedience.* Rational Debate Seminars. Washington, D.C.: American Enterprise Institute for Public Policy Research, 1967. And additional scattered portions from the aforementioned book, reprinted with the permission of The American Enterprise Institute for Public Policy Research, Washington, D.C.

To
Horace B. Davis
Ralph Spitzer
and
All others who have struggled against
The University of Kansas City Trustees

Contents

Acknowledgments

I first heard of Charles Whittaker when I was taking a constitutional law course in metropolitan Kansas City. I wondered if he might be willing to visit our class but was too shy to pursue the possibility. Two decades later I read an article in Kansas City's alternative newspaper *Pitch* (August 14, 1991) detailing the humiliations he suffered while on the Supreme Court, and found the story fascinating. More years passed, and then Jeffrey E. Thomas reawakened my interest in a man whose career had long intrigued me. Jeff's enthusiasm and encouragement made this book possible. When the going got tough on producing this volume Dr. Fred Whitehead offered the kind of personal and practical support that is in the best tradition of collegial scholarship.

Two previous students of Whittaker's life did work of such value that they merit more mention than a bibliographical note. Judith Cole and Craig Smith produced academic theses rich in recollections from Whittaker's friends and colleagues, and from Whittaker himself in Cole's work. Those volumes guided me to valuable sources and provided me with a firm foundation to stand on while reaching for understanding of the justice's life and career. No one but myself, of course, is responsible for conclusions I reached from these or any other sources of information.

Once I was a public radio producer, and in that career I discovered the value of having listeners hear what is said by a participant in an event, rather than get the information secondhand from a radio announcer. I carried that experience into my career as a scholar. I feel strongly about the value of letting readers see exact words used by participants in events, or used later by subsequent investigators. Yes, in theory those words can be paraphrased, but why deny readers an opportunity to evaluate the original language for themselves? Such evaluation allows all readers (not just those with access to distant archives) to decide whether my conclusions from the original words seem justified.

Chapter 1

Youth

Charles Whittaker was born in northeast Kansas on February 22, 1901. His grandparents were among the earliest pioneers in Kansas, moving there in 1853, the year before the Slave Power conspiracy passed the Kansas-Nebraska Act in hopes of making Kansas a slave state. Although the grandparents were from a free state, the year of their arrival meant they were not among the Yankees who moved there to claim that territory for free labor. The date of their arrival did mean, however, that their migration to Kansas was illegal, preceding federal permission to locate in what was officially Indian territory. Family tradition holds that Whittaker's grandfather purchased land near Troy, Kansas, from Indians. That land became the farm where Whittaker grew up, where he helped produce crops of wheat and corn.

Whittaker credited his mother with teaching him that success was impossible without integrity, toil, ideals, and morality.[1] "Well mannered good character," Whittaker later said, "is laid in happy homes—those homes which are the father's kingdom, the mother's haven, and the children's paradise, where the family prays together and hence stays together, and where the twig is given its direction toward the sun. . . . Such homes produce few 'teen-ager' problems."[2]

Half the year he attended a classic one-room rural schoolhouse, located on the edge of the family farm. One teacher handled students ranging in age from five to twenty. Schoolboys had limited opportunities for extra income. "Outside of the hard work on dad's farm," Whittaker recalled, "one of the most vivid memories of my boyhood was running a trap line winter mornings on my way to school. My most frequent catches were skunks, and, although their furs brought me $3 each, they didn't make me very popular at school." Whittaker noted, "Teachers sent me home several times to change my clothes."[3]

"I went to high school in Troy, Kans., and rode a pony to school through 6 miles of mud night and morning for about a year and a half," Whittaker said. "When my mother died, it broke my heart, she died on my birthday, 1917. I felt I couldn't go on and I quit high school."[4]

At school a talent for public speaking had emerged, and demand grew for the blue-eyed youth's oratory. One of his sisters recalled that while working draft animals on the family farm, he would use them as an audience for speech-making exercises.[5] His brother saw similar scenes, with Whittaker addressing horses as if they were members of a jury. He became known as a glib talker and facile persuader. Whittaker delivered comic monologues at Saturday community gatherings and served as a regular auctioneer selling off box suppers.[6]

Talking to his brother one sweaty day while shocking oats, Whittaker declared he planned to leave the farm.[7] Across the Missouri River a few miles to the east was the city of St. Joseph, Missouri. There in 1916 County Prosecutor Oscar D. McDaniel went on trial, accused of murdering his wife in a case deliciously laced with politics, sex, money, and corruption. A key contention was that McDaniel had used his experience as prosecutor to construct a perfect alibi. Whittaker avidly followed the case which resulted in acquittal.[8] "From that time on," Whittaker later declared, "I knew I was going to be a lawyer. My mind was made up. I started reading everything I could find about great trials and famous lawyers."[9]

Whittaker gained pleasure from Horatio Alger stories.[10] Their general theme involved boys from deprived backgrounds who struggled for and found worldly success. Although he was no more disadvantaged than any other rural boy, in other ways his life mimicked an Alger plot line. The first episode was his determination, in defiance of his father's wishes, to attend law school. A family member told of the father's displeasure when young Whittaker departed from the farm.[11] In addition to being a farmer, the father was also a director of the town bank, so he was familiar with white collar work. But the father refused to support Whittaker's career choice. As Whittaker could expect no family assistance in going to law school, for three years he saved money from odd jobs he did in Kansas farm country.

In 1920 Whittaker sought to enter the Kansas City (Missouri) School of Law, an independent institution specializing in night classes. That way Whittaker could earn money to supplement the $700 or $800 of savings he brought with him. As he lacked a high school diploma, his admission to law school was conditional on simultaneous completion of courses at Manual High. His success at gaining admission to law school without possessing the required high school diploma has been aptly characterized as an early example of his skill in advocacy.

His day job was as an office boy for the Watson, Gage, and Ess law firm. Before graduating and before admission to the bar he began handling trials in justice of the peace courts. Kansas City's justice of the peace courts, presided over by so-called "jackrabbit justices," were universally regarded with contempt. These establishments were not courts of record, and their judges were local political patronage appointees who typically acted as agents of businessmen, seizing merchandise from lower income customers who fell in arrears on installment payments. These courts often failed to notify defendants of proceedings against them, and thereupon awarded default judgments to merchants. Those judgments might be enforced by brutal constables who were sometimes indifferent about whether they seized property from a defendant or from an uninvolved bystander. Such tactics earned these courts a reputation as an arm of the criminal element. Judges' income derived from fees collected, so the higher the volume of business, the higher the magistrates' income. Kansas City civic leaders hailed the eventual abolition of these courts as another step in the unrelenting progress of Western Civilization.

Law students were allowed to represent clients in these courts, and no doubt such clients had better representation than most. Whittaker described the scene in such judicial assemblies:

> Not uncommonly they are housed in a small and dingy room which is a part of or adjacent to a jail or "holdover" and is often permeated by its odors. The worn wood floors are bare and usually littered. The only decorations on the dismal walls are a few framed and faded mottoes and several tattered commercial calendars. There is no rail to separate the hearing section from the remainder of the room. The forward end of the room is furnished with two ancient desks resting on a low rostrum, one of which serves as the judge's "bench", and the other serves the clerk. Before the judge's "bench" is a dilapidated table and scattered about it are a few scarred wooden chairs. To their rear, and often between two hissing radiators, several rows of battered benches and an occasional putrid cuspidor complete the furnishings.

Whittaker noted that not only middle-class clients but

> drunks and the unfortunate dregs of humanity . . . meet and mingle there. . . . Frequently there is not sufficient seating capacity, and many are required to stand for long periods—until in the numerical order of the docket earlier numbered cases of various kinds, including an interspersal of brawl and bawdy cases as well as traffic cases, are tried or otherwise disposed of and their case is reached. Naturally, decent traffic defendants are uncomfortable in this environment, and their nervousness, anxiety and eventual fatigue inevitably result in a moving and shifting about that add to the existing confusion.
>
> It is hardly necessary to say that such physical conditions and environment are not conducive to dignity and respect.[12]

One of Whittaker's fellow students was Harry Truman. "He was a year behind me," said Whittaker. "I've known him for many years."[13] Truman did not complete the courses needed for a degree, but Whittaker did. A classmate said that the law school crowd, "kicked the gong around pretty good but while everyone else was having fun, Charlie was studying."[14] Whittaker did so well at his studies that he even passed the bar exam and became a lawyer *before* graduating at the head of his class. Long afterward he showed a continuing interest in helping law students by presiding at moot court sessions and by donating hundreds of books to the law school's library.

The Kansas City School of Law classes attended by Whittaker were taught downtown at night by practicing attorneys who were part-time instructors. Four decades later Whittaker reminisced about changes in law school training:

> Some thoughtful lawyers . . . point to the displacement . . . of the seasoned lawyers as part-time teachers by full-time professors as events of mixed blessings. . . . The part-time teachings of the seasoned, successful, and prominent lawyers and judges who used to come before the students . . . often applying relevant legal principles to live concrete cases and problems that arose and were ruled that very day, and frequently giving the students practical instructions in the "do's," "don'ts" and "why's" in preparing for and conducting trials and appeals in the courts . . . were truly realistic, inspiring, informative, and educational experiences.[15]

Still, despite the high regard Whittaker eventually enjoyed from fellow lawyers in Missouri, he thought his training inadequate for the level of judicial responsibility he eventually assumed. An anonymous colleague on the Supreme Court is quoted as saying, "You know Charlie had gone to night law school, and he began as an office boy and he'd been a farm boy and he had inside him an inferiority complex, which . . . showed and he'd say, 'Felix [Frankfurter] used words in there that I'd never heard of.'"[16] While Whittaker was on the Court, Frankfurter declared, "I don't think the law school can be a substitute for, or make up for the lack of college, let alone high school."[17] One of Whittaker's sons said, "No question he was intimidated. I think he felt, all of his life, he had an inadequate education. By sheer dint of work habit he'd try to overcome that."[18]

When Whittaker entered law school, one of the era's most famous judges was Charles Evans Hughes (former Republican Presidential nominee and future Chief Justice of the U.S. Supreme Court). Law student Whittaker now dropped the middle name he was given at birth (Ernest) and began using the middle name Evans. He claimed the sound simply appealed to him,[19] but perhaps such a name change also indicated a psychological change of identity, shaking off the dust of the family farm.

Chapter 2

Law Practice

After getting his law degree Whittaker continued working at Watson, Gage, and Ess, the law firm where he had started as an office boy. Now he was an attorney with office boys helping *him*. He soon became a junior partner. As the Great Depression deepened in the 1930s, Whittaker became a full partner in Watson, Ess, Groner, Barnett, and Whittaker. The firm's name continued to change as years went by, but was known informally as Watson Ess. It was one of Kansas City's largest, and its clients included members of the Midwest's corporate elite.[1] Whittaker argued in courtrooms from coast to coast, including the U.S. Supreme Court in Washington.[2]

"Whittaker loved hard work," an acquaintance said,

> and his law firm was quick to recognize this fact, and he became involved in all types of legal situations and problems. . . . He handled practically every type of law business that could come to a Kansas City lawyer. He was equally capable in connection with a corporate problem as he was in the trial of a damage suit. He had experience in labor relations work and he enjoyed the respect of both management and labor.[3]

Whittaker's skill even attracted business from jurors who saw him in action and from litigants whose lawyers he defeated.

Whittaker was a litigator, the civilized equivalent of a hired gunslinger. His specialty is perhaps the most grueling branch of law, involving combat against skillful, well prepared, and sometimes unscrupulous opponents eager to meet in a trial of strength. Litigation is high-adrenalin activity.

Whittaker's courtroom technique made him a feared litigator. He enjoyed these encounters. "There was an extra sparkle in his eye and an extra spring in his step when he was trying a lawsuit," recalled one associate. "He had a fighter's heart and the will to win, which is so necessary for a successful trial lawyer."[4] A friend agreed: "He excels in the art of persuasion and argumentation."[5] A courtroom opponent recalled him as "a tough adversary."[6] Another associate watched Whittaker's face reddening with passion at a trial, with argument so intense that he lapsed into mild profanity. Still another associate remembered Whittaker as a demanding perfectionist.[7] A fellow lawyer noted, "He had a habit of standing kind of quietly and sort of pursing his lips when you talked to him, tighten them up a little bit, and I think that he probably was a little bit on the tense side."[8] He acted high-strung, and delays made him irritable.[9] An attorney who watched him in court remembered, "He was very serious. And he wanted to know everything that could possibly happen in the case that involved his side, either one way or the other, good or bad. In other words, he was known as a lawyer who really mastered the facts before he went into anything."[10] And he did it on a production line basis; finishing a trial and grabbing the file about the next one being held two or three days later. That era preceded the modern pre-trial discovery process by which litigants learn about each other's cases before courtroom action begins. Whittaker had to prepare surprise attacks and be able to parry unexpected blows from opposing counsel on a moment-by-moment basis in front of judge and jury.

COURTROOM TECHNIQUE

When a case was called, Whittaker was ready. An admiring lawyer in Kansas City recalled, "He was sharp, agile and always thoroughly prepared. . . . He had the great ability to perceive the weakness and strength of his adversary witnesses and he was also able to evaluate and recognize the weakness and strength of his own witnesses."[11] Justice Tom Clark: "He sensed facts—events—and mastered them as the arguments of God rather than mere words which were but the arguments of man. He could drive a quarter horse through a fallacious argument and never use a spur."[12]

Whittaker often decried efforts to rouse citizens' emotions. He called instead for calm and reasoned analysis of public policy controversies. Referring to the civil rights movement, Whittaker said in February 1964:

> Irresponsible recriminations and term usages settle nothing but only divide and confuse people and create new problems. They cannot be a good substitute for, or supplant, the cooperative, calm and responsible reasoning processes which experience has proven are the only peaceful means of solving issues.[13]

Later that year he spoke to Southern lawyers about the civil rights movement:

> Intemperate and even irresponsible, statements are made and actions taken by one side and answered in kind by the other. Frequently, in carrying on this dialogue, the practices of master propagandists are emulated in coining and using terms designed to cast ignominious aspersions on generic terms and concepts. And, on occasions, accomplishment of desired ends is sought through purposefully casting confusion upon generic terms by intentionally misusing them, or through the use, or misuse, of coined catchwords or cliches of no concrete meaning; and, whether so intended or not, those usages appeal only to prejudices and passions and arouse more rancor than reason.
>
> Surely such irresponsible recriminations and term usages settle nothing but only mislead, confuse and divide the people and create new problems. They cannot be a good substitute for, or supplant, honest, calm, cooperative and responsible reasoning processes which experience has proven are the only peaceful and permanent means of solving issues.[14]

Whittaker's sentiments may have had merit, but persons who feel they have everything to gain or lose by a public policy decision are unlikely to face dedicated opponents with the detachment advocated by Whittaker. Indeed his call for reason was, in itself, unreasonable.

Whittaker's condemnation of emotional appeals reflects his lifelong approach to litigation. He depended on facts and legal logic to win cases, a style noticed and commented upon by colleagues—not all of whom took such an approach to litigation. Said one prominent Kansas City attorney, "His keen analysis of factual and legal situations and the thoroughness of his preparation led to very successful trial results."[15] Said another bar colleague, "He was interested in fine legal logic and reasoning."[16]

Perhaps one reason Whittaker hated emotional appeals was their effectiveness against factual presentations he made in court. In a reminiscent mood he once said, "Clever counsel for the plaintiff, who was blind and suing my client for causing her blindness, concluded his examination of his client by putting his foot on the step that led to the witness stand, facing the jury, pointing his finger heavenward and asking, 'Now, then, Mrs. Robertson, from that day to this one have you been able to see the light of day?' The answer was a sob and a muffled, 'No.' Then, turning to me and bowing over-politely from the waist, he said, 'You may cross-examine.' . . . Just how did you go about cross-examining such a witness in those circumstances? I must say that I did not learn the answer to that question in that case nor in the many similar ones I was to try."[17]

Pathfinder

One measure of brilliance in a lawyer is the ability to show a path allowing judges to do something they desire to do, but which they feel is prohibited.

Whittaker's talent in that task was demonstrated in a Supreme Court conference about a coerced confession in a death sentence case.[18] Justice Felix Frankfurter insisted that the appeal should not be heard because the condemned man's lawyer had not cited the Fourteenth Amendment in arguments to the Court. Frankfurter was correct that the Court's rules required the case to be dismissed, throwing other justices into consternation as they contemplated allowing a paperwork flaw to result in a wrongful execution. Whittaker was the person who found a way out. He had all records of the case sent from Arkansas to Washington so they could be searched for an instance in which the lawyer cited the Fourteenth Amendment as grounds for appeal. The justices agreed that such a citation would be good enough to satisfy the Court's rules, and the necessary reference occurred once in the voluminous documents.[19] Once was good enough. Here was Whittaker the master litigation attorney at work, finding a way to allow judges to make the decision they wanted to make and overcoming an apparently insuperable barrier to do it. Such cleverness helped make him one of the most respected attorneys in Kansas City.

Oral Argument

Whittaker embraced rhetorical impact when strongly challenged on facts and logic. Exchanges outside the courtroom with opponents William Sloane Coffin, Jr., and William Taylor illustrate skills Whittaker must have employed when stakes were even higher in court. During such impromptu remarks, Whittaker demonstrated mastery of rhetorical persuasion. What he said might not withstand leisurely analysis for fact and logic in cold print, but he proved himself adept at hot and rapid-fire oral argument. He must have been a formidable jury lawyer.

At a public forum in 1967 Yale University chaplain William Sloane Coffin, Jr. (a prominent civil rights and anti-war activist of the era), engaged in a running debate with Whittaker.

The exchange began with this declaration by Whittaker about civil rights demonstrators: "Many of the laws they so condemn, and often flout, actually are embodiments of the laws of God, such as, Thou shalt not kill, Thou shalt love, not injure, thy neighbor, Thou shalt not steal, Thou shalt not covet they neighbor's property or possessions, and Thou shalt not bear false witness, to mention but a few of the divine laws that are embodied into our criminal laws. . . . Nor should we overlook, as is so often done, the biblical admonition that Thou shalt obey the civil authorities."[20]

In partial response Rev. Coffin observed, "Justice Whittaker mentions the biblical injunction to obey civil authority. He is referring to small sections in the writings of St. Paul and St. Peter."[21] Whittaker thereupon rejoined, "It is said here by my opponent that I have misused religion in my address."[22] Coffin made no such accusation. He simply distinguished the source of the biblical injunction in question. Whittaker now portrayed that factual distinction as an accusation of incompetence or bad faith, and forgave himself by saying, "I am not a theologian nor a cleric."[23] With that statement Whittaker rhetorically excuses possible error by admitting he is no expert while also arguing he should not be held accountable for a mistake any layman could make. This rhetorical technique slides by any error while simultaneously evoking sympathy from an audience of laymen who know they, too, could be hard-pressed on a religious topic by an expert theologian. Whittaker then shifted the debate, answering a question Coffin did not address: "What did I say of religious tenor? I said that killing, maimings by assault, coveting to the extent of burning and robbing and stealing by strong-arm or by stealth, violate one or another of the Ten Commandments."[24] In reality Whittaker had said no such thing; he had merely paraphrased some of the Ten Commandments while adding in a little New Testament. Now, in rebuttal to Coffin, Whittaker abandoned what he originally said and recast his argument into a biblical condemnation of explicit crimes—crimes that few Christian ministers would embrace, rhetorically forcing Coffin to agree with him or remain silent. Either way Coffin would appear to concede defeat.

Whittaker then administered a *coup de grâce*: "Mr. Coffin concedes that the Bible does say that thou shalt obey the civil authorities."[25] Here Whittaker concedes that his former discussion of religion did indeed go beyond the Ten Commandments, but in the heat of argument he could depend on his concession going unnoticed. "And he says this has caused the clergy trouble."[26] Coffin said this in the context of German ministers receiving commands from the Nazi regime, illustrating how circumstances could arise causing biblical injunctions to conflict (just as circumstances could arise causing laws to conflict in Supreme Court cases), with Coffin declaring that some American ministers in 1967 were experiencing the same sort of dilemma earlier felt by Germans. Whittaker evaded Coffin's moral dilemma by redirecting the audience's attention to the biblical text commanding obedience to civil authorities. "It seems a pretty plain statement to me. And for myself I see no reason to depart [from] a literal construction of it."[27] Although from the bench Judge Whittaker could be quick to say that a layman bringing a suit misunderstood the law's wording, here Whittaker argued that any layman can see what the Bible means. By implication, seminary training has clouded a theologian's ability to read the text. The Bible, like other law, simply says what it means.

Coffin made a shrewd counterattack, seizing upon Whittaker's condemnation of Martin Luther King, Jr., as a lawbreaker: "Most people think that Martin Luther King was guilty consistently of civil disobedience. But if you accept the fact that we have a kind of serried arrangement in this country so that you can disobey a municipal law in the name of a state law, and a state law in the name of a federal law, and if you accept the Supreme Court as being the final court of appeal, then, of course, we have to say that Martin Luther King has yet to break a law. Every time his case has gone to the Supreme Court he has been cleared."[28] This rhetoric was impossible to answer. Whittaker could not dispute Coffin's factual accuracy here, but neither could he admit Coffin's accuracy without destroying the foundation of his own argument against King.

Seizing upon Whittaker's silence Coffin pressed his advantage: "I still want to hear from Justice Whittaker very specifically, sir, just which criminal laws Martin Luther King has violated. I don't want this evening to end without a specific answer to that question."[29] After a few more seconds of remarks from Coffin, the discussion moderator invited Whittaker to make any concluding remarks he wished. Whittaker replied with a distraction: "I am an old trial lawyer and have argued many cases to juries and to courts and if I have learned anything therefrom it is to stop when I'm ahead."[30] Immediate laughter from the audience greeted Whittaker's good-natured declaration of victory, covering his failure to answer Coffin's challenge. Once again Whittaker performed a Houdini escape from accountability. Litigators with such talent can make a fortune.

Another example of Whittaker's powerful oral argument style came in 1967 when William Taylor, staff director of the United States Commission on Civil Rights, questioned Whittaker in a public forum:

> TAYLOR: I wonder how you can dismiss what you have acknowledged to have been gross injustices against Negroes. . . . They are subject to real physical insecurity. They are subject to terror.
>
> They don't participate in government, in their own governments, for very much the same reasons. There are always the courts but they don't have access to lawyers.
>
> WHITTAKER: I did not understand the latter statement.
>
> TAYLOR: . . . They may have access to the courts in a theoretical sense, but in many parts of the south the right to counsel is not a very meaningful right.
>
> WHITTAKER: Do you really believe that?
>
> TAYLOR: Yes, sir. In the State of Mississippi, I could count on the fingers of one hand the numbers of lawyers who are willing to take cases that may involve the civil rights—
>
> WHITTAKER: Why, the American Bar will provide counsel in any unpopular case, if they ask for it. There are many organizations—the Civil Liberties Union for one—that will provide counsel if they can not otherwise get them in the south.
>
> TAYLOR: Well, the only lawyers, sir—this I know as a matter of fact—in Mississippi, apart from a very small handful who are ready to provide counsel, are lawyers who come in from outside the state and have difficulty practicing in Mississippi courts. . . .

> WHITTAKER: If that is so, and to the extent that it is so, can you imagine a better place to be prosecuted? The prosecution would simply be for naught if they were denied counsel.
> TAYLOR: I am not thinking of criminal cases.
> WHITTAKER: Well, what are you thinking about?
> TAYLOR: Attempts to get one's civil rights redressed in the courts and the attempts to get the meaningful kinds of—
> WHITTAKER: Well, are you arguing, sir, that the way to do that is to take the law into your own hands and go out with a big club and beat people until they assent to your demands?
> TAYLOR: Absolutely not. . . .
> WHITTAKER: . . . Courts are always open, and all persons can get redress there; . . . we can not tolerate individuals or groups determining for themselves what laws they will obey and what ones they will disobey. That is anarchy.[31]

In this sequence we see an example of Whittaker cross-examining someone who has been granted expert status by the audience. First Whittaker tried to question Taylor's knowledge of facts. Thwarted in his attempt to impeach Taylor as a reliable source of information, Whittaker suddenly shifted debate from availability of *plaintiffs' counsel* in *civil* cases to availability of *defendants' counsel* in *criminal* cases. If the shift were successful, Whittaker would have rhetorically established that lawyers were indeed available to Southern blacks despite what Taylor said, thereby destroying Taylor's credibility. Taylor refused to tolerate the shift, however, and insisted on the point Whittaker was trying to evade—that the unavailability of plaintiffs' attorneys effectively closed courts to Southern blacks seeking redress of civil rights violations. Whittaker then seized a rhetorical opening provided by Taylor's stance. On the dual premise that Taylor favored civil rights for Southern blacks but also said those rights could not be enforced through courts, was Taylor thereby advocating criminal violence for a higher cause? Knowing Taylor would have to say no, Whittaker could then attempt to conclude the discussion by saying they were in agreement that legal means had to be used to achieve civil rights. Such a closure would not win the argument for Whittaker, but he would avoid losing it. The encounter would appear to be a draw even though Whittaker's cross-examination had been unable to shake the witness's testimony.

Written Argument

Whittaker's painstaking preparation of formal written remarks was legendary, and his techniques in those writings also offer insight into his courtroom style.

In public speaking Whittaker's use of quotations was supple. For rhetorical effect he often did not quote directly, but paraphrased. Use of paraphrase rather than direct quotation gave him greater leeway in cloaking his own arguments with the credibility of respected icons to which he alluded. Such a technique demonstrates a skill that Whittaker probably used in courtroom oratory.

One example is in his carefully prepared speech, "The Causes, and the Effects upon Public Order, of Planned, Mass Violations of the Law," in which he seemed to quote from the Ten Commandments but actually paraphrased them. This speech started his exchange with Rev. William Sloane Coffin, Jr., noted above.

Another example is found in "The Faith of the Free" (Juniata College version). Criticizing American workers for slothfulness during the Cold War, Whittaker said, "Just as our fathers learned, 100 years ago, that the Nation could not exist half slave and half free, we now should know that it cannot exist half weak and half strong."[32]

Here Whittaker alludes to Abraham Lincoln's famous "House Divided" speech of 1858 in which Lincoln predicted, "I believe this government cannot endure, permanently half *slave* and half *free.* I do not expect the Union to be *dissolved*—I do not expect the house to *fall*—but I *do* expect it will cease to be divided. It will become *all* one thing, or *all* the other."

Lincoln predicted a change in governmental policy, not destruction of the nation. And he said nothing at all about national character. By avoiding direct quotation, Whittaker was able to recast Lincoln's comment on government into a comment Whittaker wanted to make on national character. Whittaker never hesitated to make use of direct quotation when he wanted to, and when he chose not to, he did so for a rhetorical purpose that could not be achieved if he refreshed his audience's memory of the actual words to which he alluded.

In another version of "The Faith of the Free" Whittaker's evocation of Lincoln went beyond paraphrase: "Our fathers learned, 100 years ago, that the nation would fall if it continued to be divided against itself."[33] Here Whittaker recast Lincoln's words into the opposite of what Lincoln said. Whittaker used Lincoln's aura to strengthen an argument that Americans needed to support whatever high government officials decided to do about communism. Such rhetoric shrewdly identified opponents of government policies toward southeast Asia in the 1960s with opponents of Lincoln's policies in the 1860s. The tactic was designed not only to make current opponents look bad, but to encourage self-doubt among them (many persons who sought to end the Vietnam war felt just as strongly about promoting civil rights for black Americans). Whittaker's rhetoric was brilliant but depended upon deceit.

Evading Accountability

Litigation lawyers such as Whittaker are trained to evade efforts that opponents make to hold them accountable. Such a life-long habit seemed too hard for Whittaker to drop, and it irritated brethren on the U.S. Supreme Court who were eager to take a stand for their beliefs. In a conference about *Baker* v. *Carr*, one of the most important cases ever decided about the nature of democracy, Justice Felix Frankfurter's ire was provoked by Whittaker saying he would join a majority in the case but would not cast a swing vote to create the majority.[34] He would go along but did not want to be accountable for establishing the majority.

His litigant's skill at evasion is illustrated by what he said about gaining appointment to the district court. "I was interested in succeeding Judge Reeves, and I made this known to my friends and associates," but "fact is, I actually learned of my nomination from the newspapers."[35] Those words may be literally true but evade the fact that Whittaker orchestrated a lobbying campaign on his behalf among persons who had powerful influence with the Eisenhower White House. The same rhetorical technique is found in Whittaker's discussion of his appointment to the Eighth Circuit appeals court. "No one had spoken to me about the appointment," he stated. "The news story was the first I had heard of it."[36] Perhaps the actual nomination had not been discussed with Whittaker, but he and Attorney General Herbert Brownell had discussed the possibility of assuming the appeals bench when Brownell interviewed him for the district judge position. And while Whittaker may have learned of the nomination from seeing a newspaper story, his candidacy had already been publicly discussed. Whittaker was skilled at hiding truths in such a way that he could not be held accountable for lying, a talent that probably made him a fearsome opponent in courtroom litigation.

After retiring from the Supreme Court he made a speech ("A Confusion of Tongues") criticizing the thinking of Supreme Court justices who believed President Franklin Roosevelt's New Deal was constitutional. Whittaker's speech was widely interpreted as an attack on the Supreme Court of the 1960s. Whittaker denied it was any such thing, saying that his criticisms were not directed against the current court and that his speech even refrained from discussing incidents that occurred while any current justices were on the supreme bench.[37] This apparently forthright denial was an evasion. We know this for two reasons.

First, oblique attack upon opponents is a classic technique of political rhetoric. For example, in 1972 President Nixon said anyone who was considered as a potential president had to be someone who could handle the job's inherent pressure and stress. Everyone knew he referred to Democratic vice-presidential nominee Thomas Eagleton who was under assault for receiving psychological care for depression, yet Nixon's remarks gave him "deniability" in case anybody accused him of kicking a man while he was down.

The second reason we know Whittaker's denial was an evasion is because he actually did refer to a case involving justices who were members of the Court in 1964. His oral version of "A Confusion of Tongues" apparently did not name *Wickard* v. *Filburn*[38] when he criticized that decision supporting the New Deal, but his description of the issue left no knowledgeable person in doubt that he meant that case. We further know that he meant *Wickard* because he named that case in the speech's first draft and in the printed version published by the American Bar Association. Members of the Court who participated in the 1942 *Wickard* case included his former colleagues Black, Frankfurter, and Douglas (the latter of whom sent Whittaker a scathing letter about the speech). Even though the oral version of his speech may not have referred to the *Wickard* case by name, he intended listeners to think of that case and, despite his denial afterward, did indeed refer to a case involving justices who were still on the Court.

Whittaker's attack on Supreme Court justices who supported the policy of Roosevelt could easily be interpreted as an attack on justices appointed by Roosevelt—several of whom had been Court colleagues of Whittaker. Moreover Whittaker spoke while the Great Society program of President Lyndon Johnson was underway, a program extrapolating from the New Deal. Thus Whittaker's remarks could readily be viewed as oblique comments about current events.

While denying that he intended to attack current members of the Court, Whittaker added that his speech would have been more vigorous had it been directed toward the Warren Court.[39] That denial could be translated as, "The present Court well deserves criticism, but I shall not make any." That is a rhetorical trick, as in, "I shall not mention my opponent's criminal record." Whittaker's denial said what he denied saying.

In the 1967 speech "The Causes, and the Effects upon Public Order, of Planned, Mass Violations of the Law," Whittaker began by explicitly denying his intention to question anyone's patriotism, and then proceeded to do exactly that: "I suppose there are differing concepts of 'loyalty' and 'patriotism.' And it is not my purpose to question the loyalty or patriotism of any American. But I do wonder how those who advocate burning, and burn draft cards, impede, with their bodies, the movement of troop trains and trains carrying supplies to our troops, and who would give the enemy to understand that our country is divided and will not see the conflict through—and thus encourage the enemy to refuse all overtures of peace negotiations—can square, in their consciences, that conduct with any concept of 'loyalty' or 'patriotism' to this country."[40] By saying, "I do wonder how," Whittaker allows himself to deny that he accused anyone of anything. But the accusation is plain. It became even plainer in a speech the next year, reported by a newspaper: "He said that those persons who burn draft cards, refuse military induction, block the transport of troops and supplies, or degrade the national flag have no real chance of remaining free except 'by the exertion of others who are better men than they.' "[41]

His 1964 speech "Cliches or Fundamentals?" provides still another example of evasion. He noted as binding an 1883 Supreme Court decision under which pending civil rights legislation (which became the historic Civil Rights Act of 1964) was unconstitutional. "This is one of the bases upon which certain Senators and others are resisting passage of the presently pending 'Civil Rights Bill'. They contend and argue, among other things, that the Bill is unconstitutional under the holding of the Supreme Court." Whittaker acknowledged that proponents hoped the Court would rule differently now. "I, of course, have no information, and intend no expression, upon how that argument might fare in the Court, or even upon how it ought to fare there."[42] Although here he claimed to have no comment on how the issue should be settled, he had first explained at length why the bill was unconstitutional. And Whittaker's near-religious obedience to earlier court decisions was well known. It is difficult to see how his speech could be interpreted as "no comment," particularly when virtually the same remarks were repeated to a gathering of Southern lawyers upon passage of the Act.[43]

In his 1964 commentaries on civil rights legislation, Whittaker noted that the public accommodations aspects of the 1964 bill (requiring a business to serve customers regardless of their race) "are very like the ones contained in the Civil Rights Act of 1875, which Act, as stated, was held unconstitutional by the Court in 1883." He then went on to explain why opponents thought the 1964 bill tried to regulate *private* accommodations (businesses serving the public) as opposed to *public* accommodations (owned by government), and regulate them in a way long held to be unconstitutional. Whittaker then concluded by saying, "I do not intend to enter that controversy." But although he might contend he was simply explaining pro and con arguments about the bill, he did say the bill's public accommodations elements conflicted with "the dictionary sense" of public accommodations and were "very like the ones" long held unconstitutional.[44] Such comments were hardly neutral. And he knew his prestige as a former Supreme Court justice would bring great attention to such comments. To claim he was refusing "to enter that controversy" was an attempt to evade accountability for what he had just said.

A few months after giving the "Cliches or Fundamentals?" speech Whittaker told a reporter, "I just do not feel it would be appropriate in my circumstances to express any views concerning the constitutionality of public questions which are now before the court such as the new Civil Rights act."[45] His stated grounds for silence sounded judicious but clearly were an evasion, given his earlier detailed depiction of the Civil Rights Act's unconstitutionality.

In "Law and Order," a 1965 speech to Southern lawyers, ostensibly Whittaker simply advocated obedience to law, a sentiment that few patriotic citizens would challenge. In practice, however, Whittaker's speech advised blacks to suffer quietly and hope for the best, while the speech encouraged opponents of civil rights reforms to use all available powers of the state to defend the status quo. Indeed, the very title of his speech was a political code phrase widely used in that era by opponents of social justice reform, evading charges of racial prejudice by cloaking themselves in the guise of good citizenship.

While Whittaker's rhetorical skill at evasion demonstrated his formidability as a litigator, that skill implied he would have been stressed by demands of ultimate accountability imposed upon a Supreme Court justice. And indeed such strain was a factor in the mental and physical collapse that forced him off the Court.

DEFENDING CORPORATIONS

As a litigator Whittaker typically represented clients possessing wealth and power who sought to defeat persons of far less influence. We do not see a diverse practice in which he sometimes represented citizens with grievances against great entities, and sometimes aided the cause of such entities. He consistently promoted the interests of his society's wealthy and powerful members. Of course wealth does not equate with evil, and sometimes Whittaker's clients were clearly in the right. He particularly relished defending insurance companies against claims.[46]

Personal Injury Litigation

Whittaker's personal injury and wrongful death litigation were lucrative but "mill-run" cases. One associate spoke of "quite a bit of work for the old street and railway company. We used to have streetcars, you know, rails and streets and there were a lot of injuries. People were always getting hurt or else they were faking it. And, they had a lot of cases over at Charlie's firm . . . to defend the company."[47] Whittaker defended long haul railroads as well. One example came from a 1927 incident in which a motorist drove into the path of an approaching Union Pacific passenger train, killing himself and his wife. The incident occurred on a sunny December afternoon at a marked railroad crossing, on level ground where the approaching train could easily have been seen from about a half-mile down the track. Moreover, the highway from which the automobile turned ran parallel to the railroad tracks, and both automobile and train had been traveling in the same direction toward the crossing.

Motorist negligence would seem clear-cut, but the administrator of the deceaseds' estates claimed Union Pacific was at fault. He said the crew on the *train* should have seen the approaching *automobile* and taken necessary steps to avoid a collision. That argument was a stretch but, unfortunately for Union

Pacific, evidence demonstrated irregularity from the railroad's normal practice at that crossing. A municipal ordinance placed a speed limit of 20 miles per hour on trains passing through the city. The passenger train in question, however, was an hour late and traveling 50 to 60 m.p.h. Apparently the crossing was just outside the city limits, but trains normally were decelerating as they reached the crossing. Not only was this UP passenger train going full speed, but witnesses testified that it failed to sound any warning bell or whistle as it approached the crossing—which was the rural type without flashing lights, bells, or gates.

Judges in two courts agreed with Whittaker that people in a car ought to look both ways before driving on to railroad tracks. Regardless of the train's speed and regardless of any audible warning devices, someone in a car should be paying enough attention to notice an oncoming train in daylight on the Kansas plains. The appeals court said that train crews had no obligation to be able to stop in time to avoid road vehicles that were approaching a crossing, that train crews had a right to assume vehicles were going to yield the right of way as the law required and custom affirmed.[48]

Arkansas logging and railroad operations of Dierks Lumber & Coal Company provided Whittaker with the kind of personal injury defense work that he enjoyed. In one case[49] a Dierks foreman ordered an inexperienced and weak employee to help another worker to replace a broken railroad car coupler. The coupler was 415 pounds of steel and iron, about five feet long. One can see why the foreman thought one man couldn't carry it alone. The two workers managed to remove the broken coupler and set it aside without mishap. They reached down, grabbed the 300-pound replacement and began to straighten up. The weak and inexperienced man suddenly let go without warning. In instinctive panic his partner took the full weight "with a jerk" to avoid crushing his feet. Anyone with back trouble can appreciate the consequence, and the injured worker sued for compensation.

Whittaker argued that even though the foreman admitted that such a task required skill, the foreman had no liability in putting a worker's safety literally in the hands of a coworker known to be weak and inexperienced. Whittaker argued that the accident was the weak man's fault. But how plentiful were jobs for unskilled workers during the Great Depression? Could an Arkansas worker have defied a foreman's order in 1936 without fear of dismissal? Would Whittaker have defended a worker fired for insubordination? We should not be surprised if an advocate provides a client with vigorous defense, but Whittaker's judicial decisions show the same sort of sympathy for managers in workman's compensation cases. When handling such cases as a litigator Whittaker argued for what he believed, not simply as a hired gun.

In this case Whittaker also argued that the lawsuit should be dismissed because the injured man's attorney had not properly phrased the complaint. Whittaker's skill at ferreting out such flaws was much admired by colleagues, and as a judge he did not hesitate to use such grounds to dismiss cases. As a litigator, however, he did not always find courts receptive to this tactic. Indeed, in the present case the appeals court conceded that the worker's lawyer might have done better in stating the complaint, but ruled that a miscarriage of justice would occur if this civil case were dismissed because of such a flaw. Here the appeals court found that both law and fact supported the injured worker's claim.

A few years later Whittaker was again defending Dierks.[50] A jury had found Dierks liable for injury that a worker's wife had received in an accident involving a defective company truck. The issue at hand was injury to an employee's spouse, not injury to an employee. The couple had been ordered out of a company house on short notice because Dierks wanted them to live in a company trailer closer to the man's logging assignment. Mrs. Mabry said that the foreman who was evicting the couple ordered Mr. Mabry to use a particular company truck to remove their belongings from the house. Whittaker disputed that detail, saying that Mr. Mabry had asked to use the truck for that purpose. Whittaker admitted that the truck lacked brakes, and that the manual transmission was also defective, so the speed could not be controlled when going downhill. Whittaker admitted that Mr. Mabry had proper permission to use the truck for moving the family's household goods, but that the company had no liability for the ensuing accident in which Mrs. Mabry was injured— because Mr. Mabry used the truck knowing of its defects and because the company had not given permission for Mrs. Mabry to ride in the truck transporting the household goods. Whittaker said the accident caused by the truck's defects was Mr. Mabry's fault, that his wife had no right to be in the truck, and that the jury was wrong to hold Dierks liable.

The appeals court noted that company policy routinely allowed employees to use company vehicles to transport household goods, and that it was reasonable to assume that a wife would ride in the truck carrying the family possessions. Permission to use the truck for that purpose was permission for the wife to ride in it. The court noted that Mabry was even using the truck partially on company business, moving his belongings out of a house on company orders so the employer could turn over the house to someone else. Moreover, the court ruled, even if Mabry had been using the truck on purely personal business, the owner of a vehicle has no right to grant permission to use it if the owner knows that its operation will endanger people. On that point the court cited ample precedents with which Whittaker should have been familiar. In conclusion the court noted that the mishap with the Dierks truck was easily foreseeable. The court did not, however, make the logical inference from its reasoning: that a foreseeable event is not an accident.

Labor Relations

At times Whittaker clearly argued for interests of privilege against the interests of ordinary citizens. Such instances are illustrated by his labor relations practice.

During the 1940s Whittaker defended one corporation's activities after they had been ruled an unfair labor practice.[51] The ruling had come from a New Deal agency, the National Labor Relations board. Given the hostility Whittaker freely expressed toward Franklin Roosevelt's New Deal, we can have little doubt that Whittaker believed his client was right.

In 1942 the New Jersey manufacturer Elastic Stop Nut Corporation opened a second plant in Lincoln, Nebraska. Training began for local workers, who in turn were expected to train other workers as operations scaled up to full production. During the preliminary training stage workers began discussing whether they should join a union, either an independent one or a local of a larger labor organization. While labor unions were hardly unheard of in the Midwest, they were less familiar to Midwesterners than to their Eastern counterparts. Labor relations at the stop nut plant were highly unsettled.

A worker began circulating a petition favoring an independent union, and about two-thirds of the plant's sixty employees signed. Soon thereafter several of them got an attorney to incorporate the Employees Benevolent Association Union. The attorney thereupon presented the petition to the company; its Nebraska plant manager confirmed that a majority of workers had signed; and the company's attorney advised the manager to recognize the Association as bargaining agent for the workers even though the petition had not specified the Association as bargaining agent. The Association presented its desires in a contract, and the company agreed to all terms and signed the contract.

While all this was going on, another group of employees was attempting to form an American Federation of Labor local to represent them. An AFL official met with the plant manager, who said that the company had already recognized and signed a contract with the Benevolent Association. Employees who wanted AFL affiliation filed a complaint with the National Labor Relations Board. The NLRB voided the company's contract with the Benevolent Association due to unfair labor practices surrounding the contract's origins and signing. Whittaker appealed that ruling in court.

What exactly had the company been doing that was deemed unfair? The plant foreman had told one employee activist that Elastic Stop Nut had a "company union" in New Jersey and did not want an AFL union at the Nebraska plant. When workers filed the NLRB complaint the foreman told one worker that such "foolishness" would have to stop and indicated that another employee might be punished if he testified against plant management at the NLRB hearing. The NLRB took particular note of the unsettled nature of labor relations at the plant when these comments were made, potentially making the foreman's comments even more influential among employees. The NLRB noted that Benevolent Association organizing activity and dues collection occurred in the plant during work hours, and that handbills favoring the Benevolent Association and opposing a union were displayed on company bulletin boards. The NLRB took particular note that the employer recognized the Benevolent Association as the employees' bargaining agent even though petitions signed by workers did not specify that the Association would perform that function and, moreover, Elastic Stop Nut signed a contract with the Association as the workers' bargaining agent after being informed that the AFL was filing official charges of unfair practice alleging favoritism toward the Association. The NLRB felt that an employer who was not interfering with employees' union organizing would have refrained from signing a contract until the claims of two rival employee groups had been settled under federal labor laws governing such disputes.

Whittaker argued that the foreman was simply exercising his First Amendment right of free speech when telling employees his disapproval of union activity in the plant. Because some employees continued to seek affiliation with the AFL, Whittaker cited that as evidence that the foreman's statements had not intimidated employees. Whittaker also claimed there was no evidence that Elastic Stop Nut knew of Benevolent Association organizing and dues collecting on the shop floor during work hours, nor that the company knew about pro-Association and anti-union notices on the bulletin boards, nor that Elastic Stop Nut treated the Benevolent Association with favoritism when recognizing and contracting with it as the employees' bargaining agent.

Whittaker's arguments did not persuade the court. The court found that the foreman's statements were not isolated comments and could reasonably be considered expressions of company policy. The court believed that such comments would have to influence a new workforce grappling with pros and cons of union affiliation, and that company managers had a positive duty to refrain from comment on the question: "The Board had before it a record presenting . . . a studied hostility toward the Union and an exhibited preference for the Association, and that the remark of [foreman] Valnoski was a step in a continuous course of conduct designed to interfere with the employees in their right of self organization."[52] Whittaker argued that the foreman was simply making pastime conversation with workers planing to testify at NLRB proceedings and urging them to be truthful when he told them, "I hear you fellows are going to tell a lot of stuff about me up there. You hadn't better or its [*sic*] going to be too bad" and "You know what I told you if you went up there and lied about me."[53] The court found that Whittaker's argument was insensitive to the reality of supervisor–underling relations during labor relations turmoil, and that the foreman's comments showed that the company was threatening employees with punishment if they testified at NLRB proceedings. The court also declared that just because some employees persevered and joined the AFL did not mean, as Whittaker argued, that no coercion was being used against them.

The NLRB had also found that the company's favoritism toward the Benevolent Association meant that the contract between them could not be deemed to resolve labor issues it purportedly addressed, and the court sustained the Board's finding.

Indeed the court ruled against Whittaker and in favor of the National Labor Relations Board on all other disputed points as well. Elastic Stop Nut Corporation had to withdraw its recognition of the Benevolent Association as the employees' bargaining representative, had to repudiate most aspects of the contract signed with the Association, and had to refrain from interfering with employee efforts to organize themselves.

We do not know whether Whittaker's arguments reflected his own beliefs or whether he was simply making the best of a bad case. On behalf of a client even Abraham Lincoln was known to make arguments that he would have scoffed at outside of a lawsuit. Unlike Lincoln, however, who sometimes represented corporation interests and sometimes represented individuals seeking redress from corporations, Whittaker consistently defended monied interests when they were challenged by individual citizens. This personal preference was not just materialistic, representing the side that could pay the most: His U.S. Supreme Court decisions consistently favored company managers who were challenged by workers. In cases such as Elastic Stop Nut, Whittaker was going where his conscience led him.[54]

Commerce

Whittaker's litigations defending major corporations' commercial strategies when they ran afoul of the law probably nurtured political support that got him named as a U.S. district judge. For example, in a fight between major business interests of Kansas City, the U.S. government allied itself with one group of businessmen. The other group hired Whittaker to defend them against both their competitors and the U.S. government.[55] This was the sort of litigation that made Whittaker's reputation in elite corporate circles. An ideological interpretation of this case is treacherous because his law firm was a long-time representative of the client, but given the dislike Whittaker later expressed for the Roosevelt administration, his fight against it in court is intriguing.

In 1936 two promoters who made their money by setting up wholesale fruit and vegetable markets approached the Union Pacific railroad in Cleveland, Ohio. The railroad suggested that they consult with a Union Pacific agent in Kansas City. Two adjoining municipalities are named Kansas City, one in Kansas and one in

Missouri. On the Kansas side Union Pacific owned real estate next to municipal land called the Public Levee. The promoters and the railroad agreed that a new produce market there would boost railroad freight revenue.

No one at the time questioned the railroad's intimate role in the project, extending even to getting new laws passed by the Kansas legislature and to getting municipal financial support from Kansas City, Kansas. That latter financial support came indirectly from the railroad, which purchased municipal bonds financing the new market. The effect of this new market would be to divert substantial freight revenue from railroads serving an already existing wholesale produce center across the state border in Kansas City, Missouri. The metropolitan region, however, was not big enough to support two such markets, so Union Pacific got the city government of Kansas City, Kansas, to offer cash to key users of the Missouri market in hopes of inducing enough of them to move a few blocks west in order to make the Missouri market fail. The cash was supplied by a third party in an arrangement brokered by Union Pacific.

Up to then the activity was simply an example of ruthless business competition that made America great. The cash arrangement, however, ran afoul of the Elkins Act,[56] at least as the Act was read by the Roosevelt administration. The Act prohibited a railroad from paying selected Missouri produce dealers to move a few blocks west into Kansas, as such an effort to increase railroad revenue could destroy thriving produce businesses that were not favored by the railroad. The abuse being fought here was a railroad using its influence to destroy businesses that were not competing with the railroad—and perhaps not cooperating with the railroad. Public outcry over such abuses had eventually led to legislation such as the Elkins Act. The Act, however, did not prohibit the government of Kansas City, Kansas, from paying selected produce dealers to move from the Missouri market. The question was whether the payments were really from the city or from Union Pacific.

The federal legal action against Union Pacific was not simply a New Deal intervention in a business deal. Union Pacific competitors such as Santa Fe, Burlington, Rock Island, and Missouri Pacific joined the case on the federal government's side, as did the city of Kansas City, Missouri. When Whittaker entered on behalf of Union Pacific he entered a battle of giants.

Union Pacific had all along been open about its involvement in this project and had apparently believed that its activity was unquestionably legal. This belief may have been buttressed by the project's financing—some of the money came from the Public Works Administration, a New Deal agency. Now another Roosevelt agency was filing suit to stop the project, probably evidence less of duplicity than of the New Deal's chaos. A federal district court granted an injunction to suspend the Kansas produce market promotion. Taking advantage of a special law governing appeals, Whittaker's partner Henry N. Ess went directly to the U.S. Supreme

Court. That tribunal modified the injunction but retained its core aspects which forbade both the railroad and the municipal government from using money or reduced rents to induce produce movers to relocate. Justices Roberts, Black, and Douglas dissented. They were no enemies of the New Deal but felt that this application of the Elkins Act went farther than Congress intended, thwarting a legitimate municipal government effort to promote commerce in the city-owned market area. The majority, however, had held otherwise, and Whittaker's railroad client lost.

Despite, or perhaps because of, Whittaker's skill in defending corporations' interests (a skill that cannot be fully measured by win/loss ratios), his law firm shifted him from courtroom trials to closed-door consultations where he devised strategies to protect corporate clients. In addition he began guiding big business transactions in the Midwest, a task that made his reputation as a top attorney.[57] Years later a son reflected, "It is a somewhat heady experience to have people to whom you have tried cases to now want your business advice."[58] Whittaker was engaged in such work throughout World War II. He was strangely self-deprecating about his background: "I started trying mill-run lawsuits in June of 1928 and continued to do so until June of 1942 when I felt I had enough seasoning with mill-run cases, and then I ceased to be so active in that work and took up more office counseling, financial advising, representing banks. I tried occasional cases, but not general mill-run cases thereafter."[59]

A colleague remembered Whittaker's growing prestige. "He was hired by other lawyers to assist them in their unusual problems and he thus was truly a lawyer's lawyer. No problem was too large or too small for his guidance and counseling."[60]

One associate asserted that Kansas City's legal community of 1953 easily rated Whittaker as among the top ten attorneys in town.[61] At that time Whittaker had been with the Watson Ess law firm for three decades. Within the legal profession Whittaker's distinctive style made him one of the region's most prominent attorneys even though he was unknown to the general public.

The work provided ample financial reward. As a Watson Ess attorney just out of law school in the 1920s, Whittaker was able to afford an Oakland coupe.[62] In the early years of the Great Depression he already had an annual income of $12,000 and lived in a neighborhood known for its fine homes and wealthy residents. A lawyer colleague remembered that Whittaker never hesitated to remind his firm about the value of his services. In a profession where opulent offices were a measure of success, Whittaker's was near the top. Its opulence amazed someone who visited in the 1940s. A half century later he still recalled the fireplace (in a downtown office building) and parqueted wood floor.[63]

Although Whittaker was not insensitive to the value of money, a fellow member of the firm noted Whittaker's insistence on fair billings. Once he heard of another firm skinning a client while Watson Ess represented a second client on the same side of the case. An offended Whittaker directed the Watson Ess lawyer handling the trial to reduce his firm's fee.[64]

RELATIONS WITH FAMILY

Biographies of many prominent Americans are filled with warm anecdotes about their home life. No such stories exist about Whittaker. "The law has been my life," he said.[65] Although that summation is true enough, a few glimpses remain of his family life.

He married Winifred ("Winnie") Regina Pugh in 1928. They had three sons: Charles Keith, Kent, and Gary. Whittaker freely shared his sizable income with his wife's ailing sisters. And as World War II began, he bought several hundred acres[66] of farmland near Trimble, Missouri, just north of Kansas City, making it available to his younger sister and her husband so they could earn a living as farmers without facing the classic burden of a farm mortgage. Whittaker himself ran Herefords there, although his older sister laughed at any attempt to characterize him as a husbandman. He was a little sensitive on the point. An acquaintance said, "One time we were both over at the gas station at 62nd and Brookside on a Sunday afternoon to get some gasoline. I said, 'Charlie, where are you going?' He had on a pair of overalls or something, you know, obviously work clothes. 'I'm going up to my farm.' " When the friend expressed good-natured skepticism about the "Farmer Charlie" persona, Whittaker replied, "Look, I'm not in farming to be a gentleman, I intend to make some money out of it."[67] Nonetheless Whittaker himself once described the cattle operation as a hobby.[68] A son recalled, "He would go up there and walk through the fields and look at cattle and shuck corn and see how the ears were full."[69] An accidental but welcome side benefit to farm ownership was that lawyer Whittaker received a farmer's extra allocations of gasoline ration stamps during World War II.

Though Whittaker continued his law practice work on Sundays, on that day he typically took his family to visit his sister and her husband on the Trimble farm. The visits grew uncongenial. Mrs. Whittaker liked to take advantage of this opportunity to discuss the latest clothing fashions with someone who was interested in the topic, much to the irritation of Mr. Whittaker who saw the weekly family gathering as an opportunity for him to spend hours delivering monologues about the law. "I can remember a thousand nights," said one son, "sitting in the family room or on the porch and he would talk, and . . . I was a twelve-year-old kid, I didn't know what he was talking about."[70] Winifred finally began spending Sundays with her sisters while Charles headed north.

"There was very little exchange of gifts between my parents at Christmas, birthdays, anniversaries," mused a son. Nor did they take vacations. "I don't think he . . . could easily express affection. . . . They were both constrained. Very concerned about appearances. . . . It was a pretty platonic undemonstrative relationship." The son likened his father to the character Mr. Bridge in Evan Connell's novels.[71]

Religion was another factor that did not promote family intimacy. Whittaker once genially recalled:

> As a boy, I remember laughing at a joke about Billy Sunday and a newsboy. Billy asked: "Little boy! Can you tell me the way to the courthouse?" The little newsboy spoke right up, told Mr. Sunday the way to the courthouse, and turned away selling his papers, when Billy called him back and said, "Little boy, you don't know who I am, do you? Well, I'm Billy Sunday, the great evangelist, the man you've heard so many people talk about. You've been so good to me, you've told me the way to the courthouse, that I want to do something for you. So, if you'll come over to the tabernacle any night this week, I'll, I'll tell you the way to heaven." The little newsboy turned and said, "What're you talkin' about? You tell me the way to heaven? Why you don't even know where the courthouse is!"[72]

Winifred was an active Roman Catholic who frequently invited the non-religious Charles to attend mass with her. He preferred to stay home Sunday mornings and putter in the kitchen, preparing an after-church breakfast for Winifred and the boys. Because church membership was so important to her, he eventually attempted to mollify her by joining Central Methodist Church, where he nonetheless had little to do with religious services, although he accepted positions in the church's governing bureaucracy.

Although Whittaker exhibited no obvious piety, on occasion he spoke as if he were devout. When sworn in as a federal district judge in July 1954, Whittaker expressed hope for "God's help, upon whom I have often leaned."[73] Taking office as an appeals judge on the Eighth Circuit Whittaker said, "I have never ceased praying to God. I will never cease praying. He'll always see me through."[74] Whatever the personal significance of his religious beliefs, however, Whittaker seldom spoke of them, and outward manifestations were unapparent.

Vacations had little appeal to Whittaker, though some years he might spend a few days angling in Minnesota. He also installed a fishing lake on his Trimble farm. Such infrequent recreation was nearly solitary. One of his sons failed to recall even a half dozen occasions when acquaintances came along to Trimble.[75]

Other than Whittaker's gregariousness and his intense and driving nature, acquaintances have left few glimpses of his personality. We know he enjoyed ballroom dancing (in his earlier days), and liked to ruin good steaks by having them cooked until dried out.[76] He was an avid baseball fan and on more than one occasion described his judicial career with a baseball metaphor: "I got on; and, with the support of a good team, was enabled to touch three bases in three years. I went to first on a walk, to second on a fielder's choice, and, on the second pitch thereafter I was sacrificed to third. First base, the district court, being close to the dugout of the home team and its fans, was a perfect delight; second base, the United States Court of Appeals . . . while a little more removed from the people, was a very quiet and comfortable position. But third base, I found truly to be, as the fans say, 'the hot corner.' "[77]

Whittaker was an occasional golfer. He gave it up in the 1940s but resumed again while a member of the Supreme Court. "I love to get out in the open air and on the grass," he said. Even on the links, however, he restricted his socializing to law colleagues. His typical golfing partners in Washington were current and retired Supreme Court justices: Tom Clark, John Harlan, Stanley Reed.[78]

An old acquaintance of Whittaker mused, "I don't suppose Whittaker ever read a book on sociology, civil rights, ecology, maybe even history or literature or philosophy."[79] Although that observation was true enough, a fellow law school student recalled, "On winter nights, we often sat before the wood burning fireplace in the living room, sometimes talking about the law, sometimes quoting verses of poetry such as 'Man Without a Country'—'Face on the Bar Room Floor' and sometimes 'Grey's Elegy Written in a Country Church Yard.' "[80] His speeches are sprinkled with assorted quotations, but we do not know whether he got them from the original works or from compilations used by public speakers.

Whittaker was an early advocate of dressing for success. In a speech to young Kansas City lawyers he declared, "I would keep my clothes neatly pressed, my hair trimmed and my shoes shined."[81] He considered a three-piece wool suit to be casual summer attire. Even while tending his World War II victory garden at home he wore a starched shirt with tie. In the 1970s an interviewer described his "carefully groomed looks and straight-combed white hair of a judge straight from central casting."[82]

His long hours spent on law work caused one secretary to note that a home life was unapparent.[83] An old friend admitted amazement that a spouse and offspring even existed.[84] A son spoke of those days with his parents: "They truly would go for months without having guests in our home and were not being entertained outside the home. He went to the office in the morning and came home at night and there was dinner, which was always family; and then he either worked or read something after dinner."[85] The same son recalled their Christmases: "He was a non-participant. My mother would have bought whatever toys were going to be."[86] Shortly before Whittaker ascended to the Supreme Court, he privately mused that his boys' childhood had passed him by.[87] After that conversation, at one son's high school graduation, observers noticed Whittaker looking distracted during the ceremony and making pencil notes about legal matters.[88]

The move to Washington, DC, was hurried and hectic. The stress of making arrangements took several pounds off Winifred's body frame. A son who was a Dartmouth senior brought his red 1955 Corvette convertible to Washington and left it for his father, who used it to commute to the Supreme Court until the son could drive Whittaker's Cadillac in from Kansas City.

Observing that candidates for federal judgeships were typically persons who had achieved financial success, and that such persons typically invested in stock portfolios, after his retirement from the bench Whittaker said that judges should establish blind trusts to preserve their estates while avoiding conflicts of interest.[89] Whittaker apparently took a different approach while he was an active judge. During those years his wife Winifred routinely invested in stocks. While her husband was on the Supreme Court, for example, she purchased shares in American Telephone & Telegraph, Bethlehem Steel, Dow Chemical Co., American Cyanamid, Marine Midland, Otis Elevator, R. J. Reynolds Tobacco Co., Timken Roller Bearing Co., White Motor Co., and Yale & Town Manufacturing Co.[90] We have no reason to believe that such investments affected Whittaker's judicial work, but he obviously did not find a blind trust necessary while he was on the bench.

Winifred did not join the Washington social whirl, preferring domestic activities and community service. Her volunteer work at Georgetown University Hospital was so quiet that administrators were taken aback when President-Elect John F. Kennedy greeted her by name during a visit there.

Justice Whittaker took no more pleasure from Washington society than his wife did. At one event Whittaker spotted a friend, and they became engrossed in conversation. Their visit inadvertently became embarrassing because Whittaker had the highest social rank at the gathering. Under Washington's arcane social etiquette no one could leave before Whittaker departed, and he continued chatting with his friend, oblivious to the growing distress among guests who wanted to leave. Finally the hostess asked Winifred if she could make her husband go home.

"His entire preoccupation was with the law," Chief Justice Earl Warren said. "He refused to leave time for any diversion."[91] Justice Tom Clark agreed: "Others might leave their official duties behind as the courtroom doors closed, but for him there was no escape from their power nor flight from their presence."[92]

RELATIONS WITH COWORKERS

Apparently Whittaker got along well with fellow attorneys in the firm, but his relations with support staff were less collegial.

A secretary recalled his habitual impatience,[93] a characteristic noted by everyone who knew Whittaker. A fellow attorney remembered that as Whittaker labored to complete a brief, his vocal intensity grew with the racket from his office.[94]

He was mistrustful of support staff's competence, using only three particular secretaries and holding work until one of them was available. Whittaker refused to delegate even the simplest office tasks. Said one judge who dealt with him, "If he had himself done the work, he knew it was right."[95] Another judge concurred: "He insisted on doing everything, or checking everything, himself."[96]

Examples of this approach are numerous. He asked a research assistant to bring information about a case next week, saying there was no hurry. The following day the young man went to the law firm's library but was unable to find the necessary books. Whittaker had taken the books and done the research himself. He even refused to let his secretary affix stamps on envelopes—he insisted on determining the proper postage himself, and insisted on personally mailing letters.

He sent continual messages of distrust to persons assigned to help him. His actions implied that he had to rely on himself alone, and that he could not afford to give anyone the least amount of power over him. Was such conduct mere administrative inefficiency, or expression of a deeper personality trait? (During the Supreme Court years Justice Whittaker's Cadillac suffered a flat tire in rush hour Washington traffic. It was a hot summer day, and his traveling companion recommended seeking help from a service station. Whittaker, however, refused to delegate the task to someone else. He insisted on changing the tire himself, though he did accept help from his traveling companion.[97])

Such an approach to work vastly expanded the hours he had to spend (and bill) on preparing litigation. One of his sons remembered an oppressive work pace, with each evening devoted to legal matters.[98] Another son, who himself became a lawyer, described Whittaker's brutal occupational habits as "beyond my comprehension."[99] Whittaker expected support staff to put in extra hours as well. One secretary expressed no objection to working with him seven days a week, dropping one outside activity after another to meet his demands for more performance. She declared herself fortunate simply to hold on to her employment.[100] Associates do not recall heavy use of alcohol by Whittaker, but otherwise he was the stereotype of the chain smoking, demanding, workaholic lawyer.

Whittaker suffered from a long-standing health problem that might have excluded him from selection as a federal judge had his condition been publicly known. Throughout his adult life he struggled against crippling depression. By the end of the twentieth century such an affliction was viewed with tolerance and even compassion, but during Whittaker's lifetime the disability was stigmatized. The stigma was so harsh that Whittaker tried to hide his affliction from co-workers and the public. Fear of exposure could only worsen the burden. That he was able to achieve such a productive career under this adversity demonstrates inner strength that he failed to recognize, and suggests what victims of depression might accomplish in a more understanding environment.

Apparently Whittaker's first attack of depression began when his mother died on his birthday in 1917. "I felt I couldn't go on."[101] He dropped out of high school. His father relocated into town with the two sisters, leaving young Whittaker and his scarcely older teenager brother to live on the farm alone.[102]

When he entered the Kansas City School of Law three years later, he threw himself into an inhuman pace of work. Combining a full regimen of classes with a day job, he often worked at one followed by the other from 8:00 A.M. until 10:00 P.M., taking additional time for study and homework. While other students knocked off to have fun, Whittaker would buttonhole someone to discuss an issue encountered that day at the law firm where he was an office boy. This approach to life was commented upon by other students, who evidently ascribed it simply to excessive zeal.

Although acquaintances speak of Whittaker's amiability, they also recall his habit of turning social chit-chat in the direction of legal issues he was currently considering. Law was not only his profession but his main topic of conversation. In evenings at home he walked back and forth across the front porch, testing oral arguments in front of his bewildered children. Although Whittaker was one of Kansas City's top trial attorneys he felt "pains of inadequacy"[103] about his work. "I was almost constantly plagued with doubts about how best to cope with the arts and wiles of opposing counsel."[104] A son recalled that defeat in a case would send Whittaker plummeting.[105] Such a response can be dangerous in a profession where losses are inevitable, particularly as an attorney's reputation grows, and cases brought to him become tougher.

He suffered more than one nervous breakdown as a Watson Ess attorney.[106] Around 1937, his law firm forced him to spend a month or more on leave in Arizona.[107]

Unlike many law partnerships, the Watson Ess firm had little socializing among members. Their relations were strictly business. For lawyers in the firm, memories of socializing with Whittaker revolved around late afternoon office bull sessions on legal topics. Whittaker would come to the library as junior members of the firm finished their day's tasks. The young lawyers later emphasized how much they learned from what he had to say. They also spoke, without resentment, about his pattern of taking over the conversation by expounding upon about his cases. "Charlie always loved to argue," remembered one friend. "He was a born advocate. Often, I would be working on some legal problem and would state it to him, hoping to obtain agreement upon my views. He would invariably take the opposite side and point out every conceivable weakness of my position. Of course, he was more helpful to me in taking that attitude, but it shows his disposition and quick and fertile mind."[108]

Although many Kansas City lawyers networked with associates and potential clients through membership in the University Club, the club refused to accept Whittaker as a member. The snub continued even after he became a U.S. Supreme Court justice, because the club required members to have a university degree and refused to count his Bachelor of Laws diploma. The Kansas City Club was not so choosy, and Whittaker joined that powerhouse of community business and political leaders. He joined not for social conviviality but simply to maintain contacts with persons who could help his law practice. Indeed, both Whittaker and his wife disliked the country club set.

The main non-law socializing that fellow attorneys remember was lunch. "He always ate his lunch at a round table in a public restaurant surrounded by lawyers and personal friends. I can recall him being the leader of the discussions concerning legal problems at the Williams Restaurant, which was then located in the Gloyd Building, and later he and his legal cohorts moved to the Tiffin Room" in the downtown Wolferman's restaurant.[109] "You didn't go over and sit down at that table," recalled one visitor, "you had to be asked."[110] There Whittaker daily held forth on news of the day and on legal questions while fellow diners were seldom able to interject a comment. Yet the men kept coming back to his table because they found his monologues so entertaining. Recalled one participant, "Not everyone went every day. A lot of guys went there frequently and they had a lot of fun. And that is how they kept up on the gossip. It's like people do now in small towns over at the coffee shop at 10 or 11 o'clock in the morning. It was that kind of atmosphere. They were very prominent people who did that."[111] The daily scene became so popular that drop-ins could not find seating.[112] In that era these gatherings were all male, comprised of business and other community leaders.

As the 1950s began, Whittaker's law practice paid him over $100,000 a year. He told one colleague that he was toying with either becoming a federal judge or a transportation system's general counsel. The friend advised the judgeship: "That same system had some years prior to this killed one of my horses and never paid for it." Whittaker laughed and said he should have sued.[113]

Chapter 3

Judicial Ascent

There are three main types of federal judges. Whittaker was the first person to serve as each type.

A district judge presides at trials. This is the kind of judge most often portrayed in movies and television programs. Evidence is presented, witnesses testify, and juries render verdicts. These judges often determine the facts of cases, always find what laws apply to those facts, and direct persons in a case to do whatever the judges' findings of law require. Such a judge is like a baseball umpire, observing movements of players and the ball, and applying whatever rule is appropriate to each case.

An appeals judge examines the work of district judges. Appeals judges work without juries. A federal appeals court consists of several judges. Normally an appeals court does not reconsider evidence presented at the district trial; a person does not get a second trial in front of an appeals court. Instead this court considers whether the district judge made a mistake, most often a mistake in finding the appropriate law. If such an error is discovered, an appeals court may order a change in the district judge's ruling. If the mistake is serious enough, an appeals court may even order the case to start over again in a new trial at the district court. An appeals court is like a conference of baseball umpires responding to a dispute about whether an umpire used the right rule in making a decision.

A Supreme Court justice works without a jury and normally examines decisions of appeals courts. This examination only happens if a case "falls between the cracks," if facts of a case seem to create a paradox where applying one element of law would violate another element. All these cases are hard because in all of them the law conflicts with itself. A Supreme Court justice must not only be an expert in finding the law as it is, but must also understand the law's purpose, must have an intuitive sense of what law is supposed to accomplish even if a particular statute or previous case decision does not obviously cover the situation at hand. The nine members of the Supreme Court are like a committee revising baseball's rules to cover a game situation that never occurred before.

The work of these three types of judges has important differences.

A district judge is immersed in the hurly-burly of a case, with all the courtroom excitement familiar to movie goers. An appeals judge only examines the cold record of a trial. It is the difference between directing a theater drama and reading a newspaper review of the play.

The life of an appeals judge is not only quieter than that of a district judge, but also requires a different way of looking at cases. A district judge has to determine both the facts (what happened) and law (the consequences). In contrast, an appeals judge normally accepts the district judge's findings of fact. Instead of choosing again among differing versions of facts that confronted the district judge, an appeals judge concentrates on finding whatever law is relevant to the one version of facts accepted by the district judge.

A district judge works alone, but an appeals judge and a Supreme Court justice must continually consult with colleagues and strive to reach a joint decision with them. High court judges not only have to convince themselves of what is right but must also convince a majority of fellow judges as well. A successful appeals judge must be as adept in politics as in law.

A person well suited to being one type of judge may be miserable as another kind. Paradoxically, as Charles Evans Whittaker became more successful and powerful, he became more dissatisfied and unhappy with his career. Whittaker enjoyed being a district judge, disliked being an appeals judge, and felt wretched on the Supreme Court.

DISTRICT JUDGE

One authority notes that a district judge's main responsibility is "application of rules on which there is substantial agreement." Another authority notes that such a judge is "engaged primarily in a technical lawyer's job, applying and distinguishing precedents with relatively little freedom for the play of creative thought."[1]

Such an approach to law appealed to Whittaker. As a Watson Ess attorney he once spoke about how justice is achieved. "In the main it is, and must always be, the product of long hours of hard, diligent, painstaking labor by highly competent, experienced, careful and practical lawyers. . . . The practice of law is a deliberate science and must be recognized as such."[2] That is exactly the style of jurisprudence Whittaker followed when he was appointed as a federal district judge.

Appointment to District Judgeship

Whittaker's interest in professional advancement was demonstrated by offices held in the Missouri Bar Association: board of governors 1948–1954, secretary 1951, vice president 1952, president 1953–1954. The law profession is ruthlessly competitive, and achieving high office in large bar organizations requires ambition and political skill of high order.

Most attorneys consider a judgeship as the highest office attainable in the profession. In his decades of law practice, Whittaker was repeatedly frustrated by judges who evaded decisions of legal questions that Whittaker thought were crucial to his cases. He was also disturbed by judges who adjusted facts of a case to yield a decision the judge wanted, rather than a decision impelled by application of law to unmodified facts. "Being unable, after more than thirty years of effort at the Bar, to overcome my deficiencies in coping with such matters . . . and looking to what appeared to be vast opportunities for improved public service of the Bench, I thought it would be good to become a judge."[3] As a top lawyer in Kansas City, Whittaker knew how to position himself as a candidate when he decided to seek appointment as a federal judge. He freely admitted seeking the post.[4]

In his memoirs President Eisenhower said his search for judicial candidates "placed great value on solid common sense—a quality hard to define but well understood by most."[5] While serving as Eisenhower's Deputy Attorney General, William P. Rogers described what Eisenhower's criteria meant:

> *First*, and most important, the candidate must be an outstanding lawyer and leader in the community from which he comes. Both his personal and professional reputation must be beyond reproach.
>
> *Second*, the age and the health of the candidate must be considered. . . .
>
> *Third*, whenever a vacancy occurs in a Circuit Court or in the Supreme Court, the President has expressed his desire that outstanding judges should be carefully considered. . . . I believe all appellate courts benefit if some of the members, at least, bring an understanding of the problems of a trial judge to the conference table.
>
> *Finally*, President Eisenhower has stated that in connection with judicial appointments he places considerable weight on "the recognition [endorsement] of the American Bar Association."[6]

President Eisenhower gave the American Bar Association an institutional role in his judicial appointments, requiring the organization's approval of anyone he nominated for a federal bench. "We must never appoint a man who doesn't have the recognition of the American Bar Association," Eisenhower said.[7] He thereby assured that nominees would reflect mainstream beliefs, and that no one feared by society's power structure would have opportunity to challenge the status quo from the bench. In 1956 Justice Felix Frankfurter dryly observed, "Seven former presidents of the American Bar Association denounced Brandeis as 'not a fit person to be a member of the Supreme Court.' "[8] Eisenhower's policy gave the organization veto power over the president's proposed judicial nominations. When the Eisenhower administration expressed interest in appointing an individual, a representative from the ABA would informally ask judges and lawyers for opinions about the candidate's suitability. The Justice Department gave the ABA access to the official background information questionnaire completed by candidates.

A key question in that document asked candidates to name ten important trials they handled. The ABA in turn would interview judges and opposing attorneys associated with those cases. Trial litigation background was the American Bar Association's prime consideration in considering district judge candidates. Whittaker easily excelled in meeting that criterion.

Moreover, during the ABA investigation Whittaker was president of the Missouri Bar Association—an excellent situation when seeking a federal judgeship (as one of his law partners commented). Another person who observed the process recalled a general high regard for Whittaker among lawyers who worked with him.[9]

The chairman of the American Bar Association committee that examined Whittaker's suitability for the Supreme Court declared, "Judge Whittaker has served with distinction and to the complete satisfaction of the bar."[10] The ABA's Standing Committee on the Federal Judiciary stated at that later time:

> Prior to the President's making this nomination, the Attorney General afforded this committee full opportunity to investigate and report on the qualifications of Judge Whittaker for appointment as an Associate Justice of the Supreme Court. We found that Judge Whittaker had been one of the leading lawyers of Missouri prior to his appointment to the Federal bench, and that the performance of his duties on the bench has been marked by outstanding legal ability, industry, and judicial temperament.
>
> Our committee unanimously concluded that Judge Whittaker is eminently qualified for this very important appointment.[11]

The ABA's president-elect was even more effusive: "He will be one of the greatest justices this court ever had."[12]

In addition to ABA approval, Eisenhower also required judicial candidates to undergo an FBI investigation of their background. Upon starting his Supreme Court service Whittaker joked that he was pretty spotless after going through "J. Edgar Hoover's laundry three times in the last three years."[13]

In addition to President Eisenhower's official criteria for judicial appointments, political considerations were crucial. A generation had passed since a Republican sat in the White House, and Eisenhower wanted judges who would strengthen the long-diluted tincture of Republican philosophy in the federal judiciary. Deputy Attorney General Rogers, who was heavily involved in selecting new judges, frankly admitted that the Eisenhower administration viewed Republican affiliation as mandatory for any nominee.[14]

When the Eisenhower administration asked members of the Watson Ess firm about Whittaker's politics, a $200 contribution to the Republican cause in 1952 was the only evidence anyone could remember. Long forgotten was his one foray into political campaigning, when he made a Republican speech in the red hot Democrat community of Fulton in central Missouri:

> As a youngster in law school, I was sent by the Republican State Committee to make a political speech in the nearly 100 percent democratic community of Fulton, Missouri . . . the home of Missouri's asylum for the feeble minded. Well, on the appointed date, I made my way to the bus station in Columbia to catch the six o'clock for Fulton. When I arrived, there was the bus displaying the "Fulton" marquee, the motor was running and the door was open, so I stepped in and took the fifth seat. Soon afterward there came a group of marching men followed by a man in uniform. These men filed into and took seats on the bus. Whereupon the guard closed the door and, pointing with his finger, counted "one, two, three, four," and then, pointing to me he asked: "what's your name, where are you going, and what for?" I innocently and calmly answered, "my name is Whittaker, and I am going to Fulton to make a Republican political speech," and like a flash, he continued "five, six, ..."[15]

Evidently the experience did not whet Whittaker's appetite for such fare, and partisan politics never seemed to distract the young attorney from his law practice. Indeed, recalled one friend, "His views on controversial public questions were not on record and were generally unknown by even his closest friends."[16] (Much later Whittaker made at least one more foray into partisan politics. In 1966 he agreed to be the dinner speaker at the Missouri Young Americans for Freedom convention, an organization of political activists oriented toward 1964 Republican presidential nominee Barry Goldwater and 1968 Republican presidential candidate Ronald Reagan. "Charlie was a real down in the road conservative," an acquaintance said.[17] Said another, "At his core, he was probably a Libertarian."[18] William O. Douglas described Whittaker as "in his ideas, close to the Stone Age Man, General Curtis E. LeMay, who ran with George Wallace on the presidential ticket in 1968."[19])

Whittaker's non-existent personal political background had nothing to do with his appointment to a district judgeship. More important were his long-standing legal services for the *Kansas City Star*, where he earned the friendship of the newspaper's president and general manager Roy Roberts. News media connections gave Roberts opportunity to promote favored candidates, and in 1952 he was one of the first news executives to promote the presidential candidacy of his personal friend Dwight Eisenhower.

Roberts played a crucial role in promoting the career of yet another friend, Charles Whittaker. Whittaker had handled trials for the *Star*. Whittaker knew the influence Roberts had, and asked the newspaper executive to campaign on his behalf. Every knowledgeable observer in the era who left a comment on the subject agreed that the influential Roberts sought to make Whittaker a judge.

In addition to approaching Roberts, Whittaker also approached U.S. Senator Frank Carlson (R–KS) and former U.S. Senator Harry Darby (R–KS). They, too, were personal friends of Eisenhower, the general from Kansas. Darby was a longtime Republican National Committeeman and chairman of the Kansas delegation to the 1952 convention that nominated Eisenhower. Darby later said that his relations with Eisenhower and U.S. Attorney General Herbert Brownell assured that they would take Whittaker's candidacy seriously.[20] Darby also acted as an on-site coordinator passing endorsements from Kansas City to Sen. Carlson, who in turn could use that information in Washington conversations. Whittaker's partner John B. Gage served as a reform mayor of Kansas City, seeking to destroy municipal power wielded by the notorious Democrat Pendergast machine. Partner Henry Ess was a delegate to the 1936 Republican national convention which nominated Kansas governor Alf Landon for president. The nephew of another lawyer in the firm was Landon's son-in-law. The Whittaker law firm's Republican connections were sterling. Whittaker and the president had mutual acquaintances, and such contact with Eisenhower was important. His personal interest in judicial appointments was strong enough that years after leaving the White House he could still recount specifics about individuals he selected.[21] His staff may have handled details, but Eisenhower definitely made the final decisions.

Given that Whittaker had never been an active partisan, his ease of access to high elected officials (who in turn were willing to work on his behalf) indicates the powerful circles in which Whittaker circulated as a result of his law practice. He surely would have had similar access to elected officials in Missouri, but they were of the wrong political party to benefit his candidacy. Under the U.S. Senate's rules and traditions, Stuart Symington (D–MO) and Thomas C. Hennings (D–MO) were even in a position to halt the nomination if they chose to. Instead both were agreeable, and Hennings said, "I heartily supported his nomination as a United States district judge."[22] Indeed, Hennings would later skillfully debate a witness opposing Whittaker's nomination to the Supreme Court. Thus Whittaker had bipartisan support from the senators of his own state and senators of Eisenhower's home state. Such sponsorship helped orchestrate broader support for Whittaker.

When Attorney General Brownell recommended Whittaker's nomination to Eisenhower, Deputy Attorney General Rogers simultaneously told a White House staff member that Whittaker was a Republican and that word had been sent to the Republican National Committee. Eisenhower did not send the nomination to the U.S. Senate until the chairman of the Republican National Committee approved it.

Whittaker was by no means the only person considered for the judgeship. Marion T. Bennett was a prime competitor. Bennett was a former member of Congress from Springfield, Missouri, and was presently commissioner of the Court of Claims in Washington, DC. Bennett had powerful connections in Congress, the judiciary, and at the White House. Eisenhower's trusted chief of staff Sherman Adams was a promoter of Bennett. In the end, however, Whittaker and his friends prevailed.[23]

Headlines in the *Kansas City Star* declared: "WHITTAKER TO BE JUDGE / . . . MADE NO EFFORT / While Not Actively Seeking Post, He Was Responsive to Support Given Him." The *Star*'s Washington correspondent told readers that the *Star*'s lawyer Whittaker, unlike Bennett, "was not an active candidate for the judgeship" and that "efforts of Kansas City and outstate lawyers" were responsible for the appointment.[24]

Although disregarding the politics of selecting judges is like disregarding the politics of selecting presidents, Whittaker himself would bristle when someone tried to ask how he won his judicial appointments.[25] Such an attitude is common among successful candidates for the federal judiciary.

As a district judge Whittaker worked seven days a week. His industriousness cleared the docket of old cases and promptly disposed of new ones. His standard was to have a case completed six months after its filing. He called in opposing lawyers and urged them to settle out of court. One recalled struggling in such a meeting to avoid a summary judgment.[26] Once a trial date was set, Whittaker was merciless about adhering to it; a plaintiff's lawyer who failed to appear promptly would arrive to find the case dismissed. His court clerk recalled attorneys being beat down by the judge's strictness.[27]

A colleague reported Whittaker's frustration at being unable to pass on a friendly warning when he would see a trial advocate making a mistake, and described the new judge as a "restless, nervous, impatient sort of fellow."[28] A fellow jurist noted what happened if an attorney offered a deficient argument: "Then the severe aspect of mien and mental concentration would suddenly erupt, volcanically, and expatiate upon the law applicable to the particular facts involved."[29]

He ad-libbed instructions to juries, a feat amazing to attorneys familiar with the complexities involved. He pushed juries to render verdicts on the same day that arguments concluded. Prompt justice was his goal. He refrained, however, from commenting to juries about evidence they heard, leaving its evaluation completely to their discretion.

Years later Justice Douglas mused, "I venture to say that his greatest happiness came when he was either a lawyer or a judge in the trial court. He loved the contest; he knew the rules; he was diligent."[30]

One of his sons noticed that Whittaker spent less time on judicial duties than he did on his old law firm work.[31] Yet he felt strained. As a district judge he was afflicted by severe headaches impairing his vision, and pronouncing sentence on criminal defendants drained him emotionally. He disliked presiding over criminal cases. They revolved around questions of fact rather than logical complexities of law that he relished. Because the typical criminal defendant plead guilty, there was little for Whittaker to do other than pronounce sentence, a task that disturbed him. He was particularly disturbed by the one death sentence he pronounced. The defendant had raped and killed a woman he kidnapped from Kansas City's fashionable Brookside area, a few blocks from Judge Whittaker's home. The case was open and shut, and a jury was convened to advise on a penalty. They recommended death. Despite Whittaker's later reputation as a hardline "law and order" advocate, he was skeptical about capital punishment. He held a hearing to determine whether the law required him to pronounce a sentence that he found morally repugnant. He decided his responsibility was to the law, not to his own moral beliefs. He ordered the defendant executed. "It was an experience I have never forgotten," Whittaker said.[32] His court clerk remembered how disturbed the judge acted after the execution.[33]

Whittaker continued his law firm habit of sending implicit messages of no confidence in his staff's abilities. Other judges requested clerks to draft preliminary opinions, but Whittaker normally limited his highly trained assistants to routine trivia. Even when he told a clerk to look up a question of law, Whittaker might soon be at the clerk's side examining the same set of volumes. He insisted on absolute control of his chambers. When, in his absence, a clerk allowed another judge to borrow a law book, Whittaker angrily exclaimed that no one had a right to remove anything from his office.[34] The hapless clerk, caught between demands from two judges, brought Whittaker a copy of the book from a third judge.

Judge Whittaker was meticulous. His habit of marking up briefs and opinions, often with almost every word tagged in some way—and in different colors—was so unusual as to be commented upon frequently by persons who later examined the materials. He would transform a legal document into a Jackson Pollock canvas, and took this habit all the way to the Supreme Court. He had done the same as a practicing attorney, marking up law books in his firm's library. A young lawyer who joined the firm after Whittaker left recalled, "If you saw a case heavily underlined . . . you knew that Mr. Whittaker had used it in one of his briefs or had reviewed the case."[35] Whittaker's style of underlining implied that all parts of the material had equal importance, that he was unable to find and focus upon key elements. Such indecisiveness would become a hallmark of his tenure on the U.S. Supreme Court.

Whittaker's opinions, known for brevity, were dictated aloud to a secretary. This habit, too, he carried to Washington.

Comments preserved from lawyers and judicial colleagues seem universally favorable about Whittaker's performance as district judge, an evaluation shared by Whittaker himself. It was "a perfect delight," he said.[36]

Although a handful of cases heard by district judge Whittaker gained brief local notoriety, none has been remembered in anyone's list of notable trials. None established great legal principles, nor would we expect such a development from a judge so determined to base rulings on precedent.

A few district cases are of biographical interest. Judge Whittaker had opportunity to use his farm background in a case involving chicken catchers and clever fraud.[37] In his decision Judge Whittaker declared, "The facts giving rise to these [lawsuit] actions are indeed 'story book', and are as 'unbelievable' in this modern age as they are interesting." The case involved a swindle that was easy to accomplish but difficult to explain.

Lester N. Glover was a chicken buyer. Whittaker noted, "One of Glover's trucks, manned by a driver and accompanied by several 'catchers', arrived at Watson's place and was filled with Watson's chickens, after which the truck driver stopped at Watson's store and asked 'how he wanted his check made out', and Watson replied, 'Ottis Watson', but the truck driver, feigning feared inaccuracy, asked Watson to write on a folded piece of paper, which he presented, 'exactly how he wanted his check issued' and Watson wrote across that paper his true signature, and handed the paper back to the truck driver."[38] A similar scenario occurred with four more truckloads over the next four days. Someone pondering the scenario decades later might wonder why Watson did not become suspicious after the second or third time, but a "dumb chicken catcher" probably seemed a good enough explanation in rural Arkansas during the 1950s.

The folded papers were actually Blue Star Food drafts, which Glover was authorized to issue to chicken sellers. The five drafts, totaling $9,386.30, were "payable to the order of 'Ottis Watson' . . . signed by 'Lester N. Glover' and drawn on defendant through 'Anderson State Bank'. These drafts, bearing the name of 'Ottis Watson' on the reverse side, were each then endorsed by Lester N. Glover and were deposited by him in his bank to his credit which bank, in turn, timely presented them to defendant [Blue Star], who, having received the chickens and noting that the endorsements on the drafts appeared regular, accepted and paid the drafts."[39] The effect was the same as if you made out a company's checks to Watson, tricked him into endorsing them, then added your endorsement below his and deposited the checks in your account.

Clearly Watson had been swindled out of his money. The question was, "Who must pay for this?" The answer, according to Whittaker, was "no one."

Whittaker found that Blue Star had indeed paid for the chickens because it paid the drafts when they were presented. Moreover Whittaker found that Watson, contrary to his impression, had received all that money. The drafts were made out to him, and he had endorsed them. The legal effect, Whittaker said, was the same as if Glover's employee had handed cash to Watson, and Watson had then handed it back to the employee. Watson had possessed the money but gave it away.

Whittaker declared, "The rule is legend that where one of two innocent parties is required to bear a loss, the one whose act made the loss possible must bear it. There can be no doubt that the act which resulted in the loss—as between plaintiff [Watson] and defendant [Blue Star]—was the endorsement by Watson of these blank drafts."

Although the published record is unclear about why Watson chose to sue Blue Star, apparently the hope of recovering any money from Glover was nil, so in desperation Watson directed his effort against Blue Star. Whittaker's holding was, in essence, that Watson had been swindled by Glover, not by Blue Star, and Blue Star had no responsibility to make good Watson's loss.

Whittaker concluded about Watson, "While I have great sympathy for him, and, I think rather naturally, would like to find a way to protect him even against his own folly, . . . I have been unable to find a basis in the law."

Whittaker's farm background also assisted him in a cattle tax dispute.[40] Tax cases, of course, raised just the sort of technical procedural questions that he relished. U.S. Supreme Court justice William O. Douglas freely told Whittaker, "You know this much better than any of us."[41] Judging from opinions he was assigned to write, his colleagues on the high bench seemed glad to refer tax cases to him. His tax expertise was respected. Said Justice Felix Frankfurter: "I was thrown back to an independent inquiry of the course of tax legislation and litigation for more than a hundred years, for all of that was relevant to a true understanding of the problem presented by this case. This involved many weeks of study during what is called the summer vacation. Such a study led to the conclusion set forth in detail in the opinion of my Brother WHITTAKER."[42]

In the cattle controversy the Internal Revenue Service wanted to tax the increase of Sanderson Miller's heifers as ordinary income. Miller argued the herd's increase should be taxed as long-term capital gain, meaning the IRS owed him a refund for overpayment of taxes.

In Whittaker's words, "Roy Harris, engaged in the pasturage business, controlled a great area of blue stem pasturage in Cowley County, Kansas, and . . . plaintiffs, since the early 40's had pastured many of their cattle with him in that area." In 1947 they put newly purchased heifers in "Harris' pasture near Hoosier, in Cowley County, Kansas, to be there run and operated as a brood herd for the production of a calf crop, and with them he immediately placed a herd of bulls for breeding purposes." Later in 1947 he added cows.

> There is no contradiction in the evidence that it was the purpose and intention of plaintiffs in acquiring these heifers and cows to hold and use them for breeding purposes for the production of a calf crop, nor is there any contradiction in the evidence that they were in fact so held and used.
>
> The Government argues that there is a legitimate inference to be drawn that the plaintiffs did not in fact intend to use these heifers and cows for breeding purposes for the production of a calf crop because they had no farm and no place to care for a breeding herd, and that the Harris pastures were without trees or shrubbery except "along streams or sloughs" and were unsuited to a breeding herd of cows, and that plaintiffs merely kept these cows "to obtain the natural increase that would result from running with bulls" and to fatten them on the pasture for gain in weight and better prices. This is not only opposed to the evidence, but is also opposed to the common practice—widely known in this area, even to the Court—which is that many cattle men run herds of brood cows on rented pastures in the Blue Stem area of Kansas for the production of a calf crop and that the area—even though open—is ideal for the purpose. And the notion that cows with suckling calves will gain weight on pasture is entirely erroneous. They do mighty well if they hold their own. And, moreover, it is the inherent purpose of holding cows for breeding purposes "to obtain the natural increase that would result from running with bulls." That is what a breeding herd is kept for.

Whittaker's decision: "These brood animals having been held for more than 6 months, plaintiffs were entitled to long term capital gains treatment of those gains" and entitled to take depreciation when figuring taxes.

Although Whittaker was well regarded as a district judge, nothing about either the cases he heard or the way he handled them seems remarkable. We must look elsewhere for explanation of his ascent in the federal judiciary.

APPEALS JUDGE

Federal circuit courts consider appeals from decisions of district judges, along with appeals from decisions of executive branch regulatory agencies. Circuit court rulings govern the conduct of all district judges in the circuit. Thus circuit decisions have an impact going far beyond the parties concerned about an individual case. The Eighth Circuit Court of Appeals, on which Whittaker served, heard cases from district courts of seven states in a swath down the Midwest: Minnesota, Iowa, North Dakota, South Dakota, Nebraska, Missouri, and Arkansas.

The Eisenhower administration used approximately the same standards for appointments to appeals courts as to district courts. Although standards were the same, they made Whittaker a much stronger candidate for an appeals bench that he had been for a district bench.

In 1955 when a vacancy occurred in the Eighth Circuit Court of Appeals, about twenty-five percent of all federal judges were Republican appointees. Given Eisenhower's preference to promote sitting judges rather than recruit from outside, the pool of Republican district judges in the Eighth Circuit yielded five candidates.

Swift justice was another priority of the Eisenhower administration. Attorney General Brownell publicly warned that the backlog of district cases could worsen from annoyance into a cause for national shame.[43] The Justice Department was well aware of District Judge Whittaker's industrious clearing of the backlog he inherited and his zeal for finishing new cases within six months of their filing.

By strong tradition, fueled partly by the fact that about half the Eighth Circuit's cases originated in Missouri, one member of the appeals court was a Missourian. U.S. Senate Judiciary Committee member Hennings (D–MO) pointedly reminded President Eisenhower about that tradition when the vacancy arose upon the death of Missouri's member, and the geographic angle also received news media mention. Whittaker was the only Eisenhower appointee among the federal judiciary in Missouri. Moreover, having recently passed inspection by Republican politicians, the American Bar Association, the FBI, and the U.S. Senate, Whittaker was known to be viewed favorably by groups with power to thwart judicial nominations. In addition, Whittaker knew the Justice Department had collected a file of favorable newspaper comment about his performance.

Whittaker was such an inevitable candidate for an appeals court vacancy that Attorney General Brownell had even discussed the possibility of promotion when interviewing him for the district court position. Nonetheless Whittaker later expressed surprise at being selected as an appeals judge, saying the public learned about it before he did.[44] His recollection is unlikely to be literally true; announcing such an appointment to the public before obtaining the nominee's consent is politically implausible. At the time Whittaker told news reporters, "While I did not seek the promotion and was in no sense a candidate for it, I recognized it to be a great honor." He acknowledged awareness of "rumors" about the promotion but flatly asserted, "I must say that this comes to me as a bolt out of the blue."[45]

In the spring of 1956 President Eisenhower sent the formal nomination to the U.S. Senate, where Whittaker won easy approval.

From his experiences as a lawyer, Whittaker had a good idea of what he wanted to do as an appeals judge. "I have had my share of troubles with the courts," he told a bar association gathering.

> Often . . . when pressing a determinative mixed question of law and fact upon the trial judge, he would decline to go deeply into the matter saying, off the record, that the question was really beyond his competence, and, anyway, it would have to be determined by the supreme court of the state. But, on the record, he simply ruled against me.
>
> Then on appeal the appellate court would often . . . say . . . : "Great deference is to be paid to the ruling of the trial judge, and he is not to be convicted"—note the word—"of error in the absence of a clear and strong showing by appellant, upon whom the burden rests." And the court would then simply affirm the judgment. . . .
>
> The result was that the "buck" was passed from the one to the other and back again and fumbled at both places, and no real, considered judgment was ever given to the determinative question in the case.[46]

Clearly, appeals judge Whittaker intended to settle questions of law rather than sidestep them.

"I am moving up to the court of appeals with mixed emotions," he said. "I will miss the more active role of a district judge."[47] His expectation proved correct. The court clerk recalled how Whittaker had thrived on the hurly-burly of meetings with lawyers, courtroom action, and speculating about the thinking of jurors. In contrast, Eighth Circuit duties were quiet and contemplative.[48] "I was somewhat withdrawn from contact with people," Whittaker later reminisced. "There was lots of writing, investigating—a rather drab existence."[49] Another judge who served on the appeals court described it as "particularly fascinating, if one is inclined to be studious and likes a somewhat secluded life."[50] A district judge who refused promotion to an appeals bench declared, "While it may well be true that the highest *office* for a judge is to sit in judgment on other judges' errors, it is perhaps a more challenging *task* to seek, from minute to minute, to avoid one's own errors. And the zest of that task is enhanced by the necessity of reacting orally, instead of after the reflection permitted under the appellate judge's uninterrupted schedule of reading and writing."[51]

Whittaker kept his office in Kansas City and commuted to St. Louis, where appeals cases were heard four times a year. He was so productive in opinion writing that he became embarrassed, fearing that his elderly judicial colleagues might think he was trying to advertise his abilities.[52] Nonetheless, Whittaker appeared to get along well with fellow members of the court. They rarely dissented from opinions he wrote, and only once did he dissent from an appeals court opinion written by someone else. His clarity in opinions and his industriousness at clearing out a backlog of cases impressed the Justice Department.

As on the district court, Whittaker continued to limit contributions from his staff, preferring to devote his time to many tasks that other judges delegated to assistants. He not only did much routine research but refused to use reports from staff without first double-checking them himself. Still, Whittaker's workload lifted. One reason was that he did not run the appeals court; the Chief Judge did. Thus, for example, Whittaker could not attack the case backlog as vigorously as he did on the district court; on the appeals court he did not have authority to do so. He took part in only three or four appeals cases per month, giving him plenty of free time to sit as a supplemental judge in occasional district court cases.

Apparently a brief change for the better in Whittaker's chronic depression occurred when he became a judge on the Eighth Circuit Court of Appeals. His clerk recalled motoring with him through Iowa as summer waned. As the Cadillac's tires rolled across the miles, Whittaker mused that until now he had always needed to push hard to advance himself, but at long last the strain had eased and he could let up.[53] In retrospect Whittaker himself publicly described the job as "a very quiet and comfortable position."[54] The respite he felt from pressure ended with his appointment to the Supreme Court.

Chapter 4

Supreme Court Life

When Eisenhower chose Whittaker for the Supreme Court, Justice Felix Frankfurter quipped that the judge from Missouri's Western District arrived at the Supreme Court faster than a case could arrive from there.[1]

The Supreme Court headed by Chief Justice Earl Warren was one of the most controversial, with high-profile decisions affecting racial segregation laws, state-sponsored religious services, voter rights, alleged communist subversion, and other matters resonating with growing social unrest that exploded in the 1960s.

Daily headlines and speeches praised or denounced Chief Justice Warren, Justice William O. Douglas, Justice William Brennan, and Justice Hugo Black. An appointment to the Supreme Court is never treated as trivial, and many politically powerful groups and individuals felt they had much to lose or gain from President Eisenhower's 1957 choice to fill a Supreme Court vacancy.

APPOINTMENT

When called upon to appoint a chief justice, President Eisenhower went outside the federal judiciary and chose Earl Warren. The California governor had been the Republican vice presidential nominee in 1948 and was considered "sound" among conservatives. As chief justice he disappointed their expectations, to say the least. Eisenhower told more than one person that his biggest mistake was the Warren selection.[2] The president did not want to repeat such an error.

One reason Eisenhower now preferred to elevate lower ranking judges to the Supreme Court was the paper trail they left behind in their case decisions.[3] In theory these written opinions would reveal both the judicial philosophy and political leanings of potential Supreme Court nominees. This theory did not work with Whittaker. For a half century scholars have examined his district and appeals court opinions without finding the kind of information sought by the Eisenhower administration. Although Whittaker prided himself on logical presentations of fact and law, legal scholars often have difficulty understanding his thinking. Said one, "None of the decisions he rendered in the lower federal courts lend themselves to facile extrapolation."[4] His lower court opinions show him simply to be a legal technocrat with a businessman's general world view. In other words, his opinions indicated he was a Republican lawyer, a fact well known by the time Whittaker became a Supreme Court candidate.

Justice Douglas had a simple theory on how Whittaker became a colleague: "Whittaker of Kansas City was a protégé of Roy Roberts of the Kansas City *Star*. Roy, strong in Republican circles, got Charlie named to the District Court. In a year he got him named to the Court of Appeals. Hardly a third year had passed when Roy got him named to our Court."[5]

Although Roberts was always the "prime suspect" promoting Whittaker's career, during Whittaker's lifetime his godson reportedly maintained that Whittaker said the most influential person behind the Supreme Court nomination was a vice president of Kansas City's Commerce Trust Company, a friend named Arthur Eisenhower,[6] whose brother was president of an even larger enterprise headquartered in the White House.

Using a baseball metaphor to describe his judicial appointments, Whittaker said, "I got on; and, with the support of a good team, was enabled to touch three bases in three years."[7] Here Whittaker seemed to confirm that a coordinated effort by an organized group was responsible for all three of his judgeships. In Whittaker's rise to the Supreme Court, however, he probably benefitted as much from luck of circumstance as from power of friends.

Eisenhower considered judges from appeals courts to be ideal candidates for elevation to the Supreme Court, and Whittaker was one of the few Republican appeals judges. Moreover, just as powerful groups and individuals had asserted Missouri's claim to a seat on the Eighth Circuit, the same types of political forces noted that the Supreme Court lacked a member from the great region of middle America, between the borders of Ohio and California. Whittaker himself recognized the importance of his geographical origins.[8] In addition, given the intense political controversy surrounding the Supreme Court, someone who had recently passed close scrutiny from all groups interested in judicial appointments would have a clear edge. Attorney General Brownell said that endorsements sweeping across the political spectrum for Whittaker surpassed anything Brownell had seen for any other judge. When Justice Stanley F. Reed's retirement from the Supreme Court became known at the start of February 1957, news media speculation instantly recognized Whittaker's position of strength to become Reed's successor. Whittaker recognized his position as well.[9]

So did members of the Supreme Court. The previous autumn a young lawyer from Missouri had applied for a Supreme Court clerk position. Chief Justice Earl Warren knew that Reed would be leaving, and Warren stalled action on the Missouri lawyer's application, knowing that the same state might furnish Reed's successor, and apparently thinking that a clerk from Missouri might be a nice welcoming touch. Indeed, upon meeting Whittaker, Warren asked if he needed a law clerk, because Warren had one available from the Show-Me state.[10]

Eisenhower formally nominated Whittaker on March 1, 1957. Less than three weeks later the Senate confirmed by a simple voice vote. Considering battles endured by some nominees in later eras, Eisenhower demonstrated political shrewdness by choosing someone who had already been approved twice in recent years for other federal judgeships.

The White House announcement of his nomination was highly informal compared to such occasions in subsequent times. Apparently only five news reporters bothered to attend. In the relaxed atmosphere Whittaker enjoyed a leisurely cigarette. "I am almost rendered numb," Whittaker said. "I was just stunned. I had no indication. I had heard rumors that I might be appointed, but there was no reason to take them seriously."[11]

A month after he started his new job Whittaker decided he had made a mistake in accepting it.[12] His dissatisfaction would worsen.

METHOD OF WORK

As Whittaker began his Supreme Court duties, a reporter asked what his goal would be. Whittaker replied, "The Biblical goal—love man, deal justly, and walk humbly."[13]

Whittaker apparently referred to the King James Version of Micah 6:8, which speaks not of loving man but of loving mercy. Although we know that he was not necessarily unfeeling about the human impact of decisions (demonstrated in cases ranging from the chicken catchers up to capital offenses), a Supreme Court clerk found that Whittaker turned away from any human consequences he saw and would listen only to arguments relying upon interactions of legalities.[14] Justice John M. Harlan agreed: Whittaker "always strove against yielding up a sound legal conclusion to the compassionate circumstances of a particular case."[15]

After Whittaker had been on the Supreme Court one year, a kindly skeptic of his work noted that the justice had no discernable philosophy about constitutional principles involved in cases, and instead concentrated on sometimes minor differences in facts: "Whittaker's atomic approach to the cases has its advantages. It gives a freshman Justice time to get his bearings, to free himself from whatever elements of his past may have limited his vision, and to let his older colleagues vie with each other in promoting the mature philosophies they have come to live—and adjudicate—by."[16] With passing years, this generous interpretation faded as Whittaker's approach showed no change. A harsher critic later said, "None of his opinions seem to offer any new insight into the problem under analysis. His style and thinking were pedestrian. . . . He never offered any intellectual justification for his position."[17]

At the Court building Whittaker labored day and night in a three-room suite. One room served as his chambers, another as his secretary's work station, and the other was a law library where his two clerks had their desks and typewriters. As always, Whittaker was reluctant to accept their help.

Yet he complained that justices had too much to do, and that the quality of their work suffered because a day lacked enough hours.[18] Not all colleagues agreed. William O. Douglas claimed, "The job of an Associate Justice took four days a week. The problem was what to do with the other days."[19] On national television Douglas claimed the pace was so easily within his capability that he needed no help from clerks.[20] And during Whittaker's tenure Douglas used only one law clerk, while other justices used two or three.[21] (Of course Douglas may have been posturing to exaggerate his proficiency; after his staff finished the break they took to watch the program, they remained at work until 1:00 A.M. clearing the day's tasks.[22])

Whittaker's perception of the workload probably differed from his colleagues' perception for several reasons. His refusal to delegate work to subordinates increased the hours he labored. Also, having no judicial philosophy increased his toil. Each of his colleagues had a basic philosophy of what the Constitution was intended to accomplish. Such a feeling for the Constitution's intent expedited their work, as they looked to see whether aspects of a particular case coincided with the Constitution's purpose. Whittaker's colleagues might be able to tell at a glance how a case should be decided, and assign their clerks the task of finding rules and precedents supporting the decision. Whittaker had no such feel for cases. He examined facts of each case and provisions of the Constitution mechanically, almost attempting to use mathematical rules of formal logic to reach a decision. "If these twenty-seven facts relate to eleven different provisions of the Constitution (three of which in turn affect one another), how does all this interplay inevitably cause the plaintiff or defendant to prevail?" In such research he did not know what he was looking for, so he could not assign the task to subordinates.

That research must have been intellectually dissatisfying, as he reached no conclusions that would guide his understanding of other cases. He started from square one in every case rather than building upon a foundation of knowledge. Whittaker tried to view a painting by examining it with a microscope rather than standing back, as his Supreme Court colleagues did, and viewing the canvas as a whole. The understanding gained by Whittaker's approach might interest specialists in the technology of painting, but missed the point of what the painting is all about.

"It scared him to death," said one of his sons. "No question he was intimidated" by the great justices with whom he served.[23] If indeed Whittaker was awed by his colleagues' intellect, much of his awe must have derived from amazement that other justices discovered law so handily. To Whittaker their facile discoveries must have looked like magic, but his associates just approached the task from a different perspective than he did. Years earlier Chief Justice Charles Evans Hughes declared, "At the constitutional level where we work, ninety percent of any decision is emotional. The rational part of us supplies the reasons for supporting our predilections."[24] When writing opinions Harlan Fiske Stone would make a statement followed by a blank, with instructions for a clerk to find precedents supporting the statement.[25] Whittaker was not ignorant, and he had good grasp of the law's mechanics. But he was in the position of an expert automobile mechanic being asked to design a road system. He possessed tremendous knowledge that did him no good on the Supreme Court, and he must have been devastated to have so much trouble doing what his coworkers did with comparative ease.

One result was that he put in much longer hours than his colleagues did. Rather than trust a chauffeur, Whittaker weaved his own way through rush hour traffic in a maroon Cadillac. Although his office day began at the civilized hour of 9:00 A.M., he took less than a half hour for lunch and continued working at the Court building past 6:30 P.M. Occasionally he glimpsed Kansas City friends but often the pace was too hectic to renew old friendships. "Al Hillix of Kansas City called me one Friday morning at 10:40, but I was on my way to the regular court conference and I couldn't see him. Then one day recently I saw Jack Gage in the courtroom and dispatched a note to him asking him to drop around when court adjourned for the day, but he left before the note could be delivered."[26] One can almost hear the plaintive voice of a prisoner, able to see familiar faces from a cell window but unable to communicate. After arriving home in fashionable Spring Valley, Whittaker would continue working into the wee hours of the next morning. Puffing a filter-tip cigarette Whittaker told a reporter, "The volume and pressure of the work necessarily occupy me every day until midnight."[27] He expected his staff to join him at the Court on Saturdays, and he put in a full day of work at home on Sundays. During the Court's summer recess Whittaker studied upcoming cases. He complained about being unable to find time to think about them.[28] A reporter who spent an evening at the Whittaker home later said, "It was evident that something was troubling the justice. He was glum and preoccupied."[29]

In addition to work pressures, Supreme Court Justice Whittaker was plagued by loneliness. Even as a district judge, because Whittaker's life focused so tightly on law, most of his acquaintances had lawyer connections limiting the contact he could have with them as a judge. A Watson Ess attorney recalled Whittaker's wistful visits to the firm, with the judge longing for the old comradery with colleagues, but always having to hold back lest he stray into topics routine for law office gossip but now improper for him to discuss. Friendships with Watson Ess attorneys and clients began to wilt and fade.[30] Had his life been broader he would have had many friendships unaffected by his judicial status. One observer noted that social pleasures were virtually an oxymoron for Whittaker.[31] His concentration on law now left fewer and fewer persons with whom he could unburden himself.

By virtue of his office he was one of Washington's social elite, but he did not mix comfortably with the Eastern governmental aristocracy. His pangs were so acute that they even received a rare public mention when the *Kansas City Star* spoke of "the frustrations and disappointments, the sense of loneliness and homesickness."[32] When he crossed paths with Attorney General Brownell, who had been crucial to Whittaker's Supreme Court appointment, Whittaker remarked, "Herb, I thought you were my friend."[33] Gossips may have repeated the comment as witty, but close associates would have recognized pathos. Soon after arrival in Washington he privately began describing his Court service as a "sentence"[34] to be endured, a phrase revealing not only displeasure but his expectation that he would leave the Court after a decent interval of service.

DUTIES

Upon becoming president of the Missouri Bar Association in 1953, Whittaker bragged that except for youthful farm labor, "Working for my law firm is the only job I've ever had."[35] Although his career as an attorney was distinguished, his exclusive concentration on that task also meant he brought one of the most narrow backgrounds possible to the Supreme Court. He had no experience in managing public affairs, had never taught in a college, had never held a sales job requiring him to satisfy customers across the counter. He was like a studious monk suddenly summoned to the Vatican to serve as a cardinal overseeing a vast department of the church. Personal qualities that had served him so well in the past would now hinder his ability to perform his new assignment.

Justice Felix Frankfurter: " 'Judicial service' tells nothing that is relevant about the qualifications for the functions exercised by the Supreme Court. . . . The Supreme Court is a very special kind of court. 'Judicial service' as such has no significant relation to the kinds of litigation that come before the Supreme

Court."[36] "Judicial experience as such is not a qualification nor a desideratum for the Court's work; the problems which predominantly come before the supreme bench are of a different order from the staple business of other courts."[37] Frankfurter added, "Correlation between prior judicial experience and fitness for the functions of the Supreme Court is zero."[38] Justice Douglas agreed: "There is a popular impression that there are criteria, based on experience, that qualify some to sit on the Court more than others. A man prominent in bar association activities or a judge of a state or federal court is often thought to have special qualifications to be a Justice of the Supreme Court. Actually no prior experience, however varied, supplies the elements."[39]

Whittaker's judicial task had always been to find legal rules that already existed, not devise new ones to cover difficult cases. Such an approach frustrated him on the Supreme Court. "Precedents for almost any proposition can be found," Whittaker said, "and questions presented are often so razor-sharp that they might be decided either way with almost equal support of precedent and reason."[40] Lacking a philosophy that could help him reach conclusions guided by a particular understanding of what the Constitution sought to accomplish, Whittaker continued his familiar work habit of trying to find answers in law books instead of within himself. He exhausted himself trying to find rules governing situations that would never have reached the Supreme Court if existing rules had been adequate.

Wherever possible, he sought to avoid constitutional issues and to base his decisions on statutes and previous court interpretations. This was not possible often enough to suit him.

Whittaker's approach to Supreme Court cases included close adherence to what various courts had already said about similar cases, a principle lawyers call "*stare decisis*." One of his law clerks particularly remembered Whittaker's belief that Eisenhower had noticed that trait and was relying on Whittaker to stay the course, thereby tempering any tendency for innovative Court decisions.[41] At the time a friend of Whittaker noted concerns that the Court's decisions relied "insufficiently on conventional legal authorities and reasoning." The friend said that Whittaker, in contrast, "is adept in the use of judicial decisions."[42] While serving on the Supreme Court Whittaker himself praised an old Eighth Circuit colleague in this way: "He has always rather strictly adhered to the tried and true standards of value in forming his judgments. He has not believed that the things which are time-honored are otherwise dishonored. He has not believed in change for the sake of change alone. Nor has he thought it to be the business of the courts to arouse the conscious [*sic*] of the people or seek to cause them to alter their institutions. Rather, he has thought it to be his duty to observe the rule of stare decisis, to respect the legislative processes, and rigidly to follow and enforce the law whether he thought it to be wise or not."[43]

Although even Supreme Court justices are supposed to have due regard for decisions of other courts, Whittaker misapplied that duty. One reason cases come to the Supreme Court is because of suspicion that other courts' decisions have been mistaken. His colleagues believed they were correcting mistakes and clarifying what the law had always been. Whittaker insisted that the Supreme Court was disregarding the law and thereby derelict in its duty when it overturned prior decisions. His stance confused the duties of a district judge with those of a Supreme Court justice. A district judge is normally bound by prior decisions of other courts, and failing to apply those decisions *would* be disregard of known law. Supreme Court justices, in contrast, use anomalies in decisions of other courts to search out elements of law that have not yet been discovered. The Supreme Court's announcement of those new elements clarifies the framework for future decisions by all other courts. Whittaker, however, misperceived his colleagues' fulfillment of a core responsibility as dereliction of duty.

One duty of Supreme Court justices gets little notice, and that is their duty to decide which cases to hear. Justice Douglas considered the task staggering and was amazed by Whittaker's zeal in examining all requests: "The increase in the total number of cases on the docket is due to the rapid rise in the number of petitions from those in prisons. . . . Where the Court had only 85 cases in forma pauperis in the 1938 Term, it had 1,255 in the 1960 Term." Douglas observed, "Not many of the cases [from prison inmates] on the Miscellaneous Docket are meritorious. On the average, less than four percent are taken. Processing them is at times more difficult than processing cases on the appellate docket, for they come on typewritten or handwritten papers. Justice Whittaker—always meticulous and precise—put a special effort into these cases, as well as those on printed records. His care in scrutinizing even the humblest petition was one indication of his dedication to evenhanded justice."[44] In a reminiscent mood Whittaker once recalled the many petitions he read from convicts requesting a Supreme Court hearing. "Most of us, particularly those of us who have had some experience with such matters, also know that most convicts, and particularly those who have been represented by appointed counsel, ascribe their predicament, in post-conviction proceedings, at least partially to 'incompetence of Counsel.' Applying the light of hindsight—and sometimes twisting the facts a bit—they are frequently able to make powerfully appealing arguments in support of those claims."[45]

On oral argument days the justices took their seats on the bench at noon and listened to counsel until 4:30, with a twenty-five minute break midway for lunch.[46] Whittaker felt oral arguments were vital. Justices liked to confer quietly on the bench during those arguments, and became dismayed when their conversations became known through observations by lip readers in the courtroom. Whittaker reported the justices then switched to sending notes to one another.[47]

Observers remember Whittaker paying close attention to oral arguments. "He listened intently to the arguments and frequently interrupted attorneys to ask questions putting complex legal situations on a more down-to-earth basis. His preface to such questions often was, 'you mean to tell me that—,' then he put the specific question."[48] A contemporary newspaper found the politeness of his questions worth noting.[49] One reporter said, "On the bench, Justice Whittaker has always given the impression of deep concentration. His questions were asked in a solemn tone."[50] A Court clerk noted that such questions were the key to Whittaker's use of oral arguments. He used give and take with attorneys to clarify issues he had studied in the case.

He took the same approach as an Eighth Circuit appeals judge. Despite emphasis on written analysis of cases, oral arguments were made before the Eighth Circuit panel and were an important factor in decisions. "I think a judge has the responsibility," Whittaker later said, "of patiently hearing the presentation of the facts, making sure he understands them precisely."

Whittaker felt oral arguments were a crucial element of advocacy. He once protested, "Some Courts apparently do not welcome oral arguments. . . . I have never known a judge, worthy of the name, who has not sought all possible light, or who did not welcome well composed and helpful arguments—but remember, they are not all of that kind. And one may well wonder whether those appellate courts which have abolished oral arguments of appeals—and even whether many trial courts which have abolished oral arguments of preliminary motions—would have done so if the arguments had been better and more helpful."[51]

His enthusiasm for oral argument may have come partly from his own mastery of the art. "Everybody recognized him as a very outstanding speaker," said a judge who listened to Whittaker in action. "He was very persuasive in oral arguments."[52]

RELATIONS WITH STAFF

While serving on the Supreme Court Whittaker publicly declared, "Productivity and effectiveness of individual judges in many instances would be substantially increased by providing them with more adequate professional and clerical staffs."[53]

Whittaker had small regard for the talents of his law clerks: "They are bright but immature and inexperienced. They stay only one year generally and sometimes two but when they leave [they] have just gotten enough savvy to be of any real help to you. So you are really running a training school."[54] He saw them as having the same relation to his work that an undergraduate teenaged assistant might have to the research of a mature distinguished professor. A clerk who worked under Whittaker described the experience as "reading and typing, reading and typing, reading and typing."[55]

Whittaker's occasional brusqueness inspired one assistant to avoid speaking to the justice without a mental rehearsal of points to be covered.[56] A law clerk occasionally found him "terribly tense."[57] The staff described Justice Whittaker as a private man who generally conversed with them only about official matters. As ever, Whittaker refused to trust his staff, taking on burdens of tasks that other justices automatically assigned to assistants.

He once read that Supreme Court opinions were produced by law clerks rather than the justices,[58] and the accusation had an untoward impact; he was determined that history's record would find that opinions attributed to him were his own work. His Supreme Court brethren routinely had law clerks prepare rough drafts of opinions, but Whittaker seldom allowed his clerks to do so, and never adopted the few drafts he permitted. Clerks found their literary efforts unwelcome.[59]

When Whittaker invited his two clerks to critique his opinion in *Byrd* v. *Blue Ridge*[60] they took him at his word. One clerk pointed out excessive length of sentences and a need to tighten the relation of facts to the legal principles Whittaker had used to reach the opinion's conclusion. Whittaker became so indignant about a staff member daring to proffer invited criticism that he threw the pages at the clerk, exclaiming, "If you think you can do better, take a crack at it." In protest over his outburst, Whittaker's secretary walked out of the office and went home for the day. The hapless clerks revised the opinion through much of the night. When Whittaker read it the next morning, he told them it was excellent and sent it to the printer. One victim said that was Whittaker's expiation.[61]

Whittaker described his law clerks as useful for tracking down data, summing up litigants' requests to hear cases, and performing routine tasks. His clerks also produced condensed versions of attorneys' briefs and case records. One clerk described toiling for hours past midnight. They had no comradery with Whittaker. His idea of a sociable visit was an infrequent invitation to come with him for a fast cafeteria sandwich at lunchtime on Saturdays.[62]

Yet his staff admired him. One clerk thought him a better attorney than any other justice. Whittaker, however, sometimes seemed oblivious to admirable qualities in his work. When a clerk told Whittaker that serving with him was a peak in the assistant's career, the justice acted surprised.[63]

RELATIONS WITH COLLEAGUES

"Our Constitution and laws," Whittaker declared, "embody many of the concepts of the divine laws, including the Ten Commandments, and prescribe the minimum standards of moral and social behavior."[64] Whittaker described service on the Supreme Court as "the most solemn quest for light that can proceed from the broodings of a human soul."[65] One historian declared, "In the entire history of the Supreme Court few members labored as intensely as he did and perhaps no one agonized as much as he did over every facet of a pending case."[66] While all his colleagues took their responsibilities seriously, none shared Whittaker's peculiarly religious approach to the task. When Justice Black genially inquired of the newcomer, "Well, how do you feel about being here as a justice?" Whittaker answered, "Mr. Justice, I am scared to death." Black assured Whittaker there was nothing to worry about, "You will find that these justices are all just boys grown tall."[67] A self-sacrificing cleric entering a boys' club—the portents were not favorable.

Although Kansas City lawyers and acquaintances were unaware of Whittaker having any modesty about his talents, one of his sons said Whittaker feared he did not measure up to other members of the Supreme Court, that he felt their depth of education and breadth of experience far exceeded his own.[68] An unnamed colleague on the Court agreed that Whittaker felt outclassed.[69] At a meeting of the American Bar Association, a law student asked Chief Justice Warren if he would pose for a snapshot with the student. The law student asked a nearby gentleman to take the picture, not recognizing the gentleman as Charles Whittaker, another member of the Supreme Court. The story was told in a humorous vein at the time, but illustrates how Whittaker was eclipsed by his colleagues, an experience that had to be painful.

Paradoxically, despite Whittaker's feelings of inferiority, his opinions and dissents sometimes had hectoring passages in which he lectured his senior colleagues about their duty, which he defined in terms of responsibilities that district judges had.[70] Rather than being evidence of self-confidence, perhaps such passages were defensive reactions to situations, where colleagues were *proclaiming* their stance and he was *defending* his. Here are examples from one decision:[71]

> Neither in the Supreme Court of Appeals of Virginia nor in his petition for certiorari . . . did petitioner challenge the judgment on the ground that it was obtained in violation of the Interstate Commerce Act. I therefore respectively submit that, under our rules and decisions, no such question is presented or open for consideration here. But even if the Court properly may proceed, as it has proceeded, to decide the case under that Act, and not at all on the constitutional grounds solely relied on by petitioner, I must say, with all deference, that the facts in this record do not show that petitioner was convicted of trespass in violation of that Act [i.e., his colleagues are violating the Court's own rules, and their decision disregards facts of the case].

> There is not a word of evidence that any carrier had any interest in or control over the lessee or its restaurant. Nor is there any suggestion in the record that the lease or the lessee's restaurant operations under it were anything other than bona fide and for a legitimate and private business

> purpose. Indeed, there is not a word of evidence in the record tending to show that any carrier even had any interest in or control over the lessor corporation that owned the building. In truth, the record does not even show the name of the carrier on which petitioner was traveling [i.e., other justices are not only disregarding facts in the record but taking notice of facts not in the record].
>
> "Use" of a private restaurant by a motor carrier as results from stopping and opening its buses in front of or near a restaurant does not make the restaurant a facility "operated or controlled by" the carrier. . . . There is no evidence of any agreement, express or implied, between the proprietor of this restaurant and any bus carrier. Instead, the undisputed evidence is that the restaurant was not in any way affiliated with or controlled by any bus carrier [i.e., his colleagues are disregarding not only facts but common sense].
>
> Since the Court's opinion does not explore the constitutional grounds relied on by petitioner, I refrain from intimating any views on those subjects [i.e., since other justices are derelict in their duty, Whittaker has no comment on what they should have done].

Although Whittaker was known to lecture his brethren about failure to follow procedures governing whether a case should be heard, he was willing to look past standard procedures in order to rule on an issue he cared about. When union organizers appealed conviction under an ordinance requiring a city permit before chatting about advantages of union membership at a gathering in a private home,[72] Justices Tom Clark and Felix Frankfurter favored dismissing the appeal because the convicted persons challenged the entire ordinance as unconstitutional instead of objecting to particular passages of the ordinance. Whittaker felt the principle of free speech at issue was important enough to justify disregarding procedural flaw in the appeal. He took the opposite stance when the issue was desegregation. The decision quoted from above, involving interstate bus passengers dining at a bus terminal restaurant,[73] concerned a city ordinance relating to segregation of a restaurant serving interstate bus passengers. Here Whittaker protested that the Court majority was considering whether the Interstate Commerce Act applied, even though that issue was not raised by counsel when asking for a Supreme Court hearing. By considering the Interstate Commerce Act, the Court was violating its own rules; and unlike the union organizer case, this time Whittaker felt the rules should be followed.

From another decision:[74]

> Like the two courts below, I think it may not fairly be said, on this record, that there is any evidence that the cooperative ever did "employ" its "members," or suffer or permit them to work *for it*. . . . Like the two courts

> below, I fail to see in this any element of employment by the cooperative of its members. . . . On the basis of the amply supported findings of the two courts below, it seems reasonably clear that the cooperative never did "employ" its "members," and . . . I think the judgment of the two courts below is consonant with the facts and the law and should be affirmed [i.e., the majority not only disregards facts, but those facts are well established by other courts, with those objective observers sustaining Whittaker's opinion].

And from yet another:[75]

> Until today, I have understood it to be the unquestioned law, as this Court has consistently held, that arbitrators are private judges chosen by the parties to decide particular matters specifically submitted [i.e., his colleagues are being inconsistent, obscuring the law instead of revealing it, as they needlessly reopen a well-settled matter].

Listing a string of U.S. Supreme Court cases, Whittaker declared,

> I believe that the Court today departs from the established principles announced in these decisions [i.e., his colleagues are not enforcing the rules but changing them].
>
> This is an entirely new and strange doctrine to me. I suggest, with deference, that it departs from both the contract of the parties and the controlling decisions of this Court. . . . The Court cites no legislative or judicial authority. . . . And I respectfully submit that today's decision cannot be squared with the statement of Judge, later Mr. Justice, Cardozo in *Marchant*. [Like an angry man shouting, "I'm not angry!" Whittaker tells his colleagues that they are not finding law but inventing it, lacking authority for what they do, being dictators disregarding long established rules.]
>
> Such was the question presented to the District Court and the Court of Appeals here. They found the jurisdictional facts, properly applied the settled law to those facts, and correctly decided the case. [In contrast to Whittaker's colleagues, who by implication of his language "incorrectly" decided the case.]

At one level in such excerpts Whittaker addresses facts and standard deference to precedent, but at another level in such passages Whittaker basically says, "It is written." Though labeled a technocrat, he had an almost mystical reverence for the authority of legal texts. Any conduct deviating from his understanding of those texts disturbed him, as any fundamentalist cleric would be disturbed by conduct deviating from holy texts. And any attempt to revise the text itself was blasphemy.

Although all justices tend to be forceful, Whittaker's "school marm" scolding cannot have promoted genial relations with his colleagues. Such passages imply that anyone who disagrees with him is wrong. A fuzzy line separates self-assurance from arrogance. As a practicing attorney, Whittaker was adamant that his particular understanding of the law was the only valid one. Lawyer colleagues recalled his typical declaration, "That's the law, sure as little green apples."[76] The same attitude is expressed in his Supreme Court opinions, but often with a twist implying that other justices are not only wrong but ignorant. Whittaker declared, "The practice of law is a deliberate science and must be recognized as such."[77] Like saying Earth is the third planet from the sun, Whittaker believed he simply stated scientific fact. And those who disagree are either fools or knaves.

With such rhetoric Whittaker declared the Supreme Court should be bound by precedent rather than be respectful of it. He treated law as if it were a fact of nature existing apart from humans who make it, as if statutes and court decisions expressed the same kind of truths expressed by the laws of chemistry or physics.

Ironically, after he left the Court, Whittaker seemingly admitted that its decisions could not always be guided by past rules, a tacit admission that decisions based on personal philosophies of governance could be as legitimate as the decisions he tried to reach by searching through rules that might apply to facts in a case. In 1963 he declared, "Determination of what Congress meant by the words it used in a statute is often difficult, even when applied to subjects that Congress had in mind, for the words used generally lend themselves to different meanings in the different settings to which they are applied."[78] In 1971 he said, "Many of the constitutional provisions, congressional laws and rules of decision were devised for other times and conditions." He called them "largely irrelevant, incomplete or vague when applied to many current problems. Statutes are not often clear and the court . . . must proceed to a decision upon its best understanding of the legislative will, or upon what it thinks would have been that will if Congress had thought about the matter." He added, "Our Constitution, too, designed for the ages, is in many respects vague—some say wisely vague and hence sufficiently elastic to adapt to the changing conditions and mores of advancing times. The Constitution does not interpret itself and that burden is on the Supreme Court."[79]

Even while on the Court, Whittaker occasionally acknowledged that truth. Speaking through a cloud of cigarette smoke, he told a reporter in 1960, "Service on the Supreme court is very different from service on any other court. . . . On this court you do the blazing yourself which the lower courts have to follow. It takes some time to adjust to this type of work."[80] Apparently so, as Whittaker never made the adjustment.

Whittaker's characterization of law as scientific endeavor reflected fashionable thinking in the 1920s when he attended law school. In that era law students were taught that law was a set of rules to be followed in a neutral process that reached right, fair, and appropriate outcomes. This concept was known as legal or judicial "formalism." A new approach began percolating out of law schools in the 1930s and 1940s in which proponents of legal "realism" criticized formalism. Those critics argued that law was not built upon neutral rules; instead judges first reached a conclusion that they wanted, followed by a search for justification from authorities in precedents and other legal writings. After Whittaker's lifetime an approach called "evolution" challenged the entire edifice of legal faith which he professed. Evolutionists contended that no decision was correct in itself; when a particular issue confronted various courts, they responded in different ways. Responses that society found useful would be reproduced in further decisions. Those that were useless or harmful would fail to reproduce, die out, and have no subsequent influence. Different expressions of law could thrive in different environments (jurisdictions). The law did not express perfection but simply consisted of whatever worked in a particular environment.

Although courts were becoming comfortable with judicial realism in the 1950s and 1960s, Whittaker left no evidence that he was even aware of this shift in thinking, let alone that he accepted it. He gave no impression that he read legal journals in which such matters were explored. His legal reading seemed limited to court decisions. Those primary sources are important, but their digestion in secondary sources is significant to anyone with curiosity about a subject. Whittaker seemingly lacked curiosity about the law. Rhetorically he disguised that lack by portraying himself as an objective scientist simply trying to establish facts. His portrayal failed to recognize that science is also based on theories, through which jumbles of facts are organized into meaningful patterns revealing truths deeper than the facts. A person who has studied the ways of science noted, "If one lacks the ability to come up with a good theory, and *a fortiori* if one wouldn't know what to do with such a theory if one did, it behooves one to debunk theory in general, and claim that the safe road to truth lies in the patient and unbiased accumulation of facts."[81] That approach sounds much like Whittaker's. In jargon of a later era, he might be characterized as a customer service representative, putting in extra shifts fixing one problem after another by applying rules from a procedure manual, but having no interest in how his employer sought to achieve the company's purported mission. That lack of interest would cripple Whittaker's ability to perform as he was promoted to higher and higher positions in the company.[82]

Formalism, realism, evolution, and other views of the law have practical impact. For example, Whittaker's dedication to formalism meant that he had to expend enormous amounts of energy searching through case opinions because he did not know what he was looking for. As he claimed to have no notion of how a case should be settled, everything could be relevant. If instead Whittaker had adopted judicial realism, his search would have been streamlined because he would only have to find precedents supporting the decision he had reached prior to consulting them. It was like having a box filled with pieces from nine jigsaw puzzles. Colleagues on the Supreme Court knew what picture they wanted and only searched for those pieces. Whittaker did not know what he wanted and was overwhelmed by the mass of material.

His adherence to formalism, too, may have contributed to frictions with colleagues on the high bench. They tended to use realism rather than formalism. Whittaker seemed to view their approach as evidence of bias in their decisions. He recognized that his brethren were intelligent, therefore if they did not reach the same (and sometimes politically conservative) decision that he reached by "objective" and "scientific" application of "neutral rules" to "facts," the explanation had to be bad faith. His public implications about this were so clear that outright statement was unnecessary. Other justices, however, simply took a more modern approach to decision-making.

While on the Court his complaints about his colleagues' lack of respect for precedents could not have endeared him to other justices but, as one of his clerks noted, Whittaker placed little value on persuading his brethren.[83] He was not a politician who attempted to bring fellow justices along with him. Instead he explained what he saw as the inevitable outcome if the facts and law of a case were properly understood. Because he believed his conclusion to be the only possible one that a knowledgeable and fair-minded person could reach, he became impatient with brethren who were too dense or perhaps too biased to agree with him.

Sometimes they became impatient with him. While in joint conference about *Baker* v. *Carr*[84] Frankfurter became indignant about Whittaker's stance. Upwards of five hours Frankfurter lectured legal expert Whittaker in front of the other justices, pulling books off shelves, quoting from them while eyeing Whittaker. "Felix really berated him," Black recalled.[85]

Douglas and Whittaker clashed publicly when delivering their oral opinions in *Inman* v. *Baltimore & Ohio Railroad*.[86] Whittaker satirized the workman's compensation claim of a crossing guard who was injured by a car after obeying the employer's instructions to stand with his back to oncoming road traffic in order to inspect passing trains. A Court onlooker described Douglas as "pale with anger" as he declared in open court, "It cannot be dismissed by this attempted humor. Those of us who have read the record, as I am sure only a few of us have, recognize that the watchman did not only have to direct traffic. It was like putting a man in an inherently unsafe place and making him juggle."[87] Members of the public who witnessed the scene realized Douglas was targeting Whittaker, but probably few recognized the cutting insult when Douglas implied that Whittaker's examination of facts had been inadequate. Whittaker's painstaking examination of facts was legendary among Court insiders. Douglas told the courtroom gathering that the case examined whether injured workers could have their cases heard by juries rather than judges, and said such a question was unsuited to the "rather smart-alecky things that have been said."[88] He immediately departed the courtroom in anger.

A federal judge who was a friend of Whittaker remarked, "I know that Douglas was very unkind to him. He was heard to say through the conference room doors, 'What can you expect from a country boy from Troy, Kansas, that graduated from the Kansas City School of Law?' This was really hard on Charley."[89]

Douglas became impatient with vacillations: "Whittaker would make up his mind on argument, only to be changed by Frankfurter the next day. In Conference, Whittaker would take one position when the Chief or Black spoke, change his mind when Frankfurter spoke, and change back again when some other Justice spoke."[90] Such changes did not mean Whittaker was susceptible to flattery, favors, promises, or threats. His mind changed back and forth as new aspects of facts and law were pointed out. Once he made up his mind, however, he was immovable. Justice Clark recalled a colleague who privately sought to change Whittaker's decision and failed, finding his manner ferocious in rejecting the alternative view.[91] Justice John M. Harlan spoke of "the earthy enthusiasms of an advocate" that Whittaker took to judicial conferences.[92] Justice Clark said, "He sought for the truth as he saw it and in our conferences fought for it with all his might."[93]

Whittaker's stubborn analysis of facts and law could sometimes persuade colleagues to join his stance on a case. In *Florida Lime & Avocado Growers* v. *Jacobsen*,[94] after oral discussion Whittaker faced opposition from seven justices. Upon reading his written dissent, however, six changed their minds and adopted his viewpoint, transforming his dissent into the Court's opinion.[95]

Whittaker almost duplicated that feat in *Federal Trade Commission* v. *Henry Broch*,[96] with his dissent convincing four colleagues to support his vote. In response, Douglas altered his preliminary argument for the majority and gained back one vote, preserving the original majority.[97] This incident illustrated one difference, among many, between Whittaker and Douglas. Douglas was willing to reshape his case to appeal to desires he discovered in his audience. Whittaker, reputedly the expert jury lawyer, would not do such a thing to persuade his Supreme Court audience. Once he revealed his stance, other justices could take it or leave it. If they hesitated to adopt his reasoning, he was content to have them think about it until they realized he was right. Both approaches to building a majority opinion were honorable, but Whittaker's inevitably had to be less successful.

Whittaker's concentration on facts and rules, and his apparent lack of any constitutional philosophy, made him a prime target for lobbying efforts by other justices. "In close cases," Justice Harlan recalled, "one could never feel that he was beyond persuasion."[98] He was perceived as "reachable" by all his brethren. No matter how exasperated they might get with him, they all recognized a common political benefit in getting along with Whittaker.

Despite professional clashes, Whittaker claimed to have cordial personal relationships with his colleagues. Hugo Black he described as "a great fellow, a fine, sound lawyer and a courtly Southern gentleman" while being a "hard working justice." Black's honesty and intellectual brilliance impressed Whittaker. He was personally friendly with William J. Brennan despite their professional disputes. Harold Burton's gentle and honest nature appealed to Whittaker. Felix Frankfurter's erudition and felicity with words gained admiration from Whittaker, who privately called Frankfurter's work unsurpassed, even by Brandeis and Holmes. Whittaker felt affinity with John Harlan, admiring his legal knowledge and finding qualities of saintliness in the New Yorker.[99]

Whittaker seemed to get along particularly well with Frankfurter, regarded as leader of the Court's conservative forces. A law clerk remembered the near-awe and devotion with which Whittaker regarded Frankfurter.[100] Douglas put a different spin on this attitude: "Whittaker was duck soup for Frankfurter."[101] In the *Florida Lime* case noted above, Frankfurter had drafted the original majority opinion. When one of Whittaker's clerks pointed out how the draft could be attacked, Whittaker initially hesitated to do so. Only after more nudging about points of law was he willing to prepare and circulate a dissent that eventually became the majority opinion. His deference to Frankfurter was so great that Whittaker considered remaining silent when he observed fatal errors in Frankfurter's argument against Whittaker's stance.

After he left the Supreme Court Whittaker delivered speeches generally interpreted as attacks on decisions of that tribunal. Chief Justice Warren sarcastically commented, "Charlie never could make up his mind about decisions until he left the Court."[102]

In "A Confusion of Tongues" Whittaker condemned rulings supporting New Deal understandings of congressional power to regulate commerce. As part of his argument he said that a farmer raising wheat as fodder for his cattle was obviously engaged in a local activity beyond the scope of federal intervention. Justice Douglas became livid and told Whittaker, "The decision you are using as a cudgel to beat the Court is *Wickard v. Filburn*, 317 U.S. 111. It was a unanimous decision, both Republican and Democratic appointees joining in it. . . . It's too bad you left the Court, for up here you would at least have a chance at the proper time to convince a majority of the Court that *Wickard v. Filburn* was wrongly decided. To do so you would have to change your mind. For I note you joined in opinions that cited *Wickard v. Filburn* with approval."[103]

Here Douglas zeroed in on one of Whittaker's basic judicial characteristics. Even though Whittaker believed the *Wickard* decision was wrong, as a member of the Court he refused to attack it, considering past decisions to be settled points of law that must be obeyed whether a Supreme Court justice liked them or not. Whittaker explicitly said that he felt obligated to abide by the Court's prior decisions.[104]

Taking an engineer's approach to law, he was offended by justices who took an artistic approach, who revealed law as a sculptor reveals an image from a block of stone. Master sculptors see inside the stone, using their tools to chip away what hides the image from observers of lesser vision. Whittaker saw only the rock of law being broken apart by fellow justices who discarded obscuring precedents as rubble. He saw his colleagues destroying law, not conserving it. That angered him.

Whittaker felt he had a duty to keep bad law in force even though he had the power to change it. Yet he also felt free, once he left the Supreme Court, to criticize past decisions now that he had no power to revise them. His virtual insistence that former decisions could not be changed, combined with criticism of those decisions, was a paradox hard for observers to understand. Whittaker's stance was also curious because his speeches criticizing past decisions of the Court clearly indicated his awareness that they were created by give-and-take debate among the justices. He knew those decisions were not handed down from a deity, but were constructed by fallible human beings. Yet he acted as though once a decision was rendered, it was unalterable—as if a conclusion reached by jurists long dead had to bind the living for eternity.

In "A Confusion of Tongues" Whittaker also asserted that the Constitution was intended to create a national government with limited power—enough to protect common interests of states but not enough to intrude on states' rights to govern themselves in differing ways. States, not the federal government, were intended to exercise "all general powers of government."[105] He contended that the proper way to modify this relationship, or any other element of the Constitution, was through amendment by Congress and the states rather than twisting of words by courts. "Whether we truly have kept faith with the Constitution in all respects and have heeded the warnings of our Founding Fathers to be vigilant in protecting our fundamental law against the pressures of erosion and usurpation, are matters which I will now undertake briefly to examine."[106]

"It cannot be, and indeed is not, any longer denied that there was in the 1930's a different kind of fidelity—if fidelity it was—to the meaning of some of the plain words in the Constitution by some than by others of us."[107] Here Whittaker went beyond a simple statement that differing understandings of the Constitution existed in the 1930s, but raised the possibility that a particular interpretation of the Constitution was the product of bad faith, infidelity by judges engaged in deceit. He became more explicit as he described views of "strict constructionists" who thought all three branches of the federal government misrepresented the Constitution's meaning in the 1930s in order to increase the power of President Franklin Roosevelt's administration. In defining what he meant by "strict constructionists," Whittaker ascribed to them the views he had advocated at the beginning of his speech. So we know that Whittaker was speaking for himself, and not just theoretically, as he proceeded to attack holdings of Supreme Court justices whose understanding of the Constitution differed from his.

He labeled such justices "liberal constructionists." Whittaker could have just as easily called them lax, indulgent, permissive, tolerant, reasonable, broad-minded, impartial, unconventional, or generous. His rhetoric was significant. Although a thesaurus might suggest "liberal" as a possible antonym to "strict," such a word was loaded with political meaning, referring to supporters of Presidents Roosevelt, Truman, Kennedy, and Johnson. Whittaker's rhetoric had already implied that justices who differed with him were unfaithful to the Constitution (careless or even disregarding about its provisions), which further implied they had violated their oaths to uphold the document. By calling such justices "liberal" Whittaker was giving them a political label as well as a dictionary one, and he was also implying that liberals deceitfully violated the Constitution. A high-ranking Washington notable who desired anonymity reported conversations in which Whittaker confided his exasperation with philosophical beliefs held by a majority of his brethren.[108]

In "A Confusion of Tongues" Whittaker declared, "Hardly anyone familiar with the subject denies that the meaning and effect of the commerce clause of our Constitution has actually been changed in substantial particulars" by "liberal constructionists."[109] The commerce clause[110] gives Congress power to regulate interstate commerce. Whittaker approved of the construction given to that clause before the 1930s. Before then, the clause was considered to cover only activity that crossed state lines directly (a butcher ordering a truckload of chickens from a producer across the state line). That principle was upheld in *Schechter Poultry Corporation* v. *United States*,[111] one of the most famous cases in constitutional law. Whittaker presented his understanding of the case in some detail. Although he noted that the case struck down a key piece of New Deal legislation (the National Industrial Recovery Act) his analysis concentrated on the question of federal meddling with local business people.

Whittaker was silent about *Schechter*'s greatest issue: whether private industry cartels could establish regulations that government could force business people to obey. A society in which industry codes are developed by corporation executives and enforced by government is a fascist society. In the early 1930s fascism did not have the repellant reputation it earned over the next decade, and many Americans believed that a fascist organization of the economy could end the Great Depression. The key issue in *Schechter* was whether fascism was constitutional. The Supreme Court said no, and its holding destroyed the industrial code structure developed under the New Deal's National Industrial Recovery Act. Whittaker's lengthy explanation of issues in *Schechter* was oblivious to the greatest one.

He then went on to analyze another case classic to the history of both the New Deal and the Constitution, *National Labor Relations Board* v. *Jones & Laughlin Steel Corporation.*[112] This case asked whether the commerce clause allowed the federal government to set wages and working conditions if they touched interstate commerce only indirectly—for example, if worker disgruntlement about wages in a local business could lead to a strike affecting interstate commerce. The Supreme Court decided yes. Whittaker noted, however, that the Court divided five to four on the question. He ascribed the decision to political and economic expediency. He said the justices feared that Congress might approve President Roosevelt's plan to increase the size of the Supreme Court, allowing him to name enough justices to ensure approval of New Deal programs in future cases.[113] "Roosevelt tried to pack the court with men who thought as he thought," Whittaker declared on another occasion, "but, fortunately, Congress wouldn't let him."[114] In "A Confusion of Tongues" Whittaker also said the justices decided that the potential benefit of the New Deal law in question (the National Labor Relations Act) outweighed fidelity to the Constitution.

Despite his aversion to the doctrine of *Jones & Laughlin*, Whittaker embraced its spirit in 1967 as a constitutional basis for a federal anti-riot law, with Whittaker defining interstate travel to incite riot as interstate commerce.[115]

After saying the *Jones & Laughlin* doctrine was founded on personal cowardice and intellectual dishonesty, Whittaker went on to criticize its application in *Wickard* v. *Filburn*[116] "to sustain a federal statute imposing criminal penalties upon a farmer for growing wheat on his own farm that was fed on the same farm to his own livestock. . . . It would be difficult to imagine an activity more completely local than that."[117]

Whittaker concluded by declaring that his speech took no stand on whether New Deal programs were necessary or beneficial. "Our great national programs regulating business, labor, agriculture, education, social welfare, civil rights and other matters could not have existed under the pre–1937 conceptions of Congress's power under the commerce clause."[118] His stance was simply that the current doctrine violated the Constitution, making all those programs illegal.

Summing up, he declared that such programs had become so necessary to the orderly function of American society that they must now be retained regardless of constitutionality. His final argument, that expediency should take precedence over legality, was a stance that he had attacked throughout his speech. Thus his speech illustrated Whittaker's ability to both condemn and embrace the same policy.

Although the speech denounced what Whittaker saw as innovative interpretation of the Constitution, in a later interview he acknowledged, "Changes in our society quite necessarily are likely to compel different interpretations of constitutional provisions in their applications to these changed conditions."[119] Once again, he could both condemn and embrace the same policy.

"A Confusion of Tongues" is one of Whittaker's most puzzling literary productions. Although he portrayed it as simply a history of the commerce clause, Whittaker vigorously attacked the Supreme Court's New Deal rulings. He had to realize that such a critique would receive publicity because of the author's status as a former Supreme Court justice. And he had to know that attention would be all the greater since in 1965 the Court still included justices appointed by President Roosevelt, whose protégé Lyndon Johnson was attempting to complete Roosevelt's agenda through the Great Society legislative program. Whittaker's speech hardly broke new ground in legal scholarship, and indeed simply restated well-known arguments of New Deal opponents, arguments given a sharp twist as he virtually said that justices who ruled in favor of New Deal programs had violated their oaths of office. It is difficult to imagine what Whittaker expected to achieve beyond promoting rancor in the Court and giving ammunition to political opponents of the Great Society.

MODE OF JUDICIAL EXPRESSION

A friend recalled, "Charlie always was interested in oratory and especially oratory of the court room variety."[120] For decades James A. Reed was a dean of Kansas City courtroom oratory. Reed was also a prominent Democrat, eventually becoming a U.S. senator. Although history remembers Whittaker as an intense workaholic, contemporaries spoke of his fine dry humor. A friend recalled, "One of his best imitations is of the Senator announcing himself ready for trial."[121]

In 1960 Whittaker reminisced about his dealings with Reed:

> Business was proceeding routinely until a particular case was called and there was no answer for the defendant. A defendant without counsel, I thought—a predicament that concerned me then and that has never ceased to be a torment. With some agitation, the court asked a second time "who represents the defendant?" Presently there entered the courtroom a tall, broad shouldered, erect and graceful man, graying at the temples, who, as

> he proudly approached the bench, announced: "Your honor, *I* represent the defendant."... His magnificent presence and the manner of his announcement left no doubt in my mind that the defendant was really represented. This man I was to come to know as James A. Reed....
>
> Indelibly fixed in my mind is his closing argument to the jury in a certain bodily injury case. . . . "Back in the little town from which we came, Louis Jones and I were schoolmates, we laughed and played together, we hung our clothes on the same tree and swam in the same old swimming hole, a finer physical specimen I had never seen. But as we look at him now, torn to shreds by the negligent act of this defendant, can you wonder that my heart cries for him in sympathetic pain?" Feeling that this argument was designed to appeal more to the passions and prejudices of the jury than to the controverted issue of negligence—for we were not denying he had lost a leg—I made an objection upon that ground. And after it was overruled, improperly I thought, came this retort. "Counsel, who so heatedly objects to what I have to say on behalf of my old friend Louis Jones, must be actuated by the same motives as spurred the woman of bad repute to object to a reference to virtue in her presence because it hurt to the core."...
>
> His tongue was very versatile, and depending on the mood, which he seemed able to create at will, it could soothe like slumber or swing like a sword.[122]

In addition to courtroom oratory, Whittaker also was interested in beautiful language contained in court opinions. "He was particularly intrigued by the language of Judge Trimble in the case of Meredith v. Krauthoff. . . . As a young lawyer, he memorized a great portion of that opinion and used to recite it with fine oratorical effect and considerable emotion."[123] That case involved sufferings of a prominent Kansas City lawyer who was rejected by "better society," a theme suggesting that Whittaker's fascination went beyond the opinion's literary merit.

Passages such as those Whittaker learned by heart told a melodramatic story of a man deeply in love with a wife who told him she loved another. Her mother lived with the star-crossed couple and supported her daughter's love for the other man of higher social standing, to whom the daughter had once been engaged (they had quarreled, and she married while on the rebound). The affections and well being of a young son were caught in the middle, and that was the issue Judge Francis H. Trimble was called upon to decide:

> Herein we are asked to exercise our jurisdiction as a court of chancery in the adjudication of an exceedingly difficult, embarrassing, and important question, one that affects the most sacred feelings and reaches the profoundest depths of the human heart—which of two separated parents shall be awarded the custody of their child. It is an unwelcome task, fraught with

> heavy responsibility. In its performance, however careful and sympathetic we may be, we must walk with heavy tread into the very sanctum sanctorum of parental affection, and, laying hands upon the jewel there enshrined, make such disposition of it as, in our finite wisdom, its best interest may seem to require. It is a painful duty, from which every well-regulated mind must shrink, since its performance has to do, not only with the tender relations of parent and child, but involves the future course of a human life, and perhaps may have an influence upon the destiny of an immortal soul. One thought, however, affords some slight comfort, and that is that we are in no way responsible for the causes which have unhappily brought about the situation with which we are confronted. We are called upon to act, the heavy obligation is laid upon us, and we have no choice but to meet it. Let those whose hearts are wrung remember this when, in their pain and tears, they realize the effect of this decree.[124]

Preference for Emotionless Factual Expression

Despite Whittaker's enjoyment of flowery nineteenth-century-style oratory, he rejected such a style in his own judicial writing.

As a model for his own writing, Whittaker preferred that of Justice Louis D. Brandeis. Whittaker's praise of Brandeis could be converted to autobiographical comment. "His paramount dedication," Whittaker said,

> was to simple truth—the uncolored facts. While the doubts of many were philosophic, his were always scientific. "I have no general philosophy," he said. "All my life I have thought only in connection with the facts that came before me. . . . We need not so much to reason as to see and understand the facts and conditions." He often stated his belief that . . . an accurate determination of the facts resolve[s] the dispute.
>
> . . . He used his great powers of concentration in accurately ascertaining, marshalling, and orderly stating the facts of the case, to which he then applied, but always quite succinctly, his view of the controlling law. This method of presentation is nowhere better illustrated than in his brief in support of an Oregon statute fixing a ten-hour day for women wage earners. Ninety-seven pages were devoted to the facts, and their effects upon those workers, and only three pages were devoted to the law. This approach b[e]came known as the "Brandeis Brief" and had a profound influence on the method of presenting cases—particularly those involving social legislation.
>
> . . . His opinions were presented in a simple, straight-forward, and lucid style, without rhetorical flourish.[125]

The typical Whittaker court opinion is bland and passionless, setting up an equation of fact and law, and reporting the answer.

One clerk noted how writing was a wincing effort for Whittaker as he struggled to settle an issue by perusing one legal volume after another.[126] He composed fewer majority opinions than any other justice of his era, only eight in his five years on the Court.[127] Whittaker told associates that he was not writing on paper but instead chiseling words into stone for the ages.[128] He said the same to a reporter, "It takes some time . . . to get over becoming awed by the tremendous importance of every word written or spoken."[129]

Whittaker declared:

> When the task of preparing a proposed opinion for the Court has . . . been assigned to a particular Justice, that Justice must make a more detailed and concentrated study of the records and briefs than in the usual case, he has been able to do before, and with the assistance of his two law clerks, must do such further research as he thinks necessary, and when thus fully saturated with the case, he must prepare the proposed opinion. In most cases reaching that Court, this task, because of the complexities and importance of the cases, is a most painstaking and arduous one.[130]

(That quotation is a good example of Whittaker's written prose, sounding better if read aloud. That effect may exist because his written opinions evolved from oral presentations that he dictated to a secretary.)

When concentrating on procedural matters, Whittaker's opinions sometimes lack appreciation for ambiguities in substantive issues that troubled his brethren on the Court. Nor does his typical opinion show awareness of stakes involved in deciding a case one way or the other, stakes that inspired passionate eloquence from justices like Warren, Douglas, and Brennan. Whittaker's opinions may have resulted from intense study and thinking, but their flatness would allow them to be announced by a mechanical computer voice without losing any meaning. This does not mean Whittaker cared any less about issues than his colleagues did, but he strove to eliminate personal feeling from his legal prose. "What I miss most in Justice Whittaker's" writing, said one critic, "is any kind of agony. There doesn't seem to be any wrestling with dilemmas."[131]

The mechanical quality of his opinions was emphasized by convoluted passages in which even a knowledgeable reader could become lost. One of his clerks found the decisions overstuffed, a style more appropriate to fine details covered at the district court level than the broad principles of guidance explored by the supreme bench. Another clerk, however, saw that approach as a strength making the opinions more useful to other judges.[132]

A scholar praised Whittaker's lower court writings: "His opinions were models of orderliness, of the use of direct, exact and concise language, of logical, careful and persuasive reasoning, of the expert analysis and application of legal authorities. They were readable and to the point. There could be no doubt as to what the court had held. In short, he showed himself to be a top-flight judicial craftsman."[133]

Whittaker himself praised such style in the opinions of his appeals court colleague Judge John B. Sanborn: "Any examination of them will disclose their clarity and conciseness and that such is largely due to their simple words and structure."[134]

In contrast, Whittaker's Supreme Court opinions could become convoluted:

> Thus, even if we assume that respondent has a "status" within the meaning of 405 (a), that section by its own terms does not apply to situations "otherwise specifically provided" for in the Act. Section 241 (a) (1) specifically provides for the deportation of an alien who "at the time of entry was . . . excludable by the law existing at [that] time," and 241 (a) (4) specifically provides for the deportation of an alien who "at any time after entry" has been convicted of two crimes involving moral turpitude. And 241 (d) makes 241 (a) (1) and 241 (a) (4) applicable to all aliens covered thereby, "notwithstanding (1) that any such alien entered the United States prior to the date of enactment of this Act, or (2) that the facts, by reason of which any such alien belongs to any of the classes enumerated in subsection (a), occurred prior to the date of enactment of this Act." It seems to us indisputable, therefore, that Congress was legislating retrospectively, as it may do, to cover offenses of the kind here involved. This case is, therefore, "otherwise specifically provided" for within the meaning of 405 (a). The Court of Appeals was in error in holding to the contrary, and its judgment is Reversed.[135]

Compare the literary style of Justice Black in the same case:

> What is being done to these respondents seems to me to be the precise evil the ex post facto clause was designed to prevent. Both respondents are ordered deported for offenses they committed long ago—one in 1925 and the other in 1936. Long before the 1952 Act reached back to add deportation as one of the legal consequences of their offenses both paid the price society then exacted for their misconduct. They have lived in the United States for almost 40 years. To banish them from home, family, and adopted country is punishment of the most drastic kind whether done at the time when they were convicted or later. I think that this Court should reconsider the application of the ex post facto clause with a view to applying it in a way that more effectively protects individuals from new or additional burdens, penalties, or punishments retrospectively imposed by Congress.[136]

In *McNeal* v. *Culver*[137] the bulk of Whittaker's opinion examined facts of the case. Such attention to facts was typical in his approach to law, but could sometimes be baffling in the Supreme Court context. In this case, for example, after lengthy speculation about possible facts and their implications if true, he ordered a lower court to determine the facts. Would not such a simple order have been easier in the first place? Here his literary product reveals his reluctance to delegate work to anyone, even a fellow judge.

Whittaker's quest for precision probably resulted in an oft-noted aspect of his opinions—their emphasis on facts. Where other justices might briefly summarize facts and quickly move on to the governing law, Whittaker saw facts as determining the governing law. His opinions might construct an elaborate foundation of facts to support his edifice of law. He believed that accepting his version of the facts would force fair-minded readers to accept his version of the law, so Whittaker took pains to state them in detail and to distinguish them from similar facts that would result in far different legal consequences. Such an approach worked well on the district court level, but was thwarted by cases whose very ambiguity brought them to the highest court. There, Justice Clark observed, "Justice Whittaker believed, as did Lord MacMillan, that '. . . in almost every case except the very plainest it would be possible to decide the issue either way with reasonable justification.' "[138] Occasionally Whittaker's Supreme Court opinions have an "on the one hand, on the other hand" quality absent from what his colleagues wrote. They knew what the law should be, went out and found it among conflicting precedents. Lacking an innate sense of what the law should be, Whittaker struggled to find it in books rather than in himself. Conflicting precedents thereby left Whittaker enfeebled.

A citizenship case[139] provides a classic example of Whittaker's thinking and expression. This case involved Clemente Martinez Perez, a man who claimed different citizenships at different times, depending on what status he thought was most advantageous at a particular moment. The Supreme Court was called upon to decide his citizenship status once and for all.

One issue was his voting in a Mexican election. Speaking for the Court's majority, Justice Frankfurter noted that Congress had declared that voting in a foreign election was grounds for losing U.S. citizenship, as such an act could embarrass U.S. foreign relations. Because Perez admitted such conduct, he had obviously forfeited his citizenship. That determination having been made, it was unnecessary to address the question of whether he had also forfeited U.S. citizenship by evading military service.

For Chief Justice Warren the matter was not so simple. In dissent, he argued that voting in a foreign election was hardly grave enough to indicate someone had renounced U. S. citizenship. Justice Douglas accepted Warren's additional argument that the federal government lacks constitutional power to strip citizenship from someone.

Justice Whittaker chose to call his dissent a memorandum rather than an opinion. He agreed with the majority that Congress has power to expatriate someone, but he felt voting in a foreign election was not an act serious enough to merit expatriation. Whittaker agreed partly with Frankfurter and partly with Warren, but did not go so far as to maintain Perez was still a citizen, for Whittaker saw another possible grounds for loss of citizenship—avoiding U.S. military service. "Inasmuch as the majority have found it unnecessary to adjudicate the constitutionality of that section in this case, it would be wholly fruitless for me now to reach a conclusion on that question, and I neither express nor imply any views upon it. Limiting myself to the issue decided by the majority, I dissent."[140]

For Whittaker to have reached a conclusion would not have been *wholly* fruitless, as great dissenters often raised arguments and brought forth interpretations that later became the law of the land. Whittaker's phraseology, however, was one of his typical rhetorical traits. He says Congress has power to do something, lacks grounds (but not necessarily power) to do it in this particular instance, and may or may not have grounds in a different aspect presented to him but which he will not consider. Such a stance may be honest, but is hardly what is needed from a supreme judge. A supreme judge is supposed to say yes or no, not "maybe, depending on aspects I'm not going to examine." Whittaker's stance was almost evasive.

The fact that Whittaker brought up an issue deemed unnecessary by his colleagues, after he said Congress did not have grounds to exercise its power on an issue his colleagues *did* contend with, suggests Whittaker might have liked to rule against Perez on an issue that no one else was willing to consider. Admittedly Whittaker explicitly denied any such intent, but why else would he bring up an issue deemed unnecessary by everyone else? Particularly given his habit of stripping irrelevancies from arguments? In his dissent Whittaker never declared Perez to be a U.S. citizen, a silence suggesting that Whittaker saw grounds for ruling against Perez.

By saying the case's deciding point was insufficient to get him to rule against Perez, while saying the case was decided without considering the military service aspect, Whittaker virtually invited future litigation on that very point. Why invite more litigation if he felt the matter was settled? The only point of such invitation would be a hope for opportunity someday to join the majority who believed Congress had the power to revoke citizenship, in a future case where Whittaker believed sufficient grounds existed for Congress to use its power. Such a stance argued that the Court settled the fate of Perez but not the issue raised by the case. In 1857 when founders of the Republican party took the same approach with the *Dred Scott* case, they were accused of denying the Supreme Court's authority. Both they and Whittaker, however, were simply inviting further opportunities to settle the issue, a stance indicating that Whittaker was more of an activist justice than is commonly believed—at least if we go beyond the traditional social justice areas usually associated with activism.

Other dissenters in *Perez* held directly that the Constitution prevented Congress from revoking citizenship without the citizen's consent. In contrast, the majority held that the Constitution did permit Congress to act, and that Congress had power to set conditions for revocation. Whittaker said the Constitution permitted and Congress had power, but that Congress could not set conditions as widely as it tried to do. Whittaker was almost trying to split the difference in his decision. One can feel him straining with the case, chain smoking as he pores over precedents, trying to discover what the law is by relying on past authorities.

Douglas reported an encounter with Whittaker: "He was pacing his office, walking around his desk with pursed lips as if possessed. I asked him what was wrong. He said, referring to the five-to-four decision, that he had been trying to write the majority opinion but simply could not do it." Douglas said he thereupon offered to do it for him, and Whittaker gratefully accepted the offer.[141] Details of that account have been questioned, but one of Whittaker's clerks agreed that Douglas occasionally aided Whittaker's literary labors to some extent.[142] Given Whittaker's reluctance to trust anyone with an assignment, his acceptance of help from Douglas indicates how desperate he must have been.

When justices deliver their opinions publicly, sometimes they give summaries, with their oral presentations differing in style from their official written opinions. Whittaker, however, would read aloud his exact printed opinion, sometimes even including his supplemental footnotes.

Reading aloud from a manuscript word-for-word illustrated Whittaker's dedication to precision in expression. Having crafted the expression of his thought with such care, he did not care to deviate from that expression in the slightest. A former law partner noted that Whittaker's famous underlining tended to be a separate mark under each word rather than a single long line under a sentence, evidence that he paused to consider each word in a sentence. The old partner indicated that Whittaker strained to see their possible alternative meanings.[143]

Passionate Prose

His extreme care in choice of words makes his occasional passionate prose all the more important.

Even before Whittaker's Supreme Court years emotional passages can be found in his judicial writing. Responding to the federal government's argument that he could not exercise jurisdiction to hear a widow's plea for proceeds from her husband's military life insurance, Whittaker declared, "Upon first reading, this position shocks the conscience. Further study of the law has not changed my first impression. Servicemen who lose their lives in the service of our country, and the families of those men, are not the discretionary cestuis of a beneficent Veterans Administration, but, rather, are the beneficiaries of a grateful America, whose Congress . . . gave them a vested property right in the life insurance thereby afforded."[144] When a university faculty member protested that he was being harassed by school officials who disapproved of his extracurricular political activities, Whittaker lectured him: "The refusal of a teacher—in a most intimate position to mould the minds of the youth of the country—to answer to the responsible officials of the school whether he is a member of a found and declared conspiracy by a godless group to overthrow our government by force, constitutes 'adequate cause' for the dismissal of such a teacher."[145] The original manuscript of this passage lacks the phrase "by a godless group," but those words were added in holograph.[146] He did not pen (or, more precisely, dictate) such passages as casual throwaway comments.

Whittaker tended to avoid emotionalism, and when he shifted from his normal legal technocrat mode of expression his feelings must have been intense. Ironically, his advocacy of cold reason may have been why he occasionally grew indignant, provoked when he saw colleagues failing to use objective reasoning and thereby (in his view) betraying their responsibility to the public.

Justice Whittaker's difficulty in reaching decisions reflected his perfectionism, a demanding trait expressing fear of making a mistake. Feeling unsure of himself on the Supreme Court, and unwilling to accept in himself the errors he would refuse to tolerate from anyone else, at times Whittaker became paralyzed with indecision. His self-confident brethren on the high bench did not seem to worry as he did about the gravity of the Court's work. If they erred or later changed their minds, they simply moved on. That did not mean they lacked Whittaker's feeling of seriousness about their work, but most persons who achieve leadership positions have the quality of knowing when a time has come to make a decision, right or wrong, and act upon it. Here Whittaker's lack of experience in work involving accountability to the public (such as a legislator, an agency head, a company manager, a platoon leader, a baseball umpire) showed itself. Persons with such experience know that settling a contested matter can be more important than who prevails in the contest. Leaders may be sober indeed about their responsibility, but they do not agonize for weeks about making a decision. Indecisive persons normally cannot achieve leadership positions. Whittaker's ability to ascend to such a high leadership position suggests that either President Eisenhower's standards for judicial promotions were flawed, or in Whittaker's case Eisenhower's system slipped a cog.

Chapter 5

Flavor of the Fifties

Legal scholars have long puzzled over the court opinions of Charles Whittaker, and reasons for such confusion may well become apparent as we examine his writings. Our quest, however, is not to understand the law but to understand the man. Although his court opinions do not reveal what is normally thought of as a judicial philosophy guiding his decisions, facts and laws he cited reveal what he thought was relevant to a case. Viewed from that perspective, patterns emerge from his opinions and reveal elements of his personal beliefs. When combined with remarks Whittaker made after he retired from the high bench, the opinions he left behind take on all the more biographical significance.

"I have never defined myself," Whittaker declared. "I read the law only for understanding of its meaning."[1] He saw that meaning as dependent upon facts of a case. "Legal questions do not arise in a vacuum," he explained, "they arise only in relation to particular facts, and slight differences of fact often make wide differences in result."[2]

Whittaker's brutal work pace in search of facts and law that would reveal an inevitable decision contained deep irony. The very act of choosing and arranging facts imposed a personal order on them. In this context the facts and law he studied had no inherent meaning; he himself was deciding which facts were meaningful and what law was applicable, and other justices made different decisions. He thereby created a "truth" no more inevitable than the personal conclusions reached with much less effort by his brethren on the Court. His antagonist Justice William O. Douglas was skeptical of Whittaker's professed reliance on facts: "He enjoyed creating a decision out of the blurred, confused, elusive things that those who should know better speak of with certainty as 'the facts.' "[3] His Supreme Court colleague John Harlan distinctly remembered him as "a man of intense convictions" who continually struggled against "temptations" caused by "his personal ideologies."[4] That does not describe a mere technocrat who objectively applied rules regardless of their consequences. On the contrary, Court observers described a man who was a vigorous advocate for what he believed.

In a sense, Whittaker evaded accountability by insisting that his decisions were compelled by facts and law in a case. He was arguing, in essence, that the matter was out of his hands, that he had no choice in the decision he made. Anyone, he argued, would have to make the same decision if confronted by the same facts and law. By such reasoning, his decision and its consequences were not his responsibility. Whittaker simply certified an inevitability. Did all blanks on a form contain the requested information, yes or no?

On rare occasions Whittaker explicitly admitted he acted upon personal preference rather than discovering an inevitable scientific conclusion dictated by facts and law. District judges are far more tightly bound by *stare decisis* (respect for previous decisions of courts) than are Supreme Court justices. Even in a district case, however, Whittaker was known to say, "Defendant cites and relies upon the case of Brewer v. United States, D.C., 117 F. Supp. 842. I am unable to agree with that decision."[5] More softly, he said in another opinion, "It must be admitted that the Clarke case . . . holds. . . . But that case is out of harmony with every other case."[6] Whittaker was willing to disregard precedents if he found them too inconvenient. Indeed, the very fact that a court decision is called an "opinion" suggests that decisions are inherently far less scientific and inevitable than Whittaker claimed them to be.

COMMUNISM

Fear of communist aggression was pervasive in the United States when Whittaker served as a federal judge. Judges were in a powerful position to shape public thinking about this issue, hearing cases asking not only how much danger existed but which also asked whether the Constitution helped or hindered the anti-communist effort.

An article in *American Legion* magazine proclaimed, "On Red Monday, June 17, 1957, the Supreme Court handed down a batch of decisions which brought jubilation to the ranks of subversives all over the United States."[7] Whittaker arrived too late to be involved in those cases, but earlier decisions affected Eisenhower's search for a Supreme Court justice.

"Being a God-fearing and freedom-loving people," Whittaker said, "we sorely resent the avowed determination of the leaders of a foreign power to destroy our religious liberty, intellectual and physical freedoms, and to relegate us to serfdom in an atheist state."[8] In his 1965 speech "Law and Order" Whittaker quoted from two magazine articles:

> One saying that "increased *Communist penetration* and influence inside some sections *of the Negro movement* in the United States is a subject of growing concern to the FBI and White House." The other saying, "J. Edgar Hoover, FBI Director, and President Johnson both are increasingly concerned by the growing activity of known *Communists on the campuses of colleges around the country*. They would like to alert the country to the situation, but are concerned about being considered 'Red-baiters' if they do."
>
> I, for one, would like to lend a voice of encouragement to them to forget those fears and to alert the country fully about the facts.[9]

Moreover, in 1964 Whittaker told audiences of Rotarians, college students, and Southern lawyers that leaders of the civil rights movement threatened the nation's well-being. Part of that threat Whittaker ascribed to what he called their advocacy of communism. He said they proclaimed slogans such as "The world owes every man a living,"; "Human rights, not property rights"; "Production is for use, and not for profit"; and "The end justifies the means."[10] Perhaps civil rights leaders did believe that persons desiring work should have employment, that conflicts between property and people should be resolved in favor of people, that production of goods and services should take precedence over looting a corporation's assets, and that peaceful refusal to obey government orders (while accepting whatever punishment was meted out) could sometimes promote the community's well-being while acknowledging the law's jurisdiction. Whittaker, however, found such concepts threatening to democracy and labeled them communistic. That is the face of the enemy Whittaker saw when sitting in judgment on communist cases.

The first communist-related case decided by Whittaker was as a district judge in his hometown of Kansas City, involving people and institutions familiar to him. Questions had been raised about the patriotism and loyalty of a teacher. Americans in any era become disquieted if they belief a teacher is promoting harmful ideas in the classroom. By definition, most grade school and high school students are considered too young to apply principles of critical thinking to a teacher's presentations, and are thus considered easy victims for an unscrupulous manipulator. Although college students are considered capable of treating an instructor's pronouncements more skeptically, the public becomes just as aroused by reports of subversive college instructors as by reports of subversive high school teachers. Apparently the public wants teachers of any grade level to promote the status quo.

In 1946 the private University of Kansas City appointed Horace B. Davis associate professor of economics. His academic background was sterling: B.A.

Harvard, Ph.D. Columbia. When he began teaching Current Economic Problems at UKC the catalog described the content as "current problems of production, distribution, labor-management relations, and the post-war economy."[11] Under Davis the course content changed to "economics of imperialism and colonialism; government planning vs. private enterprise; cooperation as a social philosophy; comparative economic systems."[12] He began teaching History of Economic Thought, Consumer Economics (including "methods of protecting the consumer"), Government and Business (including "the issue of governmental control"), Labor Problems, Comparative Economic Systems, Labor and the State.[13] None of these courses had been taught at UKC before Davis arrived. All inherently had to have heavy political content, and indeed were described by the American Association of University Professors (AAUP) as "certainly among the most sensitive areas of the University's curriculum."[14] By comparison, Davis did not teach politically neutral courses such as statistics, insurance, marketing, business finance, accounting, or transportation. He soon became a target of political complaint. In 1949 his Current Economic Problems course disappeared from the university catalog and never reappeared while he was a faculty member. The university dropped his Consumer Economics course for awhile, but it was reinstated while he taught there.

Davis insisted he never penalized students for disagreeing with his political beliefs, and an investigation at the national level by the AAUP reported "impressive testimony that he had not abused his position, and that his integrity was manifested in discussions with his colleagues."[15] Davis furnished the university administration with evaluations of his teaching made anonymously by his students, and at least one student stated on the record that an objective atmosphere prevailed in Davis's classes.[16] Nonetheless some students disagreed. One who did not take classes from Davis related gossip that grades depended on how well his students mouthed Communist Party policy.[17] Even years later the communist label was freely bestowed in Kansas City. The author of this biography vividly remembers groundless accusations against one of his professors at William Jewell College in the 1960s.

Such reports about Davis attracted the attention of anti-communist activists, and in June 1953 he was summoned to testify in Chicago before the Subcommittee on Internal Security of the U.S. Senate Committee on the Judiciary. Because that experience was a quintessential example of what people were subjected to during the McCarthy era, and because such an experience was so unfamiliar a half century later, details are useful here.

The hearing was actually aimed at the University of Chicago, a target of anti-communist militants ever since Charles H. Walgreen (founder of a drug store chain) yanked his niece from the school in 1935, complaining of its political atmosphere.[18] Twenty faculty members were expected to undergo a grilling this time. Across the country the format for such hearings was the same. Witnesses would be called to testify in secret. If persons admitted and recanted communist affiliation and named their communist associates, the witnesses' identity would be kept secret and no further proceedings against them would occur. Witnesses who refused to answer questions about themselves or who refused to denounce friends and associates were forced to appear in public hearings accusing them of communist activity, accusations that could cost them their reputations and their jobs.

Somehow Davis and another UKC faculty member, Associate Professor of Physics and Chemistry Ralph Spitzer, were caught in the University of Chicago dragnet. Their pictures were printed in the *Chicago Tribune*.[19]

Spitzer had good reason to be reticent in testimony about himself. He claimed to have been dismissed from Oregon State College in 1949 due to his activism in the Progressive Party presidential campaign of Henry Wallace the previous year. Wallace was widely considered pro-communist, and Spitzer's wife was described as "the firebrand of the campus Young Progressives organization."[20] By January 1949 the president of an opposing group, the Associated Students, had attracted national attention with his insistence that "communism is a real factor on this campus" and that "there are certain people on this campus for the sole purpose of converting students to the cause of communism." College president A. L. Strand declared, "It is gratifying to see the responsible student leaders recognizing the situation."[21]

"Brilliant" and "fidgety,"[22] Spitzer became indignant over an editorial in *Chemical and Engineering News*, house organ of the American Chemical Society whose president, Linus Pauling, had recently appointed Spitzer as chairman of the Committee on Patent Legislation. Pauling, who would soon win the Nobel Prize for chemistry, was well acquainted with Spitzer, saying he belonged to "the upper group of the able younger physical chemists in this country."[23] The editorial in question endorsed an article in the *Saturday Review of Literature* by Nobel prize winner H. J. Muller, who condemned harsh repressions against scientists in the Soviet Union who did not support the genetics work of Trofim Denisovich Lysenko. Muller had given a speech at Oregon State the previous election year. School president Strand called genetics "the science of greatest political moment under the conditions of social stress in the world today."[24]

In this highly charged political climate Spitzer fired off a letter to *Chemical and Engineering News* saying that Soviet science was thriving and that condemnation of Lysenko's work was premature. Lysenko was a very public favorite of Soviet dictator Joseph Stalin. Immediately after publication of the letter President Strand fired Spitzer. The letter "showed beyond question that he was devoted to

Communist party policy," Strand said. "He goes right down the party line without any noticeable deviation and is an active protagonist for it." The letter, Strand declared, "served as a final confirmation to a conclusion long since reached." *Time* magazine, no friend to communist teachers, noted that Spitzer "stuck pretty close to chemistry" in class. Sydney Hook, an academic authority *Time* relied upon for intellectual justification of dismissing communist-tainted professors, objected to Spitzer's dismissal, as did Pauling (a chemist whose own scientific work in genetics was profound) and others whose protests appeared in *Chemical and Engineering News*. President Strand refused to reconsider. Although Spitzer's letter had not said Lysenko's work was proven, but simply that it merited further investigation, Strand told critics, "Any scientist who has such poor power of discrimination so as to choose to support Lysenko's Michurin genetics against all the weight of evidence against it is not much of a scientist, or, a priori, has lost the freedom that an instructor and investigator should possess."[25]

Despite national publicity of Spitzer's case, he soon found a new home at UKC. Seemingly the administration there must have seen the injustice in Spitzer's treatment; certainly UKC's climate was unfriendly to faculty members with suspected communist leanings. In 1949 UKC's president had stated that no communist should be allowed to teach in the United States, let alone at UKC, a statement not repudiated by the school's trustees or faculty. Because of that policy, the AAUP later found that any UKC faculty member called before a congressional committee to testify about alleged pro-communist connections had good reason to be evasive due to possible employment consequences back at UKC.[26] Indeed, a *Kansas City Times* newspaper editorial declared, "The kind of questions that presumably led two faculty members to the Senate subcommittee have been known to university authorities for some time and they have not been idle."[27] Another *Times* editorial proclaimed, "Before the Jenner subcommittee hearing . . . the Davis case had been under investigation by the university board and administration."[28]

Although Spitzer was not cooperative in Chicago, his subcommittee appearance was low-key, characterized by recollections of his weapons research during World War II (for which he received a federal government citation) and his musings regarding the chilling effect that committee investigation hearings had on scientific progress.[29]

Not so with Davis.[30] When asked to state his name, he instead questioned the committee's legality. Things heated up from there.

> Mr. MANDEL. I have here a copy of the catalog and program of the School for Democracy, dated January 1942. This school has been identified as a Communist school by various witnesses before the Senate Internal Security Subcommittee, and listed among the instructors and guest lecturers, is the following:

Davis, Horace B., instructor. American economist in the 20th century. Economic problems of the war. Ph.D., Columbia. Taught at Columbia University; Cornell University; technical director, United Shoe Workers of America; author of Labor and Steel; Shoes—The Workers and the Industry.

Mr. MORRIS. Is the information in that listing read by Mr. Mandel, correctly stated, Mr. Davis?

Mr. DAVIS. Just one moment. I would like to consult with counsel.

(Witness consults with counsel.)

Mr. DAVIS. I decline to answer on the same grounds, and I just point out that these questions, so-called, are not asked for the purpose of eliciting information, they must have some ulterior purpose. I told you I was not going to answer that kind of question.

Mr. MORRIS. How can we know whether or not the Horace B. Davis here, who had a Ph.D., is the same Mr. Horace B. Davis?

Mr. DAVIS. Well, you won't find out from me.

Mr. MORRIS. That is, other than by asking you.

Mr. DAVIS. You won't find out from me, and I don't think that you need to dodge the point. You are trying to make a record, you are not trying to obtain information.

The CHAIRMAN [Sen. JENNER]. I think we have obtained the information. I think that we have found out that the record shows you refused to answer under the fifth amendment of the Constitution. . . .

Mr. MANDEL. I have here a copy of an advertisement in the New Republic for December 27, 1939, and on the back cover it lists among the sponsors of the American Investors Union at 10 East 40th Street, New York, N. Y., the name of Horace Davis, professor of economics, Simmons College.

Mr. MORRIS. Mr. Davis, were you a professor of economics at Simmons College?

Mr. DAVIS. It would not occur to you that I might possibly refuse to answer that? . . .

Mr. MORRIS. Mr. Chairman, in view of the reaction of this particular witness, I have here a whole page of Communist activities engaged in by one Horace Davis, but in view of the attitude taken by the witness—

The CHAIRMAN. We had better make our record.

Mr. MORRIS. Very well. Were you active in the Workers Alliance of the United States, a member of the executive board, 1937?

Mr. DAVIS. I decline to answer—same grounds.

Again and again this type of question was asked, with the same response. Although printed transcripts do not reproduce mannerisms and tones of voice, the subcommittee's refusal to address Davis as "Doctor" or "Professor" illustrates the contempt with which he was regarded. Subcommittee chief counsel Robert Morris explicitly declared that Davis had been a member of a Communist Party cell.[31]

The subcommittee's questions went beyond communist affiliations and explored his writings, teaching experience, and classroom conduct. Davis repeatedly refused to answer. His lawyer Fyke Farmer later explained, "I do not understand that the Constitution confers upon the Internal Security Subcommittee, or any congressional committee, or the Congress of the United States, supervisory powers over a private educational institution."[32] By refusing to answer questions on grounds that they went beyond the legitimate scope of the subcommittee's investigation, Davis raised an issue that the U.S. Supreme Court would later consider during Whittaker's tenure on the high bench,[33] but which district judge Whittaker ignored here.

Davis also exercised Fifth Amendment rights in refusing to answer questions, a step that can be publicly humiliating but which can be necessary if a witness fears he may later be targeted by a headline-seeking prosecutor. Upon close of the hearings the *Chicago Tribune* printed a front page editorial cartoon in which a professor wearing mortarboard and robe asks, "Young man, have you prepared the lesson for today?" The student replies, "I claim the privilege of the Fifth Amendment in declining to answer on the grounds that it might incriminate me!"[34]

The purpose of the hearings became apparent in a report published soon afterward by the subcommittee.[35] "Richard E. Combs, chief counsel for the California Senate Committee on Un-American Activities . . . told the subcommittee how the college presidents of all the major California colleges cooperated with the State senate committee there, and together caused the removal of more than 100 faculty members from those universities between June 24, 1952, and . . . March 24, 1953." The report explained, "Because of the testimony of Mr. Combs the subcommittee, feeling that the exposure was being accomplished by local agencies, did not subpena any witnesses from California." Likewise when the New York City Superintendent of Schools "demonstrated to the subcommittee that local authorities were undertaking the work of eliminating subversives from the city schools, the subcommittee desisted from calling teachers under his jurisdiction." The purpose of the hearings was not to obtain information from witnesses but to get them fired from their teaching jobs. "In all but a few of the cases before the subcommittee, the university officials and local authorities suspended the teachers who invoked their privilege against incrimination when asked about Communist Party membership."[36]

The report singled out Horace Davis for special mention:[37]

> PROJECTS AND PROPAGANDA
>
> Teacher witnesses before the committee, who claimed this privilege under the fifth amendment in answer to their communist party membership, invoked a similar plea regarding their activities in recruiting students and teachers into the Communist Party or the Young Communist League, and

> their active support and promotion of Communist-front organizations, campaigns, and publications.
>
> Typical was the case of Horace Bancroft Davis, associate professor of economics at the University of Kansas City, who invoked his privilege under the fifth amendment on the subject of his support of the Stockholm peace petition, the Abraham Lincoln Brigade, Conference on Pan-American Democracy, Workers Alliance, American League Against War and Fascism, Schappes Defense Committee, New Masses, International Labor Defense, and petitions for the freedom of Earl Browder and Luis Carlos Prestes.

As background to further criticism of Davis, the report stated, "Howard Selsam has been identified by numerous witnesses in sworn testimony as a member of the Communist Party." He submitted a statement to the subcommittee on April 8, 1953 (prior to the Davis appearance) saying, "All the actions of this committee reveal its aim to be the creation of an atmosphere of repression and terror so that no teacher dare follow the lead of ideas without first asking himself what ideas or organizations this committee approves. Nearly every witness you call before you knows full well the meaning of your subpena server's knock on his door. It spells for him either the threat of dismissal from his job and his life's chosen profession, or the loss of his integrity and decency. He knows that once he seeks to maintain his honesty and freedom by standing on his constitutional grounds, his college authorities threaten his dismissal. He knows that once he begins to crawl before you, he will be dragged through the mud till he becomes an informer, a stool pigeon, or an outright liar." Selsam continued, "I employ the fifth amendment as it was originally intended to be used, namely, to protect American citizens against inquisitors, abusers of judicial power, or legislators who, under the cloak of investigation, seek to frighten our people into conformity."[38]

The subcommittee report said then, "This statement or paragraphs of it were echoed by other witnesses who invoked their privilege against incrimination when asked about the subcommittee evidence of their Communist membership, notably Horace Bancroft Davis." The subcommittee then listed seven others, and said there were more than those named. "The biased and inaccurate strictures of Mr. Selsam, whom the subcommittee considered a recognized Communist spokesman and educator, have, for reasons difficult for the subcommittee to understand, been reflected with remarkable similarity in the comments of certain educators." The report declared, "Exposure of Communists by congressional and State legislative committees has helped local authorities protect themselves against organized subversion and has given such authorities the evidence by which some hidden Communists could be removed from teaching positions."[39]

An appendix in the report entitled "Pattern of Infiltration" is comprised of a "Table showing teachers and other staff members of educational institutions who invoked the 5th amendment regarding their Communist Party membership or admitted such membership." Davis is listed as taking the Fifth and as connected with School for Democracy ("cited as a Communist school in the testimony of Dr. Bella V. Dodd") and Abraham Lincoln School of Chicago ("cited as an 'adjunct of the Communist Party' by the Attorney General"). That attorney general, Tom Clark, would serve on the U.S. Supreme Court with Whittaker.

Soon after the highly publicized Chicago hearing, Davis was called before several trustees of the university's governing board.[40] The board chairman said Davis faced disciplinary action unless he stated whether he had ever been a Communist Party member, whether he had "been active in the work of the Communist Party," and whether he had ever "supported Communist activities." The latter two questions were particularly elastic, as much opposition to Truman administration policies was characterized as communist. For example, when Truman's secretary of commerce Henry Wallace broke with the administration, Wallace was widely labeled as pro-communist.

Davis told the university trustees:

> Senator Jenner has made it clear on many occasions that he believes the Communist Party to be a subversive organization, taking orders from a foreign power and working actively for the overthrow of the United States Government by force and violence; he believes it to be a criminal conspiracy.
>
> He has implied that I am engaged in such a conspiracy and that I have commitments which would interfere with my performing the duties normally to be expected of a college teacher.
>
> I do not have any such commitments. I make up my own mind and take full responsibility for my own actions. I am not under the domination of any party or government foreign or domestic. If anyone contends that I have committed any illegal or immoral act, let him come forward and state when and where such act was committed.
>
> I do not carry on propaganda in my classroom. My philosophy of education would preclude such a thing. My students are encouraged to think for themselves. Discussion in my classes is free and disagreement is not penalized. I wish that I could say the same for the university as a whole.
>
> My refusal to answer certain questions, whether put by a congressional investigating subcommittee or by a university board of trustees, is based on principle and does not imply any disrespect either for the Congress of the United States or for the trustees as such. I recognize the authority of the United States Constitution and in my modest way hope to continue trying to make it work.[41]

In his statement Davis came as close to denying communist involvement as he could without abandoning his stance of refusing to answer questions that he considered improper. Nonetheless his phraseology did not preclude voluntary communist activity, as opposed to "taking orders" and being "under the domination." Although the legal issue was not whether Davis was a communist but rather his refusal to answer questions on that topic, Judge Whittaker is unlikely to have found the above statement to be exonerating. In a Supreme Court case involving the legal question of a defendant's Communist Party membership, Whittaker ruled that the trial judge had properly instructed the jury to use "subjective terms of a state of mind" to determine whether the defendant was a Communist Party member. Whittaker reasoned there was no other way to determine membership in a secret organization that lacks normal record keeping. "The ultimate fact of membership in such a case is almost always necessarily a subjective one."[42]

Presenting no evidence of communist activity by Davis, and acting solely on grounds that Davis had refused explicit answers to the three questions put to him, the trustees fired the tenured professor. The trustees declared, "In matters of basic social importance all members of an academic community must stand up and be counted."[43]

Citing a federal criminal statute[44] prohibiting persons from conspiring "to injure, oppress, threaten, or intimidate any citizen in the free exercise or enjoyment of any right or privilege secured to him by the Constitution or laws of the United States, or because of his having so exercised the same," Davis filed suit seeking reinstatement at UKC. Davis felt his firing resulted from persecution by Sen. William E. Jenner, subcommittee staff, and some UKC trustees who sought to punish him for freely expressing his beliefs. His lawyer Fyke Farmer later said, "We moved in that case for the university records and correspondence that passed between certain trustees and the Internal Security Subcommittee. We had that motion for the production of those documents and a motion to examine the trustees, as I recall. But we were cut off by the ruling of Judge Whittaker."[45]

Farmer summarized the case thusly:

> While under the terms of the governing rules of the university, a member of the faculty on permanent or continuous tenure could be discharged for just cause under the Missouri decisions and the general principles of the law, the courts may review such an act to see whether it was within their discretion.
>
> My insistence on behalf of Dr. Davis was that this discretion of the trustees did not extend so far as to confer upon them the right to discharge a member of the faculty for exercising his constitutional rights. If . . . the Senate Internal Security Subcommittee . . . investigation for which he was subpenaed was instituted by collusion between the university and certain trustees, and then he was called up before the board of trustees in pursuance to this collusion, of this conspiracy to get him out of the university and to injure him, and he was put the same questions [by the trustees as by the Senate subcommittee] . . . a discharge could not be based upon that because a Federal statute makes it a crime.

Farmer further explained, "There was no question at any hearing before the trustees of the university as to Dr. Davis' competency, no question of negligence of duty, and . . . the discharge was based, solely on the ground that he was under a duty to answer those questions" on communist activity.[46]

Davis was a tenured faculty member, meaning that he could not be fired without proof of incompetence or gross abuse of his position. His lawyer said of the trustees, "I think it would be within the scope of their duties to decide whether a man was in his classroom, whether he was teaching doctrines that were contrary to the laws of the United States, the Constitution of the United States, but that is not this case. There is no question about Dr. Davis' using his classroom as any forum for propaganda for any ideas he had. They just were seeking to ferret out from him ideas or acts or opinions that were, as I see it, wholly unrelated . . . to the performance of his duties as a member of the faculty."[47] The theory of tenure is to protect instructors' right to teach truth as they understand it without fear of retribution from anyone who is disquieted by that understanding of truth. In a phrase, tenure is intended to assure "academic freedom." In practice, tenure protects drones as well the work horses, but the *Davis* case addressed the core purpose of tenure—protection of academic freedom.

Normally the *Davis* case is viewed as a question of academic freedom, or the even simpler question of whether Davis was indeed a communist. His conduct, however, could have involved other elements as well. For instance, an accused person can be so indignant about charges against him and about tactics of accusers that he not only refuses to cooperate but goads his tormenters. A person may also take an unnecessary stance because he thinks it makes him look good and the other side look bad, even if a different stance is more practical. And for some people defending a principle is so important that they are willing to risk the devastating consequences of losing a case, risking their own well-being in defense of the greater good of society. Self-interest, anger, nobility. All could have been elements in the decision Davis made to sue the University of Kansas City.

The original complaint filed by Davis[48] is marked up with multi-color pencil in Whittaker's usual extravagant style. Part of the complaint included the resolution establishing the subcommittee, and in that quotation Whittaker marked "espionage," "sabotage," "infiltration by persons who are or may be under the domination of the foreign government or organizations controlling the world Communist movement." Whittaker underlined, encircled, and marked with an X that Davis "affirmed" rather than "swore" he would tell the truth. The judge also underlined quoted portions from the subcommittee report listing alleged subversive organizations that Davis was accused of aiding.

Passing in silence over the statutory grounds Davis cited, Whittaker ruled in favor of UKC's contention that the lawsuit should be dismissed because Davis stated no claim upon which relief could be granted. Whittaker declared Davis had a constitutional right to express himself but no constitutional right to be a school teacher. Davis of course made no such sweeping claim. He simply said he was dismissed as punishment for exercising his constitutional right of free speech, a punishment prohibited by statute. This issue is of great practical significance. If a private employer can fire workers for engaging in legal political activity, threat of jail is unnecessary to restrict free speech or even to decide elections. (In Kansas City, where the *Davis* suit was filed, such job dismissals by private employers were no theoretical question; they had been a key to power wielded by the notorious Pendergast political machine.)

At about the time district judge Whittaker made his ruling, the U.S. Supreme Court decided a similar case involving a faculty member who was dismissed after invoking constitutional rights at a Congressional hearing to avoid answering questions about alleged communist affiliation. Justice Clark declared, "Privilege against self-incrimination would be reduced to a hollow mockery if its exercise could be taken as equivalent either to a confession of guilt or a conclusive presumption of perjury." He continued, "A witness may have a reasonable fear of prosecution and yet be innocent of any wrongdoing. The privilege serves to protect the innocent who otherwise might be ensnared by ambiguous circumstances." Clark added, "In practical effect the questions asked are taken as confessed and made the basis of the discharge. . . . The heavy hand . . . falls alike on all who exercise their constitutional privilege, the full enjoyment of which every person is entitled to receive."[49] Such was not Whittaker's stance.

Judge Whittaker, whose precision on factual elements was legendary, misdescribed Horace Davis as a public school teacher, a misdescription allowing Whittaker to cite as precedents cases involving public schools. That the legal distinctions between public and private schools could have escaped Whittaker's notice is beyond belief. Did he merge the two as a rhetorical technique to escape facts and legal consequences he wanted to avoid? Such merging is all the more perplexing because the effect would be to impose more limits on the UKC trustees' actions.

For example, Justice Whittaker participated in a case[50] where a public school teacher was fired for failing to comply with an Arkansas law requiring teachers to list annually every group they had joined or had supported financially. A member of the Little Rock Capital Citizens Council frankly declared that such information would be used to dismiss teachers involved with the Urban League, the American Civil Liberties Union, or the AAUP. Speaking for the U.S. Supreme Court, Justice Potter Stewart conceded that classroom conduct was not the sole criterion in evaluating fitness to teach. But a "teacher's right of free association, [is] a right closely allied to freedom of speech and a right which, like free speech, lies at the foundation of a free society." Stewart continued, "Such interference with personal freedom is conspicuously accented when the teacher serves at the absolute will of those to whom the disclosure must be made—those who any year can terminate the teacher's employment without bringing charges, without notice, without a hearing, without affording an opportunity to explain."

Justice Stewart quoted from previous decisions with approval: "Unwarranted inhibition upon the free spirit of teachers . . . has an unmistakable tendency to chill that free play of the spirit which all teachers ought especially to cultivate and practice; it makes for caution and timidity in their associations by potential teachers."[51] "Scholarship cannot flourish in an atmosphere of suspicion and distrust. Teachers and students must always remain free to inquire, to study and to evaluate."[52]

Whittaker joined the dissent of Harlan,[53] who found the Arkansas statute nondiscriminatory and acceptable, at least on its face. The dissenters noted, however, "If it turns out that this statute is abused, either by an unwarranted publicizing of the required associational disclosures or otherwise, we would have a different kind of case." From a practical standpoint that is exactly the sort of abuse inflicted on Horace Davis (although legal issues in his case can be distinguished from the Arkansas one, inquiry by state statute in Arkansas versus inquiry by private school officials in Kansas City).

Judge Whittaker's district court ruling dealt with Davis's refusal to answer questions put to him by school officials and did not consider what sort of answers would have been grounds for dismissal. The questions included whether Davis had supported "communist activities," a classification covering a wide swath of behavior in that era, such as opposing the Korean War. One person who visited the Davis home recalled her shock when Mrs. Davis wondered whether North Korea had started the war. Such skepticism may have shocked typical Americans, but was an issue familiar to knowledgeable contemporary observers and later historians. South Korea and North Korea had been threatening each other with attack, and upon outbreak of hostilities the identity of whose armed forces fired the first shot was uncertain. But even though Mrs. Davis asked a reasonable question, such a question was viewed with suspicion.

In that respect Whittaker shared the common thinking of his era. His opinion in the *Davis* case showed no sensitivity for the issue of whether an employer had a right to question workers about their political beliefs. In cases involving teachers, at least, Whittaker thought "communist" sympathies were a clear and present danger overriding any right to privacy. Not only were such beliefs dangerous to the country, but they affected a teacher's job performance.

Whittaker's decision did not address the question of conspiracy between Sen. Jenner and the UKC trustees to fire Davis on grounds of his appearance before

Jenner's subcommittee. Earlier the AAUP had revealed a history of *sub rosa* conduct by UKC's president, conduct going so far as to enlist cooperative students in circulating anonymous letters attacking a colleague.[54] Jenner refused to cooperate in supplying any documentation of contact with the trustees. Fyke Farmer presented a motion seeking documents from UKC that might demonstrate contact between Jenner and UKC prior to the Chicago hearing, but Whittaker refused to accept Farmer's motion on grounds that he was not admitted to practice before the district court. Davis reported a university attorney told him that trustees Arthur Mag and Joyce Hall "had been pressing for drastic action."[55] Davis believed that trustee Raymond Hall was also seeking his dismissal. If the professor believed a conspiracy between Jenner and certain UKC trustees existed, one can well see how Davis could have been so incensed that he would refuse to cooperate with the proceedings. Such a conspiracy might even have tainted the UKC proceedings' legal standing.[56]

A conspiracy between Sen. Jenner and the UKC trustees would mean that questions put to Davis by the trustees were a subterfuge—at the least, using public shaming as a means to punish Davis for his committee performance, and perhaps (if Jenner were involved) a legal extension of questions from the committee. A conspiracy could have invalidated the trustees' questions as grounds for dismissal. Whittaker, however, chose to avoid the question of conspiracy. Instead he assumed the proceedings were legitimate and focused on whether Davis's refusal to answer the trustees' questions was adequate cause for firing him. Not only did Whittaker say the trustees had acted within their legal authority, he declared they "would have been derelict in their duties, and would have destroyed the University, had they not dismissed him."[57]

Whittaker's clerk said the judge's strong rhetoric in the *Davis* opinion, so atypical of Whittaker's legal writing, was intended to answer political liberals who might disagree with the decision.[58] Whittaker later described the case as open and shut, with his decision impelled by law governing the issues. Regardless of whether that assertion was correct, issues in the decision were defined by Whittaker. Persons with differing political values may have defined the issues differently, causing a different legal outcome. His decision's political defense of its findings exuded passion and was aimed at a particular group of people. Whittaker's handling of this highly publicized case probably did not escape the Eisenhower administration's notice. Although Whittaker claimed to have no political ideology, we may be sure one was noticed by Justice Department officials in charge of judicial promotions.

In December of 1955 Whittaker became a member of the University of Kansas City Trustees whose conduct he had just upheld. "There will always be a warm spot in my heart for K. C. U."[59]

In the later *Slochower* case[60] the Supreme Court ruled that a public college instructor could not be dismissed for failing to answer questions put by a congressional committee. That decision, however, was too late to help Davis. After leaving UKC he got a faculty position at Benedict College of Columbia, South Carolina, termed a "colored college," and received partial satisfaction from a national AAUP investigation which found his conduct unwise but his dismissal unjustified.[61] Neither he nor his old lawyer Fyke Farmer put the case behind them. Both protested Whittaker's nomination to the Supreme Court, Davis sending a letter to the senate judiciary committee and Farmer traveling to Washington to testify at the nomination hearing. Farmer dramatically appeared in Whittaker's presence and challenged his fitness for the Supreme Court. Farmer was a minor public figure of the era, well known to anti-communist crusaders. It was attorney Farmer who persuaded Justice Douglas to stay the executions of the infamous atomic spies Julius and Ethel Rosenberg.[62] Committee members had been well prepped on Farmer's leftist background, and under vigorous leadership from Sen. Thomas C. Hennings (D–MO) they invoked scorn upon him for his political beliefs and activities.

On the Supreme Court Whittaker helped decide a case brought by someone who, unlike Davis, really was a public school teacher.[63]

Herman A. Beilan had taught in Philadelphia pubic schools for almost a quarter century. In June 1952 the superintendent asked Beilan if he had served as Press Director for the Communist Political Association's Professional Section in 1944. During the year in question the Soviet Union was a military ally fighting alongside the United States against Hitler in Europe, and support for the Soviet Union was promoted as patriotic by news media and the entertainment industry. Hollywood movies with stars such as John Huston, Gregory Peck, and Clark Gable glorified the communist cause. America's political climate had changed drastically by 1952, however, and Mr. Beilan told the school superintendent that he wanted to consult a lawyer before answering. The superintendent consented. In October he summoned Beilan again, and the teacher said his lawyer had advised him to answer no questions about political beliefs. The superintendent said the subject was not politics but rather Beilan's fitness to teach, and that failure to answer could lead to termination. Denying that Beilan's loyalty to his country was an issue, the school board fired him in January 1954.

Speaking for a majority that included Whittaker, Justice Burton said the firing was legal if Beilan was an incompetent teacher. A Pennsylvania law of 1949 broadened the definition of incompetence (a firing offense) to include "advocation of or participating in un-American or subversive doctrines." That clause, however, was deleted in 1951. The issue at hand therefore, Burton said, was whether Beilan's refusal to answer a question about his political beliefs was insubordination and therefore incompetence.

> By engaging in teaching in the public schools, petitioner did not give up his right to freedom of belief, speech or association. He did, however, undertake obligations of frankness, candor and cooperation in answering inquiries made of him by his employing Board examining into his fitness to serve it as a public school teacher.
>
> . . . The Board based its dismissal upon petitioner's refusal to answer any inquiry about his relevant activities—not upon those activities themselves. It took care to charge petitioner with incompetency, and not with disloyalty. It found him insubordinate.[64]

The school board, Justice Burton said, drew no inferences from Beilan's refusal to answer questioning about his political beliefs. Such refusal itself, however, was insubordination, which was included under the definition of incompetency. Therefore dismissal did not violate Beilan's constitutional rights.

The Court majority implied that questioning Beilan about his political beliefs might have been unconstitutional, but nonetheless held that he could be fired for refusing to answer a question of doubtful legality.

In dissent Chief Justice Warren noted facts ignored by the Court's majority. "For 13 months following petitioner's refusal to answer the Superintendent's questions, he was retained as a school teacher and continually rated as 'satisfactory,' yet five days after his appearance before the House [Un-American Activities] subcommittee petitioner was suspended."[65] The Court's majority had omitted mention of Beilan's summons to the congressional committee famed for its investigations into alleged communist activities. Citizens throughout the country were called before it, and newsreels made familiar the droning voice asking one person after another, "Are you now or have you ever been a member of the Communist Party?" Mere appearance before the committee was considered a black mark against a citizen's character, and citizens whose answers and demeanor fell short of full cooperation were pilloried. Beilan cited his Fifth Amendment right as grounds for declining to answer the committee's questions fully. Details of that testimony were noted in Justice Brennan's dissent:

> Beilan testified at that hearing that he was not then a member of the Communist Party and had never advocated the overthrow of the Government by force or violence but pleaded the protection of the Fifth Amendment when asked questions directed to past party membership and activities. Five days later, on November 23, 1953, the Superintendent notified Beilan that he had been rated "unsatisfactory" because he had refused to answer the Superintendent's question and also because "[y]ou invoked the Fifth Amendment."

Brennan noted the language of the administrative appeal opinion: " '[B]y all the concepts of logic and reason the teacher admits that he has done something for which he might be prosecuted criminally.' "[66] Such language was treacherous. Given the enormous quantity of statutes, most citizens might be prosecuted for violating one law or another. Most citizens give little thought to such a possibility, but being put before cameras and sound recorders at a hostile congressional hearing can wonderfully concentrate a citizen's mind about possible consequences of any inadvertent remark. Given the power of news media and governmental authorities arrayed before a citizen in such a context, even a blameless person might feel it wise to invoke every available civil right. Clearly an inference from Beilan's refusal to answer a congressional committee's question, not an "insubordinate" refusal to answer the superintendent's question, was the basis of dismissal. Brennan noted the "Court of Common Pleas found that the administrative proceedings were actually concerned solely with the question of Beilan's suspected disloyalty."[67]

That lower court finding had been overturned by Pennsylvania's supreme court.[68] State justice Charles Alvin Jones, however, had dissented.[69] He ridiculed the school board's "professing that the Board's inquisition had nothing whatsoever to do with Beilan's 'loyalty or disloyalty'. The Board avows that it dismissed him for 'incompetency'. . . for his refusal to answer a question by the Superintendent of Schools on two occasions (June and October, 1952) . . . and for his refusal to answer questions of a similar nature by counsel for a subcommittee of the Un-American Activities Committee of the House of Representatives." The board did not allege that Beilan had violated any law. Indeed, until 1951 the Communist Party had appeared on Pennsylvania ballots as a legal political organization. Noting that *Slochower* "holds that a State school teacher having tenure may not be summarily dismissed for pleading the Fifth Amendment in refusing to answer questions of a congressional committee as to his prior political affiliations. There is left, then, as the basis of the finding of Beilan's incompetency only his refusal to answer the School Superintendent's single question. . . . The Superintendent was apparently not disturbed by Beilan's failure to answer his question. He did nothing about it from June, 1952, until November, 1953, a few days after the Un-American Activities Committee visited Philadelphia."

"A plea of the Fifth Amendment before a congressional committee," Chief Justice Warren said, "is an invalid basis for discharge from public employment."[70] After all, if a person is punished for exercising a "right," it is not a right. "Beilan's plea of the Fifth Amendment before a subcommittee of the House Committee on Un-American Activities was so inextricably involved in the Board's decision to discharge him that the validity of the Board's action cannot be sustained without consideration of this ground."[71] Here Warren took judicial notice of a fact that Whittaker chose to ignore in the *Davis* case. As with Beilan, the movement to fire Davis began with an appearance before a congressional committee. Although a private school might have more leeway in dismissals than a publicly owned school might, in the *Davis* case Whittaker did not address the issue of whether a private employer could fire an employee for exercising a constitutional right.

Douglas took up that very point in his *Beilan* dissent. He noted evidence was lacking of treasonable action by Beilan and emphasized that exercising a constitutional right must not be equated with proof of guilt. "If it be said that we deal not with guilt or innocence but with frankness, the answer is the same. There are areas where government may not probe." Douglas conceded that private employers have a broader range of action than government employers. "But government has no business penalizing a citizen merely for his beliefs or associations. It is government action that we have here."[72] Douglas noted, with Black concurring, that Communist Party membership per se revealed little about a person's beliefs; many persons belong to organizations without endorsing all elements of the group's doctrine or agenda. "Government can concern itself only with the actions of men, not with their opinions or beliefs."[73]

The core question in this case was whether Beilan was fired because of his political beliefs. The Court majority (including Whittaker) said the teacher's politics had nothing to do with losing his job. The minority said politics had everything to do with it. The *Beilan* case is a classic example of sharp division among legal experts. The case also illustrates how legal theories have direct impact on citizens' lives—in this instance determining whether a long-admired teacher could continue to pursue his profession.

A case involving a student, instead of a teacher,[74] caused the Supreme Court to rule on an issue that Whittaker had disregarded in *Davis*. Bernhard Deutch was convicted for contempt of Congress after refusing to answer questions put to him at a hearing of the U. S. House Un-American Activities Committee in Washington, DC. Deutch did not claim any Fifth Amendment right at the hearing. Instead, at his later trial he claimed that he had no obligation to answer the committee questions because they were not pertinent to the committee's inquiry, the same issue that Davis had fruitlessly raised before Whittaker.

Speaking for the Court majority, Justice Stewart upheld Deutch's claim. The ostensible purpose of the hearings was to investigate communist activity in labor unions at Albany, New York. Deutch, however, was asked about his communist activity while an undergraduate and graduate student at Cornell University. He testified freely about his own past, but balked at five questions designed to elicit information about other persons and which could have been designed to help probe political beliefs of Cornell teachers. Deutch's position was strengthened by the committee chairman's declaration that the hearing was intended to investigate labor unions, and the committee counsel's denial that the hearing was intended to investigate educational organizations.

The Court majority acknowledged that the specific grounds cited by Deutch when he refused to testify might have been legally invalid. That was beside the point, however. The point was that a congressional committee could not compel a witness to testify about a topic outside the committee's scope of inquiry, and activities of Deutch's associates at Cornell's Ithaca campus had no demonstrable connection with labor unions in Albany.

Whittaker was one of several dissenters. He argued that the committee's general inquiry topic of labor covered the questions about Cornell University because when Deutch was summoned he was told he would be asked about communist activities at Cornell, and was told that this line of questioning had been developed from testimony given at the Albany hearings. Therefore, Whittaker argued, the questions Deutch refused to answer were pertinent—the committee had said so. Under Whittaker's reasoning the committee could force answers to any question, no matter how remote from the ostensible purpose of the investigation, simply by declaring that the question followed up on other testimony or questions. Whittaker's stance implied the committee was the judge of its own conduct, and that courts should not second-guess the committee's decision.

In addition, as was so typical with Whittaker, he objected to what he saw as a procedural irregularity. He believed Deutch should have raised the issue of pertinent questions at the hearing, not at his trial. Whittaker would disallow Deutch's trial defense on grounds that he had not raised it at the committee hearing (before he was indicted and had no conduct to defend). Indeed, Whittaker contended that Deutch's failure to object at the hearing was in itself contempt of Congress because Deutch's failure deprived the committee of opportunity to defend itself to him. (The committee defending its conduct when facing a hapless, protesting witness would have been a memorable occasion.)

On its surface, the nature of Whittaker's complaint shows a litigator's mind at work, seeking to disallow consideration of facts due to defect in procedure. At a deeper level Whittaker's stance is that of a district judge, punctiliously demanding that a lay person's ignorance of court procedure should impede consideration of his case in the final court of appeal. Most important historically, however, was that Whittaker equated Deutch's appearance before the Un-American Activities Committee hearing with appearance at a trial. Ordinarily a person testifying before a legislative committee should hardly be expected to follow rules of criminal jurisprudence. In Whittaker's mind, however, a person appearing before the committee was on trial, not simply providing information to guide possible new legislation. If a sophisticated Supreme Court justice felt someone testifying before the committee was on trial, we may be sure the general public felt so as well.

That popular belief, equating committee testimony with a trial, supports the contention of many persons who lost their jobs after appearing before the committee, the contention that a connection existed between dismissal and "unsatisfactory" testimony. Job termination was the "verdict" rendered after the "trial" of testimony.

Because of close contact that teachers have with children and adolescents, concerns about the impact of such contact are understandable regardless of constitutional questions involved. In the 1950s, however, concerns about a worker's political beliefs extended throughout the world of the workplace. Americans of a later era might have difficulty understanding how a subway conductor's politics were relevant to job performance, but that was exactly the question in *Lerner* v. *Casey*.[75]

Max Lerner was a New York subway conductor. New York's Security Risk Law classified subways as a "security agency" and defined the Communist Party as a "subversive group." When asked whether he was currently a Communist Party member, Lerner refused to answer, citing his Fifth Amendment rights. He was fired for refusing to answer.

Speaking for a Court majority that included Whittaker, Justice Harlan denied that Lerner's status or non-status in the Communist Party was relevant to losing his job. Harlan maintained that Lerner had simply demonstrated himself to be an unreliable employee by failing to say whether he was currently a Party member. Such "lack of candor" was a firing offense. Lerner was free to exercise his constitutional rights, Harlan said, but was not entitled to keep his subway job upon exercise of those rights.

The Court majority's reasoning raised the question of whether a "right" exists if its exercise penalizes a citizen. The only way for Lerner to exercise the right in question was to refuse to answer his employer's question. To keep his job he had to let his government employer violate his constitutional right. Should employment be dependent on tolerating illegal conduct by an employer? That was the core question Lerner brought to the Supreme Court.

The Court majority slid around the core question by maintaining that Lerner was insubordinate and not actually exercising a constitutional right. Moreover, Harlan argued that the subway conductor was employed by a state agency, not a federal one, and that Lerner had no Fifth Amendment right in this instance because the federal right did not apply to this type of state proceeding.

The core question, however, could not be answered except by Lerner attempting to exercise a right that he believed to exist. In practical terms, the majority opinion implied that a worker should not assert a constitutional right that an employer disliked, as a good faith assertion would not protect a worker from dismissal.

A troubled Justice Brennan dissented. If Lerner's political opinions were not an issue, was it not a subterfuge to dismiss him for refusing to answer questions about his political opinions? Brennan believed that Lerner was victimized by a shell game that, at the very least, violated long established standards of due process—of fairness in legal proceedings. Brennan saw the dilemma which had trapped Lerner.

The majority's reasoning, however, was common in court decisions of that era. Again and again judges maintained that a citizen accused of communist activity was being penalized not for such activity, but for failing to provide full information about such activity. If a worker's political activity having no discernable impact on job performance (as measured by supervisor ratings) was legitimate for employers to probe, how about a worker's sex life or religious beliefs? Court rulings on communist cases opened the way for more limits on an employee's private life.

Ubiquitous government committee investigations of individuals suspected of communist leanings were a hallmark of the 1950s. Investigators operated almost without limit, but occasionally they were brought up short. Despite Whittaker's friendliness toward such investigations, in one instance he ruled that investigators had gone too far.[76]

In 1953 the Ohio Un-American Activities Commission faced some uncooperative witnesses, who refused to answer seemingly innocuous questions: "What is your husband's name?"; "What are your parents' names?"; "Where did you reside prior to September, 1948?"; "What was your name at the time you were born; what was the name given you on baptism?"; "Did you ever live in the City of St. Louis, Missouri?" Again and again the witnesses refused to answer, standing on their Fifth Amendment rights. Even after being granted immunity from state prosecution they still refused to answer, on grounds that state immunity did not provide federal immunity. The witnesses were brought to trial for refusing to answer the questions, convicted, sentenced to jail for ten days, and fined $500.

Speaking for the Supreme Court, Whittaker overturned the convictions of these suspected communists. He noted, "Instead of overruling the objection or in any way directing the witness to answer the question, the Commission gave every indication that it sustained, or at least acquiesced in, the objection by immediately passing on to the next question. That process was scores of times repeated."[77] Whittaker declared a witness could not be convicted of refusing to answer a question if the commission failed to direct the witness to answer. Such conviction would violate due process guarantees of the Fourteenth Amendment.

> As to appellants' remaining contentions, including, (1) that because the Ohio immunity statute . . . does not afford immunity from federal prosecution, they could not lawfully be compelled to answer questions over their Fifth Amendment objections to them, (2) that the questions which they

> refused to answer were not pertinent to the inquiry, and (3) that the Commission's investigation was without legislative purpose, the Court is equally divided.[78]

Given Whittaker's hostility toward suspected communists, his ruling here is a tribute to the witnesses' attorneys. They raised an issue that gripped Whittaker's attention so strongly that it impelled him to make the ruling they wanted.

Another case[79] arose when the New Hampshire legislature decided to investigate alleged subversive activities in the state, and appointed the state attorney general as a one-man committee to conduct the investigation. One target was Willard Uphaus, executive director of World Fellowship, Inc., which operated a summer camp featuring speakers on public policy questions. Camp activities had a pacifist slant. The executive director testified freely about himself but declined to honor subpoenas for all correspondence about speakers, for a list of camp employees, and for a list of guests.

The camp director declined on several grounds, including the subpoenas' apparent violation of free speech and association. A state court agreed with the director's objection to producing employees' names, and that subpoena was invalidated. At the time of the U.S. Supreme Court case, no state court decision had been reached on the subpoena for correspondence, so that issue was not considered by the high court. The matter at hand, the matter which brought the director to the U.S. Supreme Court, was his conviction for refusing to produce the guest list. He had received an indefinite jail sentence for contempt.

Speaking for a Court majority that included Whittaker, Justice Clark upheld the subpoena's validity. He said producing the few hundred names involved would hardly be burdensome for the camp director. Clark noted that the director was involved in Communist front organizations and that campground speakers were connected with groups on the U.S. Attorney General's list of subversive organizations. Clark noted the New Hampshire attorney general was pursuing a civil investigation, which "need not be constricted until sufficient evidence of subversion is gathered to justify the institution of criminal proceedings."[80] A less generous way to describe such an investigation would be a "fishing expedition."

Clark declared that citizens' right to privacy must yield to New Hampshire's right to self-preservation. Whether lectures at a summer camp endangered New Hampshire might be debatable, but Clark seemed to rely here on a state law declaring pro-communist activity to be subversive, thus by definition (if not in reality) endangering the state. Clark noted another state law requiring the camp's guest register be made available to police and sheriffs, so the attorney general was simply demanding to see records that should be freely available to other law enforcement officials. Moreover, guests should have known that fact when they signed the register. Ignorance of the law is no excuse. Clark did not address the question of whether records open to police and sheriffs were open to any other law enforcement officials, particularly an attorney general who was acting in a legislative capacity rather than a law enforcement one.

Uphaus argued that the guest list would be used to harass guests in their hometowns. Whittaker was well aware of such practices, as he had presided in the *Davis* case back in Kansas City. Clark dismissed such concerns: "The record before us, however, only reveals a report to the Legislature of New Hampshire."[81] Although Clark chose to limit his awareness, some of his colleagues (as we shall see) took judicial notice of just how such records were being used to harass people in New Hampshire. The Court majority nonetheless ordered Uphaus to obey the subpoena or be imprisoned indefinitely for contempt of court.

Speaking on behalf of Warren, Black, and Douglas, Justice Brennan took a far different view of the case, seeing the conduct of New Hampshire authorities as sinister and the conduct of Uphaus as blameless. "This record . . . not only fails to reveal any interest of the State sufficient to subordinate appellant's constitutionally protected rights, but affirmatively shows that the investigatory objective was the impermissible one of exposure for exposure's sake."[82] Brennan warned, "In an era of mass communication and mass opinion, and of international tensions and domestic anxiety, exposure and group identification by the state of those holding unpopular and dissident views are fraught with such serious consequences for the individual as inevitably to inhibit seriously the expression of views which the Constitution intended to make free."[83] He quoted from the Court's decision in *NAACP* v. *Alabama*,[84] " 'Inviolability of privacy in group association may in many circumstances be indispensable to preservation of freedom of association, particularly where a group espouses dissident beliefs.' "

The Court's minority argued that the case at hand involved "exposure . . . as a governmental sanction." Brennan noted, "The problem is one in its nature calling for traditional case-by-case development of principles."[85] Such an argument could hardly have appealed to Whittaker, who wanted to find principles of law, not develop them.

Brennan scoffed at the New Hampshire attorney general's assertion that he wanted to determine if pacifism was linked to communism.

> No evidence that any activity of a sort that violates the law of New Hampshire or could in fact be constitutionally punished went on at the camp. What is clear is that there was some sort of assemblage at the camp that was oriented toward the discussion of political and other public matters. . . . The views expounded obviously were minority views. But the assemblage was, on its face, for purposes to which the First and Fourteenth Amendments give constitutional protection against incursion by the powers of government.[86]

Brennan described the document that Clark referred to as a legislative report. It opened with assorted "essays by various authors" on communism and communist activities. "This introductory material would focus attention on the whole report in terms of 'Communism' regardless of what was said about the individuals later named." The document concluded with biographies of twenty-three individuals. The state attorney general said he did not list persons who cooperated with his investigation. In other words, he did not want to subject them to punishment of publicity. Brennan observed, "No opinion was . . . expressed by the Attorney General as to whether any person named therein was in fact a 'subversive person' within the meaning of the statute," but his report gave "names with descriptions of what had been said about the named persons."[87] His report allowed comments from other persons to serve his purpose. "A positive diligence was demonstrated in efforts to add the names of individuals to a list and then render a Scotch verdict of 'not proven' in regard to them."[88] Some speakers at World Fellowship camp "were said to have signed open letters and petitions against deportations, to have criticized the Federal Bureau of Investigation, to have given free medical treatment to Communist Party officials, and the like."[89] In that era such statements about people were damning. "Finally the report addresses itself to the remainder of the speakers: 'Information easily available to this office does *not* indicate records of affiliation with or support of Communist causes on the part of these people. . . . It is not possible for this office to guarantee that the following individuals do not have such activity in their backgrounds.'. . . The names of 36 persons with their addresses then followed."[90]

Here is a sample entry from the "legislative report" of New Hampshire's attorney general, with names deleted:

> In recent years there has been opposition to legislative investigations in some academic circles. Charges have been made, usually without an accompanying scintilla of evidence, that "hysteria" rules the country and that teachers are afraid to teach "the truth" because of the "witch hunters." This line is repeated ad infinitum in the Communist "Daily Worker."
>
> In New Hampshire, during the course of this investigation, a case did arise where rumors were circulated concerning a teacher. . . .
>
> The teacher concerning whom the rumors were circulated was [X], a teacher in the [Y city] public school system. When the rumors concerning Mr. [X] came to the attention of this office, he was invited to testify. . . .

Although the teacher denied any past or current communist affiliation, the attorney general was not satisfied. "This office was prepared to make full investigation of the facts and to make public the results of such an investigation." Rather than undergo such a public ordeal, "[X] resigned and secured employment outside the state. Had [X] not decided to submit his resignation, such a [public investigation] course of action would have been taken, but facilities were not available for inquiring into moot problems."[91] In other words, as the accused person had been run out of town, no need was seen to determine whether the accusations were true. Such was the nature of the attorney general's "legislative investigation." Black and Douglas described it as a bill of attainder.[92] (Bills of attainder are unconstitutional. They are laws passed by a legislative body, declaring a person or class of persons guilty of a crime without judicial trial and specifying punishment. Bills of attainder, by which British authorities punished American colonists without a jury trial, helped cause the American Revolution.)

Brennan noted, "The emphasis of the entire report is on individual guilt, individual near-guilt, and individual questionable behavior."[93] Brennan said the attorney general's goal was "the making of lists of persons who were either classifiable in this amorphous category, or almost so, and the presenting of the result, as a public, official document."[94]

It was after the publication of this report that the subpoenas were issued against Uphaus. That is the context in which he resisted providing the names and addresses of camp guests, although he cooperated fully in providing information about himself and his own activities.

The Supreme Court's minority believed criminal indictments against camp guests would have been shaky. So instead the legislature and attorney general decided "to reach the end of exposure [i.e. to punish] through the process of investigation."[95] Brennan found "the report discloses an investigation in which the processes of law-making and law-evaluating were submerged entirely in exposure of individual behavior. . . . If an investigation or trial . . . which is aimed at the application of sanctions to individual behavior is to be upheld, it must meet the traditional standards that the common law in this country has established."[96] The minority justices saw the state of New Hampshire punishing persons whose conduct could not be challenged in criminal proceedings. The minority saw the state punishing persons for exercising their constitutional rights.

Brennan concluded the minority's opinion with a quotation from William T. Gossett, vice president and general counsel of Ford Motor Company, a gentleman who could hardly be considered a source of radical views: "When we are frustrated by the feeling that certain people . . . have flaunted society with impunity, it is tempting to pillory them through prolonged public exposure to hearsay testimony, intemperate invective and other forms of abuse. But to try by such means to destroy those whom we are unable to convict by due process of law may destroy instead the very safeguards that protect us all against tyranny and arbitrary power."

The Court's majority, which included Whittaker, saw government taking action against presumably dangerous citizens. The minority saw government taking action against presumably innocent citizens. The majority saw dangerous subversives threatening government. The minority saw government threatening innocent citizens. This was a basic conflict of values that could not be settled by ascertainment of facts, and is one example of why Whittaker found his Supreme Court service so maddening. Too often his ability to master the facts of a case was a talent irrelevant to the issue at hand.

Fears harbored by anti-communists in Whittaker's time included fear that foreign communists were infiltrating America. In response Congress passed laws to expel such persons from the United States. Perhaps some dangerous individuals were removed, but those laws also affected persons who had lived peacefully in their communities for decades.

The human cost of such laws was illustrated when an elderly ex-communist was deported to Bulgaria just as he became eligible to collect Social Security benefits, separating him from his wife (who stayed in the United States so she could stay alive on the spouse's percentage of benefits).[97] A similar case involved a befuddled and apparently harmless old gentleman who had briefly worked in a communist book store.[98]

Ephram Nestor emigrated to the United States from Bulgaria in 1913. In 1933 he joined the Communist Party and remained a member until 1939. This political activity was legal and happened long before Cold War hostilities arose between the United States and the Soviet Union. During the Great Depression a wide variety of social and economic reforms were discussed by assorted minor political parties. Being a communist in 1935 did not have the sinister connotation it had in 1955.

In November 1955 Nestor was entitled to start drawing Social Security retirement benefits. A few months later, however, he was deported for having been a communist, and his Social Security benefits were terminated under a 1954 law cutting off benefits to anyone who was deported after that law was passed. His wife remained in America and was allowed to draw Social Security on her spouse's earnings record.

Being ejected from a country where someone has been a peaceful and productive member of society for over forty years does not nurture warm feelings of contentment for a country that would do such a thing. Rather than fight deportation, Nestor instead filed suit in hopes of retaining benefits from the Social Security system into which he had paid for so many years.

Speaking for a majority that included Whittaker, Justice Harlan ruled that membership in the Social Security system did not give members any property right in benefits from the system. Arguing that benefits were unrelated to Social Security taxes paid by members (an arguable proposition indeed), Harlan distinguished Social Security from an annuity which did depend on a holder's payments. As Nestor had no property right in Social Security benefits, the Fifth

Amendment did not prohibit cutting off those benefits without the due process of law required when government seizes property.

Furthermore, Harlan ruled that depriving Nestor of Social Security benefits was not punitive but instead "mere denial of a noncontractual governmental benefit."[99] The deprivation was based on his deportation, not on the grounds for deportation, and therefore was not punitive. As the benefit cutoff was not punitive, arguments about lack of trial, and alleged violations of constitutional prohibitions against ex post facto proceedings and bills of attainder were irrelevant.

In dissent, Justice Black noted that Nestor's Communist Party membership in the 1930s had been legal, and law in the 1930s did not make any immigrant (such as Nestor) liable for deportation on grounds of such communist affiliation. Decades later Congress passed a law making past Communist Party membership cause for deportation, and Nestor was deported on those grounds. Still later Congress passed another law cutting off Social Security to anyone deported for being a former communist. Black saw Nestor as a victim of several unconstitutional actions. Eliminating his Social Security benefits was indeed a violation of the Fifth Amendment because it took away his insurance without compensation. Black declared Social Security benefits to be an earned right, not charity. Nestor had paid into Social Security for years and was entitled to what he had paid for. Taking away those benefits in connection with deporting Nestor on grounds of political activity that had been legal when he engaged in it (Communist Party membership) was not only an ex post facto proceeding but a bill of attainder. "The fact that the Court is sustaining this action," Black said, "indicates the extent to which people are willing to go these days to overlook violations of the Constitution perpetrated against anyone who has ever even innocently belonged to the Communist Party."[100]

Black argued that revoking Nestor's Social Security was "punishment even in a classic sense"[101] and not at all the neutral proceeding portrayed by the Court's majority. Black quoted an earlier case declaring "legislative acts, no matter what their form, that apply either to named individuals or to easily ascertainable members of a group in such a way as to inflict punishment on them without a judicial trial are bills of attainder."[102] Justice Douglas agreed, describing the 1954 law as a "classic example of a bill of attainder."[103] He insisted, "Social Security payments are not gratuities."[104]

Brennan's dissent, with Warren and Douglas concurring, examined more deeply the majority's contention that Nestor had not been punished. Brennan described Nestor as "an aging man deprived of the means with which to live after being separated from his family and exiled to live among strangers in a land he quit 47 years ago. The common sense of it is that he has been punished severely."[105] Brennan argued, even if deportation is viewed as "not punishment, but as a permissible exercise of congressional power to enact the conditions under which aliens may come to and remain in this country," the statute cutting off Social Security benefits imposes a punishment on top of mere immigration rules. The statute did not terminate benefits for all beneficiaries who left the United States but only for aliens deported for particular reasons. "In other words Congress worked its will only on aliens deported for conduct displeasing to the lawmakers." The law in question "imposes punishment in violation of the prohibition against *ex post facto* laws and without a judicial trial."[106]

Charles Rowoldt was another alien who encountered the harsh anti-communist laws of that era. Rowoldt had lived in the United States since 1914. He said he joined the Communist Party in Minneapolis for about a year in 1935. To him, the group seemed to be trying to help people get jobs and food. He did not advocate violent overthrow of the U.S. government and saw no sinister party activities. He said the communists he worked with operated through the regular political system as they sought to increase employment and reduce hunger. He worked in a communist bookstore for awhile. His version of his Depression-era Party activities was not challenged by the federal government when, in 1951, it sought to deport him under the Internal Security Act of 1950, on grounds of being an alien who had once belonged to the Communist Party.

Here is an excerpt from testimony he gave about himself in 1947 when asked about his political beliefs, testimony that the federal government found damning in 1951:

> Any government that exists today has a right to exist as it is—by the power of the majority of a nation's people. Nobody in the world can say there are no changes. We must always consider changes. They can be made when the people see that it is the right time for it, and at that time they will have their representatives which will take care of it. I am absolutely against sudden dictatorship and overthrow of government. . . . My belief is a different thing than communism is. According to Marx and Lenin and as I have seen the Communists working, since I knew of them, they are aiming, more or less, with forever methods to set up an economic system to get the people out of a monopoly control on to their own economic feet. That is the way I see them working now.[107]

Justice Frankfurter delivered the Court's decision on Rowoldt's appeal of the deportation order. Frankfurter noted that an amendment to the Internal Security Act absolved anyone who was a Party member simply to get a job or food or for any other innocuous purpose. Rowoldt's Party membership provided him with a job at a legitimate bookstore. Frankfurter described Rowoldt as an "old man who has lived in this country for forty years"[108] and exempt from deportation.

Speaking for dissenters who included Whittaker, Justice Harlan said the

Internal Security Act amendment that Frankfurter relied upon applied only to aliens seeking admittance to the United States, not to aliens already living here. The dissenters said if the effect of such a statute was harsh, that was a matter for Congress to remedy, not the Supreme Court.

Here we see Whittaker joining in a real life expression of judicial conservatism, of refusing to encroach on a congressional prerogative. Although the principle is usually stated as absolute, in practice it is elastic. At some point a statute can be so harsh as to be unconstitutional, and at that point justices who refused to intervene would be derelict in their duty. In the case at hand, however, such a decision did not arise because the majority ruled that an amendment to the harsh law exempted Rowoldt from the harsh provisions.

As Whittaker's later speeches showed, his judicial conservatism was not absolute. When the question was whether Congress had gone too far in regulating the national economy through New Deal reforms, Retired Justice Whittaker did not hesitate to brand such statutes as unconstitutional. His willingness to disregard the will of Congress when it regulated the conduct of great business enterprises, contrasted with his respect for the will of Congress when it devastated the lives of harmless individuals branded as communists, provides a glimpse of his political philosophy. Although he described himself as nonpolitical, his stance on the two questions was typical for conservative Republicans of that era.

Nonetheless, just as he always claimed, that stance did not dictate what a decision would be if he found facts compelling him to lay aside personal inclinations. He sometimes refrained from using McCarthy era laws to deport immigrants possessing communist backgrounds. In one case he allowed a Spanish Civil War veteran to remain in the United States,[109] and in another prevented deportation of an immigrant who was caught between conflicting laws and bureaucrats.[110]

Frank Bonetti entered the United States in 1923 at the age of fifteen. He joined the Communist Party in 1932, leaving the party in 1936. The next year he fought in Spain with the Republican Army, saying if Hitler was not stopped there, world war would result. Bonetti's courage cost him a foot, amputated as a result of a war wound. By going to Spain to fight Hitler's fascist forces Bonetti gave up his residency rights in the United States. He reentered the United States in 1938 as a quota immigrant and was granted permanent resident status.

In 1950 Congress passed a law (Internal Security Act[111]) authorizing deportation of any alien who was a member of the Communist Party upon or subsequent to entry into the United States. The Eisenhower Administration sought to deport Bonetti.

Whittaker delivered the Court's opinion. He did not consider the ex post facto nature of applying a 1950 law to something a person did in the 1930s when there was no penalty for the action (although if he had, Whittaker might well have argued that deportation was a civil proceeding not prohibited by the Constitution's ban on criminal ex post facto proceedings). Whittaker stated the question as whether Bonetti's 1923 or 1938 entry governed the case. If the 1923 entry governed, then Bonetti could be deported because he joined the Communist Party subsequent to 1923. If, however, the 1938 entry governed, Bonetti could not be deported because he was not a communist in 1938 or thereafter.

Whittaker ruled that the most recent entry governed because Bonetti had given up his residency rights in order to fight Hitler and had to go through the immigration process to return to America in 1938. Given Whittaker's hostility toward anyone with a communist background, his decision is an example of allowing himself to be governed by legal reasoning regardless of where it led.

His decision is even more remarkable because an alternate path was available. Justice Clark spoke for dissenters who argued that Bonetti's 1923 entry governed the case. They said the law referred to an immigrant's first entry; Bonetti's departure and return in the 1930s were irrelevant. The dissenters noted that the 1950 law operated retroactively (was ex post facto in nature), and that no question existed about the right to deport Bonetti under that law if he had never made his Spanish sojourn.

Although Whittaker refrained from a direct riposte, he surely would have responded that facts determine the law of a case, and that his dissenting colleagues were simply arguing that different facts would lead to different controlling law—a point Whittaker surely would have granted. But the dissenters could not change the facts, so they could not change Whittaker's decision.

Another deportation case[112] relied on the same statute used against Bonetti. The Internal Security Act of 1950 said any alien who became a Communist Party member after entering the United States was subject to deportation. Knut Einar Heikkinen was a Finn who emigrated to Canada in 1910 and became a Canadian citizen. From 1916 onward he made his home in the United States. He was a Communist Party member from 1923 to 1930, took a lengthy trip to the Soviet Union in the 1930s, and apparently was a Party member again for a year or two after World War II. The Immigration and Naturalization Service started to deport him in 1950 but canceled the proceedings. Subsequently the INS began proceedings again, and a deportation order was sent to him in April 1952.

Under the Internal Security Act Heikkinen was indicted and convicted for failing to leave the United States within six months after receiving the deportation order (count 1) and for failing, in that time frame, to apply for travel documents necessary for leaving the United States (count 2). He received a five-year sentence on the first count, with imposition of sentence for the second count postponed until prison time was served under first count.

Speaking for the Supreme Court, Justice Whittaker found those convictions wrongful. He noted a complete lack of evidence that any country was willing to let Heikkinen move there, an excellent excuse for not leaving the United States. In addition, U.S. immigration officials told Heikkinen to wait to hear from them on arrangements they were making for him to leave the country. Given that agency's stance, Whittaker and the Court could not see how Heikkinen was willfully trying to evade the deportation order by remaining in the country. His convictions were reversed. (During World War II Japanese Americans had been put in a similar dilemma, with contradictory orders that could not be obeyed without violating one of them, with disobedience providing an excuse for incarceration.)

As typical with Whittaker, he made his decision on the narrowest ground possible. He had no comment on a basic philosophical issue rumbling through the case, the ex post facto nature of penalizing someone for an act (joining the Communist Party) that was not prohibited at the time it occurred.

RACE RELATIONS

Along with fear of communism, turmoil surrounding racial desegregation was the greatest social controversy of the 1950s. Racial prejudice had long been a facet of American life, but not until the Warren years did the Supreme Court begin to find constitutional ways to promote racial equality. Such cases were numerous, but from a biographical standpoint (trying to understand Whittaker rather than trying to understand the law), two cases bring out his approach to questions of racial discrimination.

One of the great civil rights disputes of the 1960s was "public accommodations." Did the owner of a restaurant or hotel or theater have the right to refuse service to a potential customer because of skin color or some other factor having nothing to do with proper decorum and ability to pay? If a restaurant was privately owned but open to the public, which right was greater: the owner's right to choose customers, or a hungry person's right to pay for a meal? And what was a public accommodation anyway? At what point, for example, did a private club serving members become a restaurant open to the general public? Did a bus terminal restaurant have to serve any passengers who were engaged in interstate travel? That latter question arose in *Boynton* v. *Virginia.*[113]

Speaking for the Court majority, Justice Black framed the key question of the case: "Whether an interstate bus passenger is denied a federal statutory or constitutional right when a restaurant in a bus terminal used by the carrier along its route discriminates in serving food to the passenger solely because of his color."[114]

Bruce Boynton stepped off a Trailways bus on forty-minute layover in Richmond, Virginia, during an interstate journey and ordered food at the Trailways bus terminal restaurant. Boynton was in an area reserved for "whites," and the restaurant's assistant manager told him to move to the "colored" section. Boynton declined. He was arrested and convicted for remaining in the restaurant unlawfully after being told to leave. Boynton, who was a law student, argued that as an interstate passenger he had a lawful right to remain in the "whites" section of the restaurant. His attorney Thurgood Marshall agreed.

Justice Black said the Court would consider two constitutional questions explicitly raised in Boynton's appeal: rights of interstate bus passengers (persons engaged in interstate commerce) and application of the Fourteenth Amendment's guarantees of due process and equal protection of laws. Noting that Virginia tribunals had examined whether the restaurant violated the Interstate Commerce Act, Black said the U.S. Supreme Court would do so as well.

The Court ruled that if restaurant services were provided by Trailways, services had to be equally available to all passengers. Although the bus company did not own the restaurant, its service was primarily to bus passengers. The bus terminal had legal authority to dictate the manner in which food would be sold to bus passengers, what food products could be sold, and even what equipment the restaurant could use. And Trailways had half ownership of the terminal and thus indirectly had partial control of the restaurant. The Supreme Court majority conceded that if a Trailways bus stopped near a restaurant then the restaurant did not necessarily become part of the bus company's interstate transit business. In this particular instance, however, the restaurant inside the Trailways bus terminal was part of the company's system and subject to federal regulation of interstate commerce that guaranteed equal service to all passengers.

Whittaker dissented explosively. He began by saying the Supreme Court violated its own rules by considering the Interstate Commerce Act's relation to the case when the Act's relation was not raised in Boynton's petition of appeal. Certainly an argument can be made for Whittaker's viewpoint. He was saying, however, that the judicial system's final court of appeal should disregard a relevant factor if that factor was not raised in the proper procedural format. Here was the stance of a supreme technocrat who was, in essence, willing to rule against a litigant because a form was improperly filled out. Certainly court procedures are established for good reason, and exceptions should not be made lightly. But even parliamentary procedure allows for suspension of rules in order to be sure justice is done.

Stating his protest about consideration of the issue, Whittaker proceeded to argue Boynton's conviction was legal under the Interstate Commerce Act because the Trailways bus company did not own or control the restaurant. Casting aside definitions of "ownership" and "control," we see here a basic philosophical clash between Whittaker and the Court majority. He saw ownership and control as the governing factor. The majority said that was irrelevant. For those justices the bus company's use of this restaurant was the key factor, making this food service part of the Trailways interstate transportation system, thereby obligating the restaurant to conform to the Interstate Commerce act regardless of who owned or controlled it.

Whittaker conceded that the bus company's partial ownership of the terminal gave it partial control of the restaurant that leased space there.[115] He argued, however, that this fact was not considered at the state court level and thus could not be considered by the U.S. Supreme Court. Here we have a scholastic view of jurisprudence indeed. Whittaker admits facts of ownership and control that contradict his argument but says those facts must be disregarded because they were not part of the Virginia Supreme Court of Appeals record. He thereby makes his argument logically valid but admits it is untrue. Good logic, poor law. Normally Whittaker was fanatic about determining facts of a case. Does his disregard of facts here express a personal philosophy opposed to desegregation? That question is particularly apposite if we consider Whittaker's stance in *Elkins* v. *United States*.[116] There he concurred in Frankfurter's dissent maintaining that the quest for truth obligates courts to consider evidence illegally acquired by prosecutors. Surely the same quest entitles courts to consider legal evidence even if not acquired under standard rules.

In *Boynton*, Whittaker said he could find no demonstration that Trailways had made the restaurant part of its transportation system. He could find no evidence in wording of contracts, perhaps, but there was also evidence of bricks and mortar: of Trailways buses halting at a building labeled as a Trailways terminal, where the terminal (owned in part by the bus company) was legally named "Trailways Bus Terminal, Inc." and was leasing space to an entity legally named "Bus Terminal Restaurant of Richmond, Inc." Could not one reasonably infer that the restaurant had something to do with bus passengers?

Whittaker's opinions exhibited a litigator's mind, invoking rules to hinder consideration of unpalatable facts, and invoking facts to justify disregard of unpalatable rules.

In 1966 he spoke about the sorts of issues he considered in *Boynton*:

> Property that is privately owned and operated is "private" property, to which only those who are expressly or impliedly invited by the owner may of right come and enter and surely this implies that any such invitation may be revoked by the owner at any time for any reason satisfactory to him. Yet almost daily we see efforts, some of them successful, to expand the concept of "public" to include that which is "private"—such as a citizen's privately

> owned and operated store, shop, restaurant, motel, farm, medical or law office—and to make those "private" facilities subject, as of right, to use and enjoyment by the public.[117]

Desegregation, whether of public accommodations or public schools, was but one civil rights issue that repeatedly came to the Supreme Court's consideration. Voting rights were another.

A classic case[118] arose when the Alabama legislature altered the boundaries of Tuskegee in a complicated geometrical figure that shifted about 395 of Tuskegee's 400 black voters out of the city. They could still vote, but not in Tuskegee elections. Had their right to vote been taken away?

The Supreme Court said yes. Justice Frankfurter ruled that the legislature had violated the Fifteenth Amendment's guarantee of voting rights. Justice Whittaker concurred but on different grounds. He agreed that Tuskegee's blacks had been unconstitutionally deprived of voting rights but did not see a violation of the Fifteenth Amendment, because the blacks could still vote somewhere. Instead he thought their Fourteenth Amendment rights to equal protection of laws had been violated by the gerrymandering.

Whittaker's stance in this case is interesting when viewed against his subsequent harsh rhetoric against civil rights agitators. That rhetoric can be glibly dismissed as expressing ingrained racial prejudice common to many citizens of that era, particularly if gauged by standards of a subsequent time. The Tuskegee case, however, offers a deeper understanding of Whittaker's later rhetoric that became so popular with opponents of the civil rights movement. His speeches and articles continually attacked civil disobedience, action which by definition is unlawful and which would offend a person whose life was defined by law. Victims in the Tuskegee case carefully abided by law, so Whittaker was not hostile to their plight. If he were against civil rights per se he could easily have accepted and defended the subterfuge used by Alabama, that the legislature has power to establish city boundaries regardless of consequences.

During and after Whittaker's service on the Supreme Court, linkage between civil disobedience and the civil rights movement was so strong that criticism of the former could easily be interpreted as criticism of the latter. The Tuskegee case, however, challenges such an interpretation of Whittaker's speeches and articles.

Such interpretation was nonetheless easy to make. Discussing the Fourteenth Amendment, Whittaker referred with approval to "contemporary" community standards defining what sort of conduct was constitutional,[119] suggesting awareness that what was constitutional in 1864 might not be in 1964. Discussing civil rights, however, he cited an 1883 Supreme Court decision that he called binding and told a college audience in February 1964, "There is no Federal—distinguished from State—legal basis for compelling 'integration'." He further declared that pending civil rights legislation (which became the Civil Rights Act of 1964) was unconstitutional. He singled out for particular criticism the bill's public accommodations section requiring businesses to serve customers regardless of their race, noting its similarity to an 1875 law that was ruled unconstitutional in 1883. He stated, moreover, "No concrete meaning can be ascribed to a 'Civil Rights Act'. The term . . . is virtually meaningless."[120] Upon passage of the Act he repeated those remarks when speaking to a group of Southern lawyers in July 1964, in a speech entitled "Immutable Moral Values."[121]

In "Immutable Moral Values" Whittaker complained, just after passage of the 1964 Civil Rights Act, that illegal civil rights demonstrations had gained "apparent approval . . . in high places." He granted that demonstrations obstructing use of private and public property were often peaceful but "in many cases constitute common trespasses and disturbances of the private and public peace."[122] Here Whittaker is making his way forward to a stance he would express in "Law and Order," where he would define an illegal demonstration as inherently violent and therefore unprotected by First Amendment guarantees of peaceable assembly.

Whittaker was angered that Martin Luther King, Jr., "was recently publicly honored—some say rewarded—by an old and highly respected American university through its conference upon him of an honorary degree—not in some new political science but in law."[123] The source of Whittaker's anger about such an award would not be explained until his later speech "The Causes, and the Effects upon Public Order, of Planned, Mass Violations of the Law," (discussed below) in which he argued that King and other civil rights leaders advocated lawlessness.

One can almost hear the disbelief in Whittaker's voice as he told his audience of Southern lawyers, "Federal authorities have not only failed to punish such trespasses and violence but, instead, have frequently restrained local authorities from doing so."[124] Such comments must have been well received by Southerners who had long fought civil rights advocates and who viewed the new Civil Rights Act as a violation of states' rights. (Indeed this welcome reception is documented through insertion of assorted Whittaker remarks into the *Congressional Record* by representatives and senators from the South.[125])

The speech concluded with warnings about persons who used religious references to cloak their desire for socialism or communism. Here Whittaker picked up on a broader theme running through the civil rights movement led by blacks such as Rev. King and whites such as Rev. William Sloane Coffin. That theme was a call for social justice that went beyond new statutes and which sought to reduce the income gap between the very rich and the very poor. Whether that call was a demand for communism is debatable, but Whittaker's belief was clear.

In June 1965 Whittaker gave a speech to the Tennessee Bar Association. His remarks were reprinted in publications ranging from the *Chicago Tribune* and *Philadelphia Inquirer* to *U.S. News and World Report* and *F.B.I. Law Enforcement Bulletin*. The discourse was entitled "Law and Order," a code phrase used by opponents of statutory reforms intended to promote social justice in general and racial concord in particular. In "Law and Order" Whittaker was speaking to an organization of Southern lawyers during turmoil surrounding passage of the bitterly contested Civil Rights Act of 1964.

In that speech Whittaker shoveled scorn upon "*self-appointed leaders of minority groups*" who advocated civil disobedience. His rhetoric was particularly harsh about an unnamed civil rights leader who Whittaker described as recipient of both an honorary law degree and a peace prize. Listeners of the era clearly understood he meant Martin Luther King, Jr. Indeed, after King's murder Whittaker refused to record the speech for radio broadcast. "No man," Whittaker told the Southern lawyers, "or any group or race of men, can be permitted, in a government of laws, to take the law, or what they think ought to be the law, into their own hands, for that is anarchy, and sure to result in chaos." Grievances should be settled in courts, not in the streets.[126] After further consideration, Whittaker published a revised version of that speech in which he described civil rights demonstrations as "organized crime,"[127] a choice of rhetoric unlikely to fulfill his oft-stated desire for calm discussion of public policy controversies.

In "Law and Order" Whittaker portrayed the civil rights movement as an organized crime conspiracy influenced by communists. He began by describing conduct of citizens who demanded service at racially segregated lunch counters and other businesses.

> At the beginning, those "demonstrations" consisted of episodic group invasions and appropriation of private stores, first by sitting down and later by lying down therein, and, eventually, by blocking the entrances thereto with their bodies.
>
> Seeing that those tre[s]passes were often applauded in high places, were generally not punished but, rather, were compelled to be appeased and rewarded, those racial leaders and their groups quickly enlarged the scope of their activities by massing and marching on *the sidewalks, streets and highways*—frequently *blocking and appropriating them to a degree that precluded their intended public uses.*
>
> And *that conduct, too, being nearly always appeased,* the process spread areawise, as might have been expected, from one Southern city to another, and then into many Northern cities.[128]

Whittaker's rhetoric about "appeasement" referred to granting Adolf Hitler's demands in hopes of preventing war in the 1930s. That "misguided appeasement" was being cited by U. S. government leaders as justification for the Vietnam War that raged while Whittaker spoke, a war opposed by many persons who supported the civil rights movement. Here Whittaker indirectly chided the federal government for failing to follow an anti-appeasement policy at home while the government argued such a policy was crucial overseas. For listeners of Whittaker's era, his rhetoric had fierce emotional impact—likening civil rights demonstrators to Nazis (of the 1930s) and communists (of the 1960s) who had to be opposed at all costs lest democracy be destroyed. In at least one respect, of course, Whittaker's analogy was incorrect. Hitler continually escalated his demands. The civil rights movement's goal was the same in 1965 as in 1955—to eliminate discrimination against citizens on basis of race.

Whittaker continued his analysis of civil rights demonstrations by saying:

> That conduct is not protected by the peaceable-assembly-and-petition provision of the *First Amendment.*
>
> That provision says: "Congress shall make no law . . . abridging . . . the right of the people *peaceably* to assemble and to petition the Government for a redress of grievances."
>
> *Nothing in that language grants a license to any man, acting either singly or in a group, to violate State criminal laws.*[129]

Here Whittaker declared that defiance of an unconstitutional state law was violent by definition, and that suppression of such conduct was legitimate. "That conduct cannot properly be termed 'peaceable'," he said.

> Mob actions . . . have *proven*—as certainly we should have expected—to be tailor-made for infiltration, take-over and use by rabble-rousers and Communists who are avowedly bent on the breakdown of law, order and morality in our society and, hence, in its destruction.[130]

Whittaker's depiction of civil rights advocates as doing the work of communists, at a time when United States military personnel were dying in combat against an Asian communist regime, could not fail to promote anger among both supporters and opponents of the civil rights movement. He could not have been unaware of such rhetoric's effect, and such a choice of language repudiated his own frequent calls to tone down the emotional level of public policy debate.

Whittaker acknowledged that some state authorities had been unconstitutionally suppressing citizens who attempted to exercise civil rights guaranteed by the federal Constitution. Nonetheless he condemned these citizens for their defiance of unconstitutional state laws: "The fact that the provocations may have been themselves constitutionally unlawful cannot justify unlawful means for their resolution. Both types of conduct are wrong—constitutionally wrong, the one as much as the other. And, obviously, two wrongs cannot make a right."[131] If citizens refused to obey illegal orders from state authorities and held protest marches in defiance, such defiance threatened the well-being of society:

> The causes are plain. We have, in high places, tolerated and even encouraged preachments to break the law. . . .
>
> The remedy is equally plain. It is simply to insist that our governments, State and federal, reassume and discharge their first duty of protecting the people against lawless invasions of their persons and property and from assaults upon their liberties by demanding and commanding respect for law and legal processes through the impartial, evenhanded, vigorous, swift and certain enforcement of our criminal laws and the real and substantial punishment thereunder of all conduct that violates those laws.[132]

Whittaker's criticism of civil rights activism became even more blunt in 1966:

> "Integration," a term of no constitutional significance . . . embraces the concept of amalgamation, well illustrated by the transfer of schoolchildren from their home district to a distant district for the purpose . . . of affirmatively "mixing" or "integrating" the races when indeed no provision of the Constitution so requires. . . .
>
> We also hear much confused argument about "civil rights.". . . Webster says that . . . in the United States the term means "rights secured by the Thirteenth and Fourteenth amendments to the Constitution, and by certain acts of Congress abolishing the incidence of involuntary servitude."
>
> Thus, the only meaning of the term in the abstract that even approaches concreteness is that civil rights are the rights of all men in the United States to be free from the "incidence of involuntary servitude.". . .
>
> No minority group that has settled in our land has obtained, or likely ever will obtain, general acceptance and amalgamation here until, by long years of exemplary conduct, a majority of its members have earned the respect and liking of the people generally. Any effort to compel social acceptance would be a step in the wrong direction and self-defeating.[133]

Here Whittaker used one of the most inflammatory terms in the history of American race relations, "amalgamation." As always, his choice of language allowed him to dance away from its connotations if he were challenged, but the term's historical implication of sexual contact between black males and white females was inescapable. Although Whittaker relied on Webster to argue that civil rights encompass no more than the absence of chattel slavery, one wonders how Judge Whittaker would have treated a litigant whose definition of a legal principle was based on Webster's dictionary.

In the 1968 presidential election campaign Richard Nixon decried the Johnson administration for inadequate law enforcement, and Whittaker agreed in an election day speech to the National Institute of Municipal Law Officers: "We must have respect for the law or have the fear that compels obedience to the law." Nixon had used the phrase "Law and Order" as one of his main slogans—a code phrase for suppression of unruly black citizens and an end to the "War on Poverty," a Johnson administration program designed, in part, to reduce black unrest. On election day Whittaker agreed with foes of that program, assuring listeners that poverty did not promote civil unrest.[134]

Whittaker's portrayal of the civil rights movement as a violent threat to democracy, deserving suppression by armed force, was not universally endorsed by his fellow Americans. But neither was his view universally condemned. On the contrary, many opponents of the civil rights movement blamed it for violent riots sweeping American cities in the mid-1960s, and saw connections between outbreaks of mass violence and incidents of individual violence such as street robberies. In other segments of "Law and Order" Whittaker articulated those concerns as well. Evening strolls around one's neighborhood are difficult to enjoy when every approaching stranger causes fear. Whittaker and his wife personally suffered from such an experience when their Kansas City residence was burglarized; Winifred was so upset by the violation of their home that they put it on the market immediately and moved away.[135] Many Americans responded sympathetically to Whittaker's call for a society where people could quietly enjoy their property and their lives. Whittaker, however, seemed oblivious to factors generating turmoil throughout America in the 1960s. Americans needed far more than police and courts to liberate themselves from anxieties causing social unrest.

Another Whittaker speech, called "The Causes, and the Effects upon Public Order, of Planned, Mass Violations of the Law," was the first event in a series of discussions between him and other persons, sponsored by the American Enterprise Institute in Washington, DC.

Mass protest, Whittaker declared, "whether it be called a 'demonstration' or something else, waged for the avowed purpose of 'forcing' the grant of 'demands' outside the law, the legislature, and the courts, cannot be any peaceable petitioning for a redress of grievances."[136] Under such reasoning, protestors were not exercising their right of free speech (because Whittaker defined their conduct as violence, not speech), and authorities thereby could use whatever level of force they deemed necessary to break up those "violent" assemblies. Such reasoning, too, implied that government agencies provided the only acceptable venue for conflict resolution.

Speaking of persons who engaged in civil disobedience, Whittaker said, "Many of the laws they so condemn, and often flout, actually are embodiments of the laws of God. . . . Nor should we overlook, as is so often done, the biblical admonition that Thou shalt obey the civil authorities. I wonder how those who advocate violation of, and violate, our laws—civil or criminal—can square their conduct with that biblical admonition."[137] Whittaker declared that preachings by one of the "self-appointed Negro leaders," Martin Luther King, Jr., typically resulted in riots, looting, arson, and murder. Whittaker quoted a Chicago police official about King: "Wherever he goes and preaches nonviolence, violence erupts."[138] Whittaker, an expert in facts, said that high federal officials—including President Lyndon Johnson, Vice President Hubert Humphrey, and Secretary of State Dean Rusk—endorsed and encouraged such riots.[139]

Whittaker claimed the core reason for urban unrest was unemployment caused by recent mass migration into Northern cities by "many millions" of blacks who were formerly self-sufficient in the rural South. Population figures contradicted his assertion, and he cited none. Instead Whittaker claimed his "personal observations over a good many years" proved that the "many millions" of Southern blacks recently moving into Northern cities

> had lived in rural or semi-rural areas, in rented houses, of poor quality by our standards, surrounded by a few acres of land, for which they paid small rents, and upon that land they produced vegetables, tubers, and pork ample to their needs. With their trusted shotgun, dog, and fishing pole they could, and often did, augment their provisions with plentiful game, fowl, and fish from the nearby fields, forests, and streams, and hence, without cash, they could always have plenty of substantial and nourishing food. With their trusted axe, they were able to get from nearby forests ample firewood, for the chopping, to heat their homes. Their small needs for cash were primarily supplied by tending a small "patch" of cotton, "on the shares," on the rented acres mentioned, and any further need of cash was supplemented, as needed, by episodically "working out." They did not live well by our standards, but they were nearly always filled and warm, were highly free and independent, enjoyed much leisure and generally were a happy lot.[140]

The contentment long observed by Whittaker was less apparent to the Ku Klux Klan, White Citizens Councils, and local constables who had been struggling against a disgruntled and fearful black population for years.

Whittaker and Professor Daniel Berman of American University had this public exchange about Whittaker's speech:

> BERMAN: What is a Negro to do in a society where crime against him goes unpunished, where those who are charged with the enforcement of the law make it quite clear that he is not welcome to bring complaints, that the bringing of complaints by him will meet with terrible consequences?
> WHITTAKER: Well, don't you think that the opinions of the Supreme Court have been sufficiently clear on that matter? Do they not hold that any such treatment of a Negro by a state in the south or elsewhere in our nation is the denial of due process under the Fourteenth Amendment, and therefore cannot be tolerated?[141]

For Whittaker, injustice in society could be remedied by justice in a courtroom. His religious devotion to law resulted in judicial detachment from reality, leaving him oblivious to circumstances immune to the law's commands.

Although Whittaker was famed for basing his opinions on careful examination of facts, his speeches indicate no awareness of several facts relevant to the situation he condemned. For generations black citizens had been excluded from the political process, especially in the South where King concentrated his efforts at that time. Through schemes that even Whittaker had declared unconstitutional (such as gerrymandering election districts) blacks were prevented from voting for public officials who could reform the laws. Since blacks could not seek reform of discriminatory laws through influence in city councils and state legislatures, the only way to challenge discriminatory laws was to violate them in order to create court cases in which the laws could be challenged. Although Whittaker said blacks should seek court relief if they felt aggrieved, the only access to such relief was through civil disobedience. Whittaker was well aware of this; as a judge he had urged that courts refuse to hear "theoretical" grievances that did not involve law violations. In *Poe* v. *Ullman*[142] Whittaker joined a majority finding no need to determine constitutionality of a state law forbidding physicians from providing married women with contraceptive devices and instructions on their use, holding the question was moot until a physician violated the law and was prosecuted. Under Whittaker's reasoning, physicians had to engage in civil disobedience if they wanted to protect the rights of themselves and their patients. How did this differ from a black person sitting at a whites-only lunch counter? In speeches Former Justice Whittaker condemned people for doing what Justice Whittaker said they had to do in order to assert their rights, namely violate laws that they felt to be unjust in order to determine if the laws were constitutional. If blacks had followed the advice of Former Justice Whittaker they might have been denied access to mayors, city councils, governors, legislatures, and courts forever.

Frustrated by such denial of access, large non-violent gatherings demanding reform assembled in the 1960s, sometimes in defiance of orders from governmental officials. Whittaker declared that such non-violent meetings were by definition (*his* definition) not peaceable if conducted in defiance of orders from government officials (perhaps the same officials who denied these citizens access to legislatures). By defining such gatherings as not peaceable, Whittaker excluded them from First Amendment protections and supported both mass arrest of participants and disregard of their grievances.

In essence, the combined rhetoric of Whittaker's speeches advised victims of racial segregation laws to stay home and stay quiet, while telling local police to move against citizens who defied that advice.

Chapter 6

Lingering Aftertaste

Although our understanding of law changes as decades pass, that change is usually slow. As the twenty-first century began, some aspects of American jurisprudence would still be familiar to Jefferson and Lincoln. To view law as timeless, as Whittaker did, would be an extreme viewpoint. Yet he was certainly correct to think that his decisions could affect his profession and ordinary citizens long after his judicial service ended. Such effect can be seen in cases dealing with civil liberties and with relations between employers and workers.

CIVIL LIBERTIES

Most questions about civil liberties arise in criminal cases. In that category one venue common to Whittaker's time largely disappeared in later decades: prosecutions for communist activities. Other venues, such as violent crimes and drug offenses, were still familiar court controversies when this book was written. These cases are trip wire warnings of possible threats to democracy. The significance of such threats depends on the significance of democracy. Because the issues are so often raised by convicted criminals, many persons view civil liberties as technicalities liberating thugs and swindlers so they can continue to prey upon ordinary citizens. In issues that Whittaker had to decide, however, we shall see that respect for civil liberties did not necessarily release convicts whose rights were violated. Moreover, in some cases strict observance of civil liberties resulted in firmer punishment, and all cases established principles affecting lives of law-abiding citizens far more often than lives of criminals.

First Amendment

Said Whittaker, "I think a number of First Amendment rights are absolute and some are not."[1] This comment is a rare expression of judicial philosophy from him. Nothing in the First Amendment's text indicates what elements, if any, are limited and what ones are unlimited. Reaching such a determination requires a person to go beyond the text. Although Whittaker would probably claim to be guided by case precedents, in a case reaching the Supreme Court precedents typically conflict. In such circumstances Supreme Court justices must be guided by personal beliefs about the Constitution's intent. Whittaker's brief comment about the First Amendment implies that he sought some answers from within himself instead of from within the law. Everything we know about Whittaker indicates that searching for answers inside himself instead of inside books would have been unnatural and excruciating. In such a search within himself he had to seek something whose existence he liked to deny.

Whittaker was unfriendly to First Amendment guarantees of peaceable assembly.

> GEORGE HERMAN, CBS News: What to me, as a non-lawyer, as a plain citizen, what you seem to be saying . . . is that if I make a protest which may bring nasty consequences I shouldn't have made that protest.
> WHITTAKER: That is very largely true. If you make the march with knowledge that it is likely to ignite a squib, then you are the one who must be deemed to have intended that consequence.[2]

Here Whittaker says that members of a violent mob that attack a peaceful protest are not responsible for those acts; the victims they attack are responsible. In his view citizens had no right to assemble if that assembly might be violently attacked by persons who opposed it. In his view such an assembly was not peaceful and thereby not protected by the First Amendment. In essence, if people wanted to meet in protest against violent oppression, Whittaker's advice was to stay home and stay quiet. Law enforcement authorities had no responsibility to protect such citizens.

If no question of violence arose, Whittaker could be more friendly to claims of First Amendment protections, as he was when labor union activists were prosecuted for visiting with citizens in their homes.[3] The city of Baxley, Georgia, required a city permit to be obtained by anyone recruiting memberships in a dues-paying group. Rose Staub and her associate Mamie Merritt were organizers for the International Ladies' Garment Workers Union. They visited with several Baxley women in their homes about joining the union. Before day's end, they were questioned by the police chief while in a restaurant. The interrogation resulted in a charge of failing to obtain the city permit, and the women were duly convicted. Did the city of Baxley have the right to prevent such personal conversations in private homes?

Justice Whittaker delivered the Supreme Court's ruling. He swept aside all protestations of states' rights, and said the city ordinance was impermissible infringement of free speech.

Although some of his colleagues on the Court might have seized this case as an opportunity to deliver a resounding defense of liberty and condemnation of governmental intrusion, Whittaker's argument was a calm recital of facts and governing precedents. In his prose he followed the ideal he advocated—dispassionate discussion of public controversies.

Yet he was no absolutist on protection of peaceable free speech, as demonstrated in his acceptance of police censorship of movies in Chicago.[4] In this era Chicago police were allowed to censor any movies shown to the public in that city. On First Amendment grounds a film distributor refused to submit movies for censorship, generating a case that went to the Supreme Court. There, Justice Tom Clark spoke for a majority including Whittaker. Clark ruled that the question was not whether the Chicago censorship board's standards were unreasonable, but whether the state of Illinois had a right to limit what the public could see. The Court upheld that right regardless of facts regarding Chicago's censorship, and the movie distributor thus lost the case.

Although Whittaker was uncharacteristically silent on facts, dissenters Earl Warren, Hugo Black, William O. Douglas, and William J. Brennan were not. The seven-page opinion was followed by thirty pages of dissent.

Warren's indignation was clear:

> The Chicago licensors have banned newsreel films of Chicago policemen shooting at labor pickets and have ordered the deletion of a scene depicting the birth of a buffalo in Walt Disney's *Vanishing Prairie*.... Before World War II, the Chicago censor denied licenses to a number of films portraying and criticizing life in Nazi Germany.... A member of the Chicago censor board explained that she rejected a film because "it was immoral, corrupt, indecent, against my . . . religious principles.". . . A police sergeant attached to the censor board explained, "Coarse language or anything that would be derogatory to the government—propaganda" is ruled out of foreign films. "Nothing pink or red is allowed," he added.... The police sergeant in charge of the censor unit has said: "Children should be allowed to see any movie that plays in Chicago. If a picture is objectionable for a child, it is objectionable period.". . . Between the Court's decision in 1952 in *Joseph Burstyn, Inc.* v. *Wilson* . . . , and the filing of the petition for certiorari in 1960 in the present case, not once have that state's courts upheld the censor when the exhibitor elected to appeal.[5]

Fourth Amendment

Unreasonable search of buildings and people by British agents was one governmental abuse that brought about the American Revolution in the 1700s. People minding their own business could be accosted day or night by government agents and forced to endure lengthy and abusive inspections. Memories of such abuses were still fresh when the U.S. Constitution was adopted, and popular sentiment quickly inserted the Fourth Amendment to guarantee that the federal agents could not oppress citizens in the same way that the king's agents did.

Many questions about Fourth Amendment protections arise from drug cases. Typically drug offenses generate no complaint, so law enforcement officers must pursue cases with a zeal that is unnecessary in crimes with cooperative witnesses. While attempting to enforce drug laws, law officers are continually tempted to violate the Constitution, violating a higher law to defend a lower one.

In one case,[6] a landlord made a social call to a tenant's house. No one was home, but before the landlord departed he noticed an odor of whiskey mash. He summoned local police (state agents). With his permission as owner of the house, police entered through an unlocked window and discovered an illegal still. They summoned federal authorities (federal agents) who entered and documented the situation.

None of these law enforcement officers bothered to obtain a search warrant, and the tenant who was convicted of violating liquor laws objected to that lapse. Permission from the owner of the property was irrelevant; permission to search without a warrant had to come from the resident, who was not home and gave no permission. Speaking for the Court majority Whittaker noted that officers had plenty of time to get a magistrate's warrant without any danger of evidence or a suspect disappearing. Whittaker declared a search to be impermissible without a warrant from an objective magistrate. Even if police think a warrant would be issued if they asked, they cannot proceed without a warrant. Whittaker overturned the tenant's conviction.

Such overturning is important and necessary if the Constitution is to be defended. If government officials can violate the Constitution to obtain convictions, then Constitutional rights would no longer exist. The point in such cases is not to protect a petty criminal but to protect blameless citizens from abuse of power by government agents. Agents who disregard law when they find it constricting have the same attitude as the criminals they hunt. Unless agents can be held accountable for their actions, arbitrary search abuses that provoked the American Revolution could return. A mere reprimand is not enough to prevent abuses; government officials have to know that they cannot do their jobs (in this case law enforcement) without obeying the Constitution.

In a similar case Whittaker took an opposite stance.[7] A paid informant with a record of reliability told a Federal Bureau of Narcotics agent that James Draper would be arriving by train from Chicago with narcotics. The informant described in detail Draper, his mannerism, and his carry-on luggage. On one of the two specified days for arrival, law officers saw Draper alight from the train. They arrested him, finding heroin and a hypodermic needle on him. With this evidence, he was convicted of concealing and transporting narcotics. He appealed, arguing that the arrest and search violated the Fourth Amendment, meaning evidence obtained in the search should have been disallowed at the trial.

If "probable cause" existed, that is, if officers had reasonable grounds to believe a crime was being committed, the arrest and search and evidence were valid. Whittaker delivered the Court's opinion. Noting that before the arrest, the Bureau of Narcotics man "had personally verified every facet of the information given him . . . except whether petitioner had accomplished his mission and had the three ounces of heroin on his person or in his bag,"[8] Whittaker found that the Fourth Amendment's requirements had been satisfied.

Douglas dissented. He believed the things confirmed by the drug officer (Draper's presence, appearance, mannerism, and luggage) were all legal and unsuspicious. The only basis for believing a crime was underway was a paid informer's hearsay. This was not an emergency; the federal agent had ample time to get an arrest warrant beforehand. Yet this was not done. Why? Because "the arresting officers did not have a bit of evidence, known to them and as to which they could take an oath had they gone to a magistrate for a warrant, that petitioner had committed any crime. . . . If they went to a magistrate to get a warrant of arrest and relied solely on the report of the informer, it is not conceivable to me that one would be granted."[9]

Douglas acknowledged that the standard of probable cause was lower than proof, but until now the mere word of an informer (without any corroborating evidence) had not been considered probable cause for making an arrest. Until this Supreme Court decision, probable cause had required a law officer to personally observe something suspicious in order to make an arrest. Douglas saw no reason to abandon that standard.

Abandonment of that standard would eventually have far reaching effects. One of the most dramatic involved application of a legal process called civil forfeiture. Under Whittaker's ruling, the word of an accuser whose identity was hidden from the courts became probable cause, which is sufficient grounds for prosecutors to seize property associated with a crime described by the informant. Those civil forfeiture proceedings became a financial windfall for police agencies across the country, allowing them (for example) to seize and sell a car if an informant claimed a passenger carrying marijuana had ridden in it.

In theory law enforcement officers who lack a search warrant cannot enter a home against a resident's wishes. The extent of this protection against unwarranted search was tested when a municipal health inspector demanded entry into a home to determine if it harbored rats.[10] If the purpose of a search was not to check for evidence of criminal conduct (though such evidence certainly might be observed upon entry), could a government official enter a home without a search warrant?

Speaking for the Court, Justice Frankfurter said yes. He declared that the power to search without warrant in defense of community health was needed and proper. Regardless of whether Frankfurter's legal reasoning was correct (and four justices disagreed with him), Whittaker's concurrence is interesting from a biographical standpoint. Rather than address the philosophical purpose of the Fourth Amendment, Whittaker concentrated on the more technical question of whether the reasonableness of the search exempted it from the Fourteenth Amendment's application of the Fourth Amendment to the conduct of state and municipal officers.

While sitting as a federal appeals judge Whittaker heard a case involving warrantless search of U.S. mail.[11] A wife in Kansas City mailed a first class package containing heroin to her husband in Denver. A mail carrier, who knew the wife, was also an undercover Federal Bureau of Narcotics agent. He considered her a narcotics suspect and voiced his suspicions at the post office. The post office station superintendent had the package opened, revealing two envelopes containing heroin. On basis of this warrantless search she was convicted for mailing poison, illegal purchase of narcotics, and illegal possession of narcotics.

But should a warrant have been obtained before officials opened someone's first class mail? The package was in the government's possession. No one was going to spirit it away. No urgency required a split second decision from officials.

Whittaker ruled that contents of first class mail cannot be examined without a warrant. He overturned the wife's convictions.

Here Whittaker stood by a basic principle distinguishing American democracy from dictatorship. Citizens have a right to private communication, whether by phone or by mail. In either case, that right to privacy cannot be violated on a whim by police to satisfy their idle curiosity. Police cannot intrude on such aspects of a citizen's private life without convincing a judge that the public interest overrides a citizen's expectations of privacy. Here Whittaker defended the right to be left alone. As always, the issue was not whether criminals have such a right but whether blameless law-abiding citizens have such a right. We may be sure that a man such as Whittaker was not inclined to protect crooks.

Fifth Amendment (Double Jeopardy)

The Fifth Amendment prohibits double jeopardy. "Double jeopardy" allows a person to be tried more than once for the same offense. If such a practice were permitted, acquitted persons could be tried again and again until they no longer have enough strength or resources to defend themselves. This tactic is a favorite among dictatorships, which often use trumped up criminal charges to clothe political harassment (even in a democracy rigid law enforcement could convert upstanding citizens into violators of one obscure statute or another). The Fifth Amendment's prohibition of double jeopardy is considered a key guarantee of democratic liberty, protecting persons found innocent by a jury of their peers.

In one case[12] Whittaker had to decide if an accused bank robber who was acquitted in a federal trial suffered double jeopardy when federal officials subsequently organized a state trial about the bank robbery. The decision narrowed the definition of double jeopardy and gave governmental authorities more opportunity to imprison particular individuals.

The case arose when a federal district court jury acquitted a defendant of bank robbery charges. The defendant had been fingered as a confederate by two robbers who confessed. Movie watchers are familiar with the prosecutor technique of promising leniency in exchange for information. In this case the crooks pointed to a defendant with an alibi that the jury found persuasive—he claimed to be having a haircut miles from the bank at the time of the heist, a claim supported by several witnesses. Federal officials who brought the trial were indignant that the jury dared to disagree with the prosecution's version of events. Passion ran so high that the trial judge declared to another jury after the verdict:[13] "A man who sat here on the witness stand who was charged with robbery and admitted when he took the stand—he did not have to take the stand, but he took the stand and admitted himself that he had been convicted of larceny, and then he admitted that he had pleaded guilty to robbery before, and the jury saw four deputies necessary, sitting around him during the whole time." Relating the defendant's story of his movements with a car in specified times to specified places, the trial judge said, "It sounded to me like you would have had to have Aladdin's magic carpet to have moved around over the city of Chicago. . . . It was so impossible and improbable." The judge sputtered, "In a case like that, a man that confesses that he was guilty of robbery but he just didn't do this one."

The thwarted federal prosecution team then approached state officials and convinced them to bring state bank robbery charges against the defendant who had been acquitted of the federal charges. Federal officials not only turned over their files to the state, but reopened their investigation and obtained new evidence not considered in federal court. The federal team also provided crucial witnesses to the state. State prosecutors openly conceded that they operated under direction of the federal team, which inspired and developed the case.

This time the defendant was convicted. Had he been a victim of double jeopardy? In one aspect, the case was a classic example of what the Fifth Amendment was supposed to guard against: A person vilified by federal officials was tried again for bank robbery after being acquitted the first time. The issue was clouded, however, by the fact that the first trial had been by the federal government and the second trial by a state government. One action by a person can violate multiple laws on both the federal and state levels. If someone is tried twice as a result of one act, once by the feds and once by the state, is that double jeopardy? Moreover, if the state trial is engineered and conducted by federal authorities who lost the first trial, is the second trial truly a state action or merely a disguise to cloak a second attempt by federal officials?

Speaking for a Supreme Court majority that included Whittaker, Justice Frankfurter ruled that double jeopardy had not occurred, as the defendant had not been tried twice on the same charge; one act (alleged bank robbery) merely resulted in more than one charge.

Frankfurter noted that cooperation between federal and state prosecutors was natural and fitting, and he considered whether a state's ability to preserve order would be impaired if federal prosecution for an act prohibited a subsequent state prosecution for the same act. On that issue Frankfurter declared that states' rights would be violated if a federal prosecution impeded a state's ability to enforce its laws. Here we have leakage from civil rights controversies, in which states' rights advocates protested federal interference in state law enforcement. "Some recent suggestions that the Constitution was in reality a deft device for establishing a centralized government are not only without factual justification but fly in the face of history," Frankfurter proclaimed. He worried that federal authorities could impair states' rights by conspiring to try defendants on a minor charge for which they would be acquitted, thereby preventing under double jeopardy subsequent trial for an act which had also violated state laws. Frankfurter viewed such a hypothetical and historically nonexistent conspiracy as violating the Fourteenth Amendment: "It would be in derogation of our federal system to displace the reserved power of States over state offenses by reason of prosecution of minor federal offenses by federal authorities beyond the control of the States."[14] Although Frankfurter said he was helping to define the scope of the Fourteenth Amendment his argument sounded more like he was addressing the Tenth Amendment.

Justice Black (joined by Warren, Douglas, and Brennan) dissented. Black argued that the defendant had indeed been tried twice for a particular bank robbery. In Black's view bringing a new charge deriving from the same act was double jeopardy. By implication in such reasoning, a defendant could be tried on multiple charges in one trial, but could not be put to a series of trials on one charge after another. Such a series would be a subterfuge to disguise double jeopardy. Looking to broader implications of the Court's decision, Black declared, "The power to try a second time will be used, as have all similar procedures, to make scapegoats of helpless, political, religious, or racial minorities and those who differ, who do not conform and who resist tyranny."[15]

Dissenters objected to the majority's implication that state and federal governments attempt to subvert each other's laws, thereby necessitating trials in each jurisdiction to protect both levels of government. In reality, the four dissenters noted, state and federal governments traditionally cooperate to protect each other's interests without bringing a person to trial in each jurisdiction. Black denied that "successful operation of our dual system of government depends in the slightest on the power to try people twice for the same act."[16] He declared, "The Court's reliance on federalism amounts to no more than the notion that, somehow, one act becomes two because two jurisdictions are involved. Hawkins, in his Pleas of the Crown, long ago disposed of a similar contention made to justify two trials for the same offense by different countries. . . . It was discarded as a dangerous fiction then, it should be discarded as a dangerous fiction now."[17]

Brennan penned a separate dissent in which Warren and Douglas joined. "To set aside this state conviction because infected with constitutional violations by federal officers implies no condemnation of the state processes as such." In Brennan's view a state could bring a truly independent prosecution after a federal acquittal. "The conviction is set aside not because of any infirmities resulting from fault of the State but because it is the product of unconstitutional federal action. I cannot grasp the merit of an argument that protection against federal oppression in the circumstances shown by this record would do violence to the principles of federalism."[18] To Brennan the question was not the state's independent power but instead was the limit of federal power.

Whittaker first joined a majority overturning the conviction as a violation of double jeopardy. Whittaker said he found the prosecutors' conduct shocking. Given his scruples about never commenting to a jury about evidence, Whittaker must surely have been offended by the district judge's tirade to a jury as well. Then Whitaker began to vacillate. "Felix really went after Whittaker in *Bartkus*," said one Court clerk about Frankfurter's lobbying. Whittaker finally decided the Fifth Amendment applied only to federal prosecutions, and did not prohibit states from conducting multiple trials for the same offense. Brennan argued that federal participation in the state trial made it a second federal trial in fact regardless of legal pettifogging. In hopes of winning back Whittaker, an exasperated Black exclaimed, "It doesn't say twice put in jeopardy by the same government, but for the same offense." Black declared, "When the 'feds' do what was done here, we have a direct violation of the Fifth Amendment or it is so shocking to the conscience that we can't take it under the Fourteenth."[19] Whittaker nonetheless became the swing vote sustaining prosecutors who kept bringing an accused person to trial until he was finally convicted.

On its face another case[20] discussed the same interplay between federal and state laws in prosecutions, but dissenters to the decision argued that core dispute involved lawlessness by federal law enforcement officers.

As happens so often, restriction of civil liberties deriving from this case began with drug law enforcement. Federal drug agents arrested Bernard Wilson and found narcotics on him. A later commentator noted that the search had been illegal.[21] Although the arrest and search were by federal officials, Wilson was indicted on state charges. He argued that evidence seized by the federal agents should be excluded from the state trial, an exclusion that would have made conviction unlikely.

Speaking for the Court, Whittaker rejected Wilson's plea but (as was so typical with Whittaker) on narrow grounds avoiding the key question of whether prosecutors had violated Wilson's rights—in other words, whether they had chosen to violate one set of laws they disliked in order to enforce another set they did like. The official case summary correctly described Whittaker's thinking: "Since the complaint [from Wilson] did not allege that the arrest was without probable cause and since the arrest and incidental search and seizure were lawful if respondents had probable cause to make the arrest, the complaint failed to state a claim upon which relief could be granted."[22] Such an approach treated technicalities of pleadings as more important than issues that pleadings attempted to raise. Even Justice Potter Stewart, who agreed with the effect of Whittaker's decision, disagreed with his reasoning. Said Stewart, "I could not base affirmance of the judgment upon the ground that the petitioner's motion was technically deficient in failing to recite the talismanic phrase 'without probable cause.' "[23]

Whittaker touched upon the issue of federalism examined earlier in the bank robber case, saying in *Wilson*, "We live in a jurisdiction of two sovereignties. Each has its own system of courts to interpret and enforce its laws, although in common territory. . . . By this action, petitioner not only seeks to interfere with and embarrass the state court in his criminal case, but he also seeks completely to thwart its judgment by relitigating in a trial *de novo* in a federal court the very issue [suppression of evidence] that he has already litigated in state court." Whittaker declared that Wilson sought impermissible interference of one jurisdiction with another.[24] Whittaker's stance here differed sharply from his earlier stance in the bank robber case, where he joined a majority that had no problem with *prosecutors* in one jurisdiction revisiting an issue that had already been decided in the other court's jurisdiction. Seemingly, defendants could not rely upon a principle established for prosecutors.

In *Wilson*, dissenter Douglas, joined by Warren and Brennan, believed involvement of federal agents clearly gave Wilson a right to seek involvement from federal courts. Wilson asked for a ruling on whether his arrest and search were illegal and, if they were illegal, asked the federal judiciary to eliminate that illegal evidence from his trial. The dissenters viewed Whittaker's reasoning, by which technicalities of pleadings were used to evade the issue Wilson sought to raise, as unjust: "At most, the defect complained of would justify his being required to amend his pleading," not throw out his case because his pleading omitted allegation that probable cause was lacking.[25] "This is rigid law at its worst," said a commentator who analyzed such thinking in nineteenth century cases. Such rulings "to put it bluntly . . . reveal an approach by the judges which suggests that they themselves were insecure and incompetent as lawyers and that they found it necessary to indulge in hypertechnicality to prove that they understood the mysteries of their art."[26]

Douglas focused on the core issue: Federal courts must assure that federal law enforcement officers obey law.[27] They must not attempt to evade federal law by using state courts to run prosecutions that would be impermissible in federal courts. "The tender regard which is expressed [by Whittaker] for federal-state relations will in ultimate effect be a tender regard for federal officials who flout federal law. Today we lower federal law enforcement standards by giving federal agents *carte blanche* to break down doors, ransack homes, search and seize to their heart's content—so long as they stay away from federal courts and do not try to use the evidence there. This is an invitation to lawlessness which I cannot join."[28]

In another case Whittaker pondered circumstances defining whether double jeopardy occurred with simultaneous prosecutions for several law violations pertaining to one act.[29] A single action can violate multiple laws. For example, a bank robbery might include theft, carrying an unlicensed firearm, and threatening someone with a deadly weapon. An accused person might be tried for several such offenses without violating double jeopardy, but at some point the prosecutions might become double jeopardy. Whittaker had to face that issue when a court verdict found McKinley Gore had made a single sale of narcotics on one day and a single sale on another day, with each sale violating three laws. He was convicted on six counts (three laws times two instances). Was this double jeopardy?

Whittaker went along with the Court majority that found no double jeopardy in the proceedings.

Four dissenters disagreed. Chief Justice Warren noted that Congress's purpose in passing three different laws applicable to Gore's conduct was to let prosecutors choose one path from three different possibilities, to provide prosecutors with a range of possibilities for punishing a single act and not to provide multiple punishments for a single act. Justice Brennan explained further with a quotation from *Blockburger* v. *United States*:[30] "Where the same act or transaction constitutes a violation of two distinct statutory provisions, the test to be applied to determine whether there are two offenses or only one, is whether each provision requires proof of a fact which the other does not." Brennan observed, "The Court's decision today is inconsistent with the principles of *Blockburger* because it allows separate offenses to be proved and separate punishments to be imposed upon the proof of a single fact." For example, "Proof of the single fact of possession of unstamped narcotics suffices to convict the defendant of offenses under either § 4704(a) [selling narcotics "not from the original [tax] stamped package"] or § 174 [unauthorized sale of narcotics]."[31]

Normally double jeopardy is considered in terms of being found not guilty of an offense, and then being tried over and over again until a person is so drained that he can no longer defend himself, and a guilty verdict is finally rendered. In *Gore* v. *United States* the question was more subtle: Is a person put in jeopardy twice if the same set of facts is used to convict the person of two law violations? Here the situation is that a person cannot violate one law without simultaneously violating the other (unlike a bank robber who might or might not use a firearm and therefore could not be automatically convicted of the weapon offense if he were convicted of taking the money). The question in Gore was whether one law that could not be violated without automatically violating another law was a trick to evade the prohibition against double jeopardy.

Under the majority's decision a single act could be defined as violating dozens of laws, allowing a person to be imprisoned for decades or for a few months, all depending on a prosecutor's whim on how many laws to use.

Another case involved complicated sequential prosecutions.[32] The power and glory of the nation's capital had long bypassed Everett Green when his landlord decided to evict him, separating Green from an ailing long-time woman friend who lived in the same apartment building. Both apparently fretted about the situation, wondering if she could care for herself. Fire broke out in the building. Firefighters found the despondent Green injured. The woman was dead from the blaze. Prosecutors surmised a murder/suicide scenario and charged Green with arson. Under Washington, DC, law someone who died in an arson fire was considered a first degree murder victim of the arsonist, and Green was so charged.

Even prosecutors conceded tragic overtones in the situation and did not portray Green as a bloodthirsty killer. He was convicted of arson. The judge informed the jury that if it found Green guilty of murder, the jury had the option of finding Green guilty in the first or second degree. He was found guilty of second degree murder and sent to prison.

Green had aggressive lawyers. They found a flaw under which Green could get a new trial, but a new trial carried a risk of ending in a verdict that would carry the death penalty. Should Green serve out his prison term, or take an everything-or-nothing gamble on a new trial? Only he could make that choice, and he chose to risk all.

This time he was convicted of first degree murder, a death penalty offense. The situation, however, was not as straightforward as it appeared.

Green's initial appeal covered his conviction for second degree murder, but the new trial was under the original indictment for first degree murder. Here, Green's lawyers now argued, prosecutors erred. Because he had already been tried once for first degree murder and found innocent of that (when the jury chose the option of convicting him of second degree instead of first degree), his lawyers argued that a second trial on the first degree murder charge was double jeopardy. A new trial for second degree murder would have been permissible, as it was by Green's request. He had not asked, however, for a new trial on the first degree murder charge of which he had been acquitted.

Green's lawyers prepared as thoroughly as possible for oral arguments before the Supreme Court. They noted Harvard Law School was holding a moot court session arguing a case with the same facts and law as the Green appeal, and Justice Brennan was participating. They dispatched an observer who sent along a detailed report on Brennan's questions and remarks.

At oral argument Whittaker was concerned about reversing Green's conviction. Whittaker asked if, at this point, Green could be tried again on second degree murder or some other charge. The attorney for the prosecution conceded that such options were no longer available. Either the first degree murder conviction would be sustained, or Green would have to be freed.

The case troubled Whittaker. After thorough discussion at the closed conference that justices held among themselves each Friday, the vote was divided four to four, with Whittaker undecided. Week after week he was asked for his decision, and each time he was unable to give one.[33] He got the case held over from his first term to be reargued. At first he refused to join Black's majority decision because it overruled *Trono* v. *United States*.[34] Black thereupon dropped that element of the opinion, and Whittaker joined. Although he disdained Douglas for adjusting an opinion to get more votes, Whittaker was willing to give Black just that sort of opportunity.

Speaking for a majority including Whittaker, Justice Black ruled that Green's second trial for first degree murder violated double jeopardy. The U.S. Court of Appeals had already ruled that no evidence existed for a second degree murder charge, so Green could not be tried on such a charge. His time in prison already covered the sentence he received for arson. The Supreme Court ruling made him a free man. He had paid his debt to society. He lived out his days in Washington and died in 1961.

Fourteenth Amendment

Cases involving the Bill of Rights (first ten amendments to the Constitution) commonly touch upon the Fourteenth Amendment as well, which often requires states to comply with Bill of Rights' provisions that always apply to the federal government. "When the judgment of the state court is found to be so lacking in principles of fundamental fairness as to shock the contemporary community conscience," Whittaker told a reporter, "it is thought to violate the 'due process' provision of the fourteenth amendment and it is the duty of the Supreme court to strike it down. The fourteenth amendment, of course, applies only to action by a state. It does not apply to discriminatory action by individuals."[35] In cases involving the Fourteenth Amendment Whittaker not only had to consider due process in general but also the right to counsel in particular.

"Due process" refers to all the elements of litigation necessary to maintain fairness, to ensure that defendants have every opportunity to make their cases while ensuring that powerful plaintiffs are unable to abuse their strength by preying upon the defenseless.

In criminal cases the stakes are high, and despite his reputation for strict law enforcement, Whittaker claimed to seek justice rather than convictions. He told a bar association gathering in 1960:

> I visualize a dark-skinned youth sitting at the counsel table, accompanied only by his appointed and unpaid counsel. . . . The black-robed judge formally calls for trial the case of "United States of America against Willie Jones." Surely that announcement of the impending contest sounds one-sided. . . . Do you feel that . . . it would be conscionable for the court to give the Government the "breaks" of the trial—for "breaks" there surely will be—or should the defendant get them? I must confess a sympathy for the latter view. The Government needs no breaks, and they, like doubts, should go to the accused defendant.[36]

Perhaps that image was in Whittaker's mind when he wrote the Court's opinion in a case involving a coerced confession.[37] A few weeks after Frank Andrew Payne started working for a Pine Bluff, Arkansas, lumberman, the merchant was discovered at the store with his head smashed, and several hundred dollars had been emptied from his cash drawer. A search for the murderer began.

Arkansas law enforcement officials made a warrantless arrest of Payne, afterward failed to bring him before a magistrate for a hearing, deprived him of food, kept him barefoot on a ninety-mile round trip for a lie detector test, failed to tell him he had a right to a lawyer let alone a right to say nothing, and (while refusing to let him see family, friends, or lawyer for three days) told him that thirty or forty persons were attempting to storm the jail to lynch him but that officials would protect him from the mob if he confessed. The nineteen-year-old Payne, who only had a fifth grade education and was described as "mentally dull," said he believed the police chief would let the mob take him unless he confessed, so he produced the confession the chief wanted.

Questions arose about whether law enforcement officials had disregarded due process requirements of the Fourteenth Amendment. The state of Arkansas argued that circumstances surrounding Payne's confession were irrelevant as evidence aside from the confession would have convinced a jury of Payne's guilt.

Speaking for a Court majority, Whittaker declared that a coerced confession in a state criminal trial, whether the applied pressure had been physical or psychological, was forbidden by the Fourteenth Amendment. As to the argument that the jury would have reached the same verdict without the confession, Whittaker declared, "No one can say what credit and weight the jury gave to the confession." He concluded, "admission in evidence, over objection, of the coerced confession vitiates the judgment." In other words, the guilty verdict was set aside.

When Payne was tried again he was convicted again, once more receiving a death sentence.[38] Such an outcome illustrates the truism that civil liberties protect the blameless without allowing criminals to escape. Because violation of civil liberties is sometimes grounds for reversing convictions, an impression exists that civil liberties let hoodlums go free. On the contrary, enforcing all laws, both criminal statutes and civil rights, assures that citizens can go about their business while criminals are apprehended and held accountable.

In the *Payne* case Whittaker's careful language said that the coerced confession had been admitted into evidence over objection from the defense—language illustrating how important access to a lawyer can be. Would Whittaker have refused to find a violation of the Fourteenth Amendment if the issue had not been raised at the appropriate point in lower court proceedings?[39] Would Whittaker have allowed a man to be executed if the man's attorney had not followed the right procedure in raising a point so compelling that it overturned a jury verdict? Would Whittaker let a man die because he did not protest violation of his rights at the bureaucratically appropriate time? Given Whittaker's technocrat approach to judgeship, perhaps we should be grateful if he was never called upon to answer those questions.

In another case dealing with coerced confession Whittaker was less sympathetic to the convicted man's plea.[40] The official case summary described the situation: "A mentally retarded 19-year-old youth with no criminal record, was arrested in 1936 on suspicion of stealing bicycles. After being held virtually incommunicado and interrogated by groups of police officers for nearly four days while sick and faint, inadequately fed, without a hearing and without the advice of counsel, family or friends, he confessed to participation in a murder." Was such a confession coerced and therefore invalid? Speaking for the Court, Justice Stewart said yes, the confession was coerced and violated due process guarantees of the Fourteenth Amendment.

Whittaker disagreed, and joined in dissent with Clark, who wrote, "The Court second-guesses the findings of the trial judge and those of the only other trial court that heard and saw any of the witnesses, both of which courts impartially declared the confession to be entirely voluntary."[41] Clark noted that the prisoner did not ask for an attorney or relatives or friends or food. "In what case, I ask, has a court dealing with the same extrinsic facts, a quarter of a century after conviction, overturned so many decisions by so many judges, both state and federal, entirely upon psychological grounds?"[42] In the same spirit, one might ask how Whittaker could expect a mentally retarded, ill, and apparently docile youth to make vigorous assertion of legal rights that Supreme Court justices disagreed about. The fact that so many lower judges could see nothing questionable is more a commentary on their eyesight than their infallibility. The grounds for overturning were not psychological but legal, involving the fundamental validity of court proceedings based on a confession from an intimidated young man who could not understand what was happening.

This case is a classic illustration of Whittaker's legal technocrat approach to law. If all the forms were filled out correctly he could find no grounds for complaint or redress.

A case seeming very similar to *Payne* provided Whittaker with an opportunity to do the kind of flip-flop that so often thwarts persons seeking to find his judicial philosophy.[43] Arthur Thomas was a twenty-seven-year-old "itinerant Negro laborer" accused of murdering a woman who owned a grocery store located near his residence. An Arizona sheriff's posse of about a dozen men arrested Thomas in the midafternoon soon after the crime. He denied committing the crime and accused Ross Lee Cooper. Cooper was nicknamed "Baby John" and was a young mentally retarded resident of the old barracks where Thomas lived. A mounted rancher thereupon lassoed Thomas around the neck and started yanking him toward some trees. The rancher was not a member of the posse, though his lack of official status was probably unapparent to the accused man who had the rope around his neck. The sheriff swiftly halted that incident.

The sheriff took Thomas along as Cooper was arrested. As both suspects were standing next to each other, a rancher lassoed them (reports vary as to whether the rope was around their shoulders or their necks) and dragged them to a kneeling position. Once again the sheriff intervened.

At 4:30 P.M. Thomas was taken barefoot to the nearest town where a justice of the peace resided, as required by Arizona law. The gentleman being unavailable, Thomas was taken the county attorney's home at 6:00 P.M. The county attorney told Thomas that he had no reason to feel threatened. Thomas adamantly insisted that Cooper was the murderer. The next morning the sheriff brought Thomas, still barefoot, before a justice of the peace. Whether the judge informed Thomas he could have a lawyer is unclear; the judge later testified both ways. Thomas confessed and plead guilty. The sheriff then took Thomas to the county attorney's home, where the confession was repeated with more detail. The county attorney said, "You don't have to talk to me if you don't want to, but you can, if you will, tell me in your own words, in your own free will, just what took place." That statement was hardly a vigorous communication of Thomas's rights. A reporter who visited Thomas in jail soon thereafter found him "nervous and afraid." Thomas "indicated that he'd been 'roughed up' and that the Sheriff had saved his life." A third confession was obtained from Thomas at the county attorney's office, and a few days later at the request of a deputy U.S. marshal Thomas initialed each page of that confession as true.[44]

The trial judge ruled that the two written confessions had been coerced under threat of lynching, but that the oral confession before the justice of the peace was in a proper judicial setting and voluntary. The question before the Supreme Court was whether the oral confession had been coerced as well.

Whittaker was among the Court majority, whose spokesman was Justice Clark. Clark ruled the confession was voluntary and valid. He noted, "No mention or threat of lynching was heard."[45] Being roped around the neck and yanked toward some trees was not threatening enough to Clark, nor did Thomas telling a reporter soon afterward that he believed the sheriff had saved his life indicate to Clark that Thomas had any fear for his life during the incident. Perhaps no mention of lynching was made, but if someone points a pistol at you and cocks it, you can sense a threat even if none is stated aloud. Clark admitted that a state patrolman present at the incident recalled the sheriff saying, "Will you tell the truth, or I will let them go ahead and do this." That did not count as a threat, Clark said, because the sheriff denied saying it. Only undisputed testimony, Clark said, could be considered. That an experienced trial judge such as Whittaker could go along with such an argument is surprising. One wonders if he would have accepted it from a prosecutor or defense attorney arguing before him in district court.

Clark also ruled that Thomas was well aware of his legal rights because he had a criminal record, demonstrating his familiarity with the criminal justice system.[46] Clark had one opinion, yet anyone who has been churned through the criminal justice system, if it even be on a matter as simple as a non-injury traffic offense, might feel a need for professional assistance despite that familiarity. It is hard for readers in a later era to understand how a judge could think that a casual laborer had enough understanding of law to make an informed decision to dispense with an attorney while facing a murder charge.

The general situation of alleged intimidation in this case is similar to that in *Moore* (discussed below), in which Whittaker joined with a majority granting a new trial. Yet in the present case Whittaker agreed with a majority denying a new trial. Despite the similar atmosphere of intimidation in the two cases, however, a legal technocrat such as Whittaker could focus on a difference in the question before the Court. The basic issue in *Moore* was the right to an attorney. In *Thomas* the basic issue was coerced confession. Such a technical distinction could allow Whittaker to grant a new trial to one prisoner and refuse a new trial to the other even though both cases evolved from alleged coerced confessions.

It is harder to see how Whittaker could write the Court's opinion in *Payne* and deny a new trial to Thomas. A judge primarily concerned with protecting civil liberties would probably have looked past any fine factual distinction between the two cases, and would probably have concentrated on the similar patterns of police conduct. Whittaker, however, was famed for his exacting inquiry into facts of a case, by which he tried to find applicable law. This approach allowed him to decide differently on cases that ostensibly involved the same principle. Such an approach led to decisions that seem like flip-flops to persons concerned more with broad constitutional principles than with narrow distinctions of facts. Whittaker's approach had its own internal consistency but led many observers to conclude that he lacked any constitutional philosophy to guide him on the Supreme Court.

Whittaker once reminisced about his early days as a lawyer in the 1920s, observing a proceeding in which a defendant had no lawyer—"a predicament that concerned me then and that has never ceased to be a torment."[47] Four decades later Whittaker noted with approval that anyone accused of a serious crime finally had a right to counsel. "It is difficult to believe that any intelligent person, at all familiar with the intricacies of the law and its practice—and surely no lawyer—would deny the good reasons for such a rule."[48]

Yet, when confronted with a real case[49] rather than legal theory, Whittaker let a defendant be sent to death after officials denied the defendant's request for an attorney before the trial. In a later case[50] Whittaker ruled otherwise. Although Whittaker is hardly known for originating innovative legal doctrine, in these two cases he seemed to argue that a defendant's intelligence should be the determining factor on whether a defendant accused of a crime was entitled to representation by an attorney: As a defendant's intelligence rose, the right to a lawyer declined. Such a doctrine has not found a place in American jurisprudence.

The first case arose when California authorities arrested a man suspected of murder. John Russell Crooker repeatedly requested an attorney, but police interrogators disregarded those requests and continued to grill him until he broke down and confessed. By denying the suspect's request for a lawyer, the police officers committed a crime. A California official who refused to allow a defendant to have a lawyer upon request was guilty of a misdemeanor. The larger question was whether police violated the federal Constitution as well. Speaking for a majority joined by Whittaker, Justice Clark said that preventing this particular murder suspect from having a lawyer did not violate due process requirements of the Fourteenth Amendment because this suspect was intelligent enough to know his rights without advice from an attorney.

Four incredulous dissenters (Douglas, Warren, Black, Brennan) protested that even an intelligent and well-informed person needs professional representation when caught up in rules of criminal prosecution. The Court's minority believed constitutional rights protect everyone, regardless of whether a person's intelligence is low or high.

The dissenters implicitly noted the danger of making constitutional rights dependent on a citizen's intelligence—at what point is a citizen too smart to have constitutional rights? How is that intelligence or awareness to be measured? The dissenters explicitly contended that law enforcement officers have an obligation to obey the law. If the law does not apply to police and prosecutors, then they are lawless. The result in dictatorships throughout the world is too familiar to need repetition.

The minority's stance implicitly raised the issue of allowing government agents to disobey laws they find inconvenient. In this case law enforcement officials' violation of California law was uncontested; the Court majority simply contended that violation was permissible under the Fourteenth Amendment. The minority felt otherwise. Implicitly the dissenters understood the only way to stop denial of counsel was to prohibit convictions that depended in part on denial of counsel.

The point was not whether denial was unnecessary to obtain a conviction and therefore permissible because it did not affect the outcome of prosecution. The point was that all defendants are presumed innocent, so innocent citizens (including both those who are found not guilty and those against whom charges are dropped) are deprived of fundamental rights when deprived of professional legal advice in criminal proceedings. If government agents can prevent blameless people from exercising one type of right that authorities find inconvenient, how can authorities be stopped from depriving citizens of other fundamental rights as well?

After Crooker was sent to his death, the Court revisited the issue of an accused person's right to counsel; *Crooker* v. *California* was overruled and the right to counsel affirmed.[51]

Whittaker's thinking was called upon in still another case involving right to counsel. In the words of a state judge,[52] Elijah McNeal, Jr., "had an altercation with the proprietor in an establishment that appears to have been a 'jook', called the 'Blue Chip', he withdrew to his quarters, and, more effectively to renew the feud, reappeared armed with a shotgun loaded with fine shot. When he was within range of his late adversary he fired missing his target and wounding four other persons. His aim was wretched despite six years service in the army where, he says, he became a sharpshooter." He was convicted of assault with intent to commit second degree murder and sentenced to twenty years imprisonment.

McNeal appealed on grounds that he had been denied a lawyer during that trial. Although the state supreme court held that he was old enough to represent himself in what that tribunal called a simple case, the U.S. Supreme Court disagreed. Speaking for the Court, Whittaker did not go so far as to say McNeal was entitled to legal representation, but did rule that a hearing should be held to determine if he deserved a lawyer to defend him. The official summary of Whittaker's opinion said good reason existed to accept that McNeal was "indigent, ignorant and mentally ill." The summary noted "abundant evidence of his ignorance and his inability to question witnesses and otherwise conduct his own defense." Whittaker suggested McNeal "might have a good insanity defense" (but no one raised it) and said the trial involved "highly complex legal questions, beyond the comprehension of almost any layman." The Court did not say McNeal's rights had been violated, however, only that a hearing should be held to determine whether he had a right to a lawyer.

At this hearing personnel on the state supreme court were the same as when McNeal's appeal had been denied; but after Whittaker spoke, their portrayal of the situation was now starkly different.[53] The same judges now noted, "Petitioner was . . . compelled to conduct his own defense though he had never appeared in court charged with a felony, was ignorant of court procedure and unequipped to represent himself." The judges noted McNeal had been "financially unable to employ counsel and being unaware that he had any right to counsel furnished by the State did not request the trial court to appoint one." The judges also noted that "'Petitioner was incapable of questioning witnesses and otherwise unable to conduct his defense'; and that the petitioner received head injuries while he was in the armed services, experienced amnesia spells and developed emotional instability to such extent that he was confined in the Veterans' Hospital at Bay Pines where he was a patient for five months." Citing these facts and Whittaker's order, the state justices ordered a new trial for McNeal, at which he must be informed that he had a right to an attorney and at which his mental state would be examined.

Concurring in the result of Whittaker's ruling, Justice Douglas commented on the history of the issue. "The Court held in *Betts* v. *Brady*, 316 U.S. 455, . . . that a state court in a criminal case need not appoint counsel to represent an indigent defendant, unless the failure to furnish counsel results in a conviction lacking in 'fundamental fairness.'. . . I cannot believe that a majority of the present Court would agree to *Betts* v. *Brady* were it here *de novo*." Douglas thought "the result of our decisions is to refuse a State the power to force a person into a criminal trial without a lawyer if he wants one and can afford to hire one, but to deny the same protection to an accused who is too poor to retain counsel." Douglas observed, "It is a burden placed on an accused solely by reason of his poverty. Its only sanction is *Betts* v. *Brady* which is so at war with our concept of equal justice under law that it should be overruled."[54]

Such a comment from Douglas was sure to perturb Whittaker, who had a fanatical commitment to abide by past court decisions.

Still another case[55] arose when, twelve years after Willie B. Moore pleaded guilty to murder, he appealed his conviction on grounds of not having a lawyer when he pleaded. The state circuit court and Michigan supreme court denied his appeal. In contrast, a U.S. Supreme Court majority including Whittaker ruled that Moore had been tricked into going to trial without a lawyer, and the Court granted a new trial.

Moore had been held in jail several days before confessing in 1938. A judge at that time asked Moore if he wanted a lawyer, and he said no. The trial judge consulted privately with Moore for a few minutes and decided the guilty plea was voluntary. Moore was told he had a right to counsel but waived his right. He said nothing at the hearing and asked no questions of witnesses. The judge imposed the maximum penalty allowed under Michigan law for first degree murder, solitary confinement for life at hard labor without parole.

In 1950 Moore sought a new trial. He explained that in 1938 the sheriff had told him that if he didn't plead guilty, the sheriff might be unable to protect him from mob violence. Moore said he had seen no alternative but to plead guilty. At the 1950 hearing the man who had been sheriff in 1938 concurred that he had told Moore that his life was in danger through mob violence unless he plead guilty so he could be sent out of town before mob violence erupted. The circuit court denied Moore's request for a new trial, saying that no threat of mob violence had existed. Moore appealed, and the case eventually went to the U.S. Supreme Court.

Speaking for a majority that included Whittaker, Justice Brennan noted Moore was seventeen years old when convicted and had possessed only a seventh grade education. Brennan noted assorted reasonable defenses that a trial lawyer could have raised on Moore's behalf, such as insanity, mistaken identity, the degree of murder. Such matters involved technical knowledge of law that Moore did not possess.

Brennan said the point wasn't whether mob violence against Moore was an actual possibility in 1938, but rather the point was Moore believed such a threat existed. Good reason existed to think that Moore refused counsel in the interest of getting out of town as fast as possible. Brennan said that Moore's fear, his age, and his possible mental abnormality made representation by counsel imperative. The Supreme Court granted a new trial.

The result of his new trial? He was convicted again, this time of second degree murder, and no credit was allowed on the years he had already spent in prison.[56] Despite claims to the contrary, generally civil liberties simply protect ordinary citizens and do not let guilty persons go free.

Although Whittaker here supported the claim of a defendant who had been intimidated into refusing a lawyer, in *Thomas* (discussed above), involving even greater intimidation, Whittaker ruled against the defendant. That sort of inconsistency has baffled students of Whittaker's career, but the "inconsistency" depends on what a person sees as the key issue. If the key issue is intimidation that prevents an accused person from exercising his rights, then Whittaker's rulings do appear inconsistent. The *Moore* and *Thomas* cases can be distinguished apart, however. *Moore* involved right to an attorney; *Thomas* involved a coerced confession. To a legal technocrat, those distinctions might well be more important than the issue of intimidation.

RELATIONS BETWEEN EMPLOYERS AND WORKERS

During the 1960s Whittaker asserted, "In recent years the status of the majority of our people has changed from that of owners and operators of millions of small and independent enterprises scattered throughout the country *to* that of employees of our great corporate industrial complexes based in large urban centers."[57] That assertion was incorrect. No such shift had occurred recently; indeed reasonable doubt exists that most Americans were ever business operators (unless one defines subsistence farming for one's own immediate needs as commercial enterprise). Nonetheless Whittaker believed a profound and novel change had occurred, creating an unfamiliar situation ripe for exploitation by unscrupulous agitators.

"Employees," Whittaker proclaimed to an audience of Kansas lawyers, "through their organized Unions—encouraged by the Federal government and aided and preferred by its laws—have acquired almost dictatorial powers over wages." Even in the heyday of labor activism, rather few wage earners set their own wages. Revealing as Whittaker's statement was about his attitude toward organized labor, his feelings were not supported by historical fact. "Looking more to self-interest than to national interests, these Unions have used their economic power to command substantial annual wage increases." Those high wages, Whittaker said, "carried the actual cost of making our products to a height far above the price that those products will bring in the world market, and consequently that market is largely closed to us."[58] He assured his listeners, "There appears to be no reason why we cannot or should not immediately stop further annual increases in wages and prices before getting so deeply into the mire that we cannot extricate ourselves." He closed the topic by saying, "I leave to you whether there is or can ever be any other permanent solution."[59] Opposition from corporation managers was one reason why the wage-price spiral could not immediately stop. When President Kennedy proposed that the steel industry accept a deal in which wages could be held down if prices were held down, steel company managers said no. Whittaker ignored one time-honored method of promoting international price competitiveness of American goods—adjustment of tariff and other import–export regulations. Experts in international trade, as opposed to an audience of lawyers, might well have been able to offer additional alternatives that were unapparent to Whittaker.

While serving on the Supreme Court, Whittaker expressed skepticism about the industriousness, dependability, and patriotism of American workers:

> The chips are down and the stakes are high, yet we are preoccupied with a shorter working day and week, with fringe benefits and early retirement. In other words, with the "easy life." "Life without effort," says Admiral Rickover, "appears to be our national goal." We seem to have developed the false and dangerous complex that the ephemeral thing called the "Government" has an inexhaustible treasury, and having established it, it should now establish, protect and sustain us in the comforts "to which we have become accustomed." Even worst [*sic*], we frequently "fiddle while Rome burns." We tolerate ruinous work stoppages, slow-downs and disruptions at our military and industrial plants whose production is vital in our "race" for the instruments of survival, while those avowedly out to "bury" us work around the clock.[60]

Attacking the civil rights movement's demonstration tactics, which he called criminal and Communist-infiltrated, Whittaker declared that such demonstrations, "*did not have their origin in that [racial] strife, but, rather, in the labor strife, sit-ins and lie-downs of an earlier era.*"[61]

Workman's Compensation

During Whittaker's tenure the Supreme Court considered several cases touching upon the Federal Employers' Liability Act covering job-related injuries. The cases typically involved deciding questions of fact in which the Supreme Court was supposed to defer to findings of the district court. For that reason Whittaker was skeptical about the wisdom of hearing such cases. In addition, these proceedings were often decided by a narrow vote, inflaming the minority justices who lost over and over again.

As a Watson Ess lawyer Whittaker enjoyed defending insurance companies against claims. When confronted with workman's compensation cases on the Supreme Court Whittaker examined facts with a gimlet eye. His inclination to find ways for employers to avoid paying workman's compensation claims was so blatant that it once earned a public rebuke from Justice Douglas.

In that case, *Inman* v. *Baltimore and Ohio Railroad*,[62] a railroad crossing guard was hit by a drunk driver and contended he was entitled to compensation under the Federal Employers' Liability act due to alleged negligence by his railroad employer. In a jury trial the employee was awarded compensation. An appeals judge reversed the jury's verdict. After the case reached the U.S. Supreme Court, Justice Clark delivered the majority's opinion, affirming the appeals judge. The jury verdict was thus thrown out, and the employee received no compensation.

Part of Whittaker's Kansas City reputation was based on labor relations litigation, including what one of his sons called "terribly difficult labor negotiations . . . where he represented the *K*[*ansas*] *C*[*ity*] *Star*."[63] Specifics about that work are scanty, but the *Inman* case may reveal his general attitude on the topic. Whittaker was often silent in Supreme Court decisions, but in this instance he decided to add his own opinion ridiculing the employee's claim: "About the only way, as I perceive, that respondent could protect its crossing flagmen against injury from such lawless conduct by third persons would be to provide them with military tanks and make sure they stay in them while within or moving about crossing-intersections in the performance of their duties—and I am not even sure that this method, though ironclad, would be certain protection to a flagman against lawless injury by third persons, for someone might shoot him. . . . How this can be thought to square with any known concept of 'negligence' by respondent is beyond me."[64]

It was not beyond Justices Warren, Black, and Brennan, who concurred in the dissent of Douglas. Douglas noted that the crossing guard's duties went beyond stopping traffic. He was supposed to inspect the passing train for hotboxes and notify the conductor of any observed. He was also supposed to watch for trains coming from the other direction. To perform these duties the employee had to turn his back to traffic on a heavily traveled street where drivers were notorious for moving across the crossing before the signalman gave them the all clear. The Court minority argued that a reasonable employer could anticipate routine danger from motorists in such conditions, danger that could be reduced if a second employee were stationed at the intersection, or by installation of a mechanical crossing gate. Criminal intervention by third party was not the point. The point was that such third party intervention was easily foreseeable, and being so, the employer had obligation to protect employees from it. An analogy would be a city having funds to furnish police with bullet-resistant vests requested by officers, but refusing to do so because there was no obligation to protect police officers from criminal intervention by third party.

Whittaker's opinion was uncharacteristic in that it contained not a single citation of law to support his contention. Normally he relied heavily on precedents and authorities, but here he stood on his own authority as a Supreme Court justice. His opinion's prose also exuded passion that was unusual for his legal writing. Clearly the *Inman* case touched his emotions. Perhaps his sympathy for the railroad reflected his Kansas City law firm's work for large railroad corporations.

Justice Whittaker's response was similar in another railroad employee injury case, *Moore* v. *Terminal Railroad*.[65] The similarity extended even to vocabulary in which Whittaker referred to the absence of a "scintilla" and "iota" of evidence. In *Moore*, the Supreme Court *upheld* a jury verdict that railroad negligence contributed to the employee's injury. Whittaker strongly dissented, taking a position similar to the one he would later take in *Inman*. In *Moore*, Whittaker said the accident was solely the employee's fault.

> The simple facts recited do not show even a "scintilla" or an "iota" of evidence, to say nothing of any substantial evidence, of negligence by respondent. Instead, I insist, they affirmatively show that it was petitioner's own act in turning the [baggage] cart at such an angle as brought its south end into collision with the moving train that was exclusively "the cause of the injury.". . .
>
> To hold that these facts are sufficient to make a jury case of negligence under the [Federal Employers' Liability] Act is in practical effect to say that a railroad is an insurer of its employees. Such is not the law.

This dissent is among the most lucid prose Whittaker ever produced in his legal writing, easy to follow and with minimal citations that do not choke his text. Perhaps the easy flow meant his private law practice had made him comfortable with such a labor law issue.

In another case[66] Whittaker felt the facts of injury were irrelevant, and instead argued the issue of compensation should be decided on whether the injured person deceived the employer when applying for work. Justice Black delivered the Court's decision: A person who obtains employment under false pretenses is nonetheless an employee. The fraud could invalidate the employment contract, but the person is performing tasks under orders from the employer. Those orders mean the employer is liable for injuries received while performing those tasks. The key factor is the employer ordered the person to do something that resulted in injury.

Whittaker dissented. He advocated "the age-old and sound proposition that fraud in the inducement of a contract vitiates the contract."[67] Despite Whittaker's rhetorical implication, the Court majority did not contest that principle. Although the person in question accepted supervision, performed assignments, and accepted a paycheck, Whittaker contended the person was a "putative" employee, not a real one. Since the person was not an employee, the company was not liable for injuries received in the course of employment—as no employment existed. His argument would seem to hold also that no liability for damages existed; for example, a manufacturer could not be held accountable if a "putative" employee turned a wrong valve and flooded a community with poisonous emissions.

Whatever the validity of Whittaker's stance, it allowed him to find that the company had no liability for injury received while a person was performing a task on the company's orders. In all these Supreme Court cases, Whittaker always found that the employer had no liability for an injury received while someone was on the job. In one case Whittaker argued that the injured person was not technically an employee. In another Whittaker argued that there was no way the employer could have prevented an injury. In still another he argued that the injury was the worker's own fault. Whittaker's findings sometime required impressive legalistic acrobatics, so impressive as to let us speculate that his findings were based on personal philosophy rather than legal mandate. At least two times Whittaker was the sole member of the Court to support the employer.[68]

Whittaker's personal values are suggested by his typical stance that workman's compensation cases under the Federal Employer's Liability Act should not be heard by the Court because they simply required determinations of fact, and those determinations had already been made at the district court level.

Wages

In another case[69] with biographical interest, an employer sought to avoid paying overtime rates to workers. The company engaged in an unusual mix of business—local interior decorating and manufacture of airplane parts for interstate sale. The company argued it should benefit from the Fair Labor Standards Act provision exempting retailers from paying overtime rates to employees. Speaking for a nearly unanimous Court, Chief Justice Warren ruled that the exemption did not apply to a company whose business included non-retail activity.

The sole dissent came from Charles Whittaker.

Whittaker agreed with his colleagues that the employee had been producing airplane parts, and that his overtime had been paid at a straight hourly rate without an overtime bonus. Whittaker, however, distinguished that labor from the employee's work in the company's interior decorating business, and argued that the employee was not entitled to an overtime bonus for interior decorating labor. The core of Whittaker's dissent rested on his understanding of facts, a district judge's approach to a case rather than an appellate judge's.

In his dissent Whittaker rejected the district Court's finding of fact. The district court had determined the facts warranted an overtime bonus for all hours of overtime labor the employer had received from the worker. Perhaps Whittaker's understanding of the facts was as reasonable as an opposite understanding, but Whittaker typically argued that the Supreme Court should accept a district court's finding of fact. On this point the language of his dissent was revealing: "I would, therefore, dismiss the writ [in which the Supreme Court agreed to review the appeals court finding] as improvidently granted, or, at the very least, remand the case to the District Court for a new trial and for proper findings of fact."[70] Here Whittaker seemed to specify what the result of a new trial had to be, as a ruling on facts could force a particular verdict. Interesting, too, in this context was Whittaker's suggestion that the appeals court finding (supporting the employer) should be allowed to stand. Here we see a litigator's mind at work, creating fallback positions for a client. If the appeals finding could not stand, then a new district trial should be held. If a new district trial were held, a new finding of fact should be imposed to affect the outcome.

In the case at hand, Whittaker's deviation from his normal scruples (which should have compelled acceptance of district court findings of fact) suggests a sympathy for company managers. Indeed Whittaker seemed irked that the district court not only awarded an overtime bonus but ordered the employer to pay the worker's attorney fees.

In addition to overtime questions, the Supreme Court was also called upon to decide how far the federal minimum wage law reached. The case[71] arose over operations of Whitaker House Co-operative (spelled differently than Whittaker and no relation to him). Co-op members produced fabric items at home: knitting, crocheting, and embroidery. These items were made to the co-op's specifications, could be sold only to the co-op at whatever price it gave, and members were subject to removal from the rolls if their work did not comply with co-op standards or if they offered their inventory to any other buyer.

Were the workers independent contractors, or did their relationship with co-op management make them employees in fact regardless of what co-op managers called them? If they were employees they were entitled to the protection of federal minimum wage law.

Speaking for the Court Justice Douglas found the workers to be employees. In addition to provisions of the Fair Labor Standards Act of 1938 Douglas cited the Code of Federal Regulations, saying "no industrial homework, such as respondent's members do, shall be done 'in or about a home, apartment, tenement, or room in a residential establishment unless a special homework certificate' has been issued. Respondent's members have no such certificates."[72] Douglas noted the purpose of such laws and rules was to prevent homeworkers from being cheated of a minimum wage. "The members are not self-employed; nor are they independent, selling their products on the market for whatever price they can command. They are regimented under one organization, manufacturing what the organization desires and receiving the compensation the organization dictates."[73]

Co-op members, Douglas noted, can also be co-op employees, just as factory employees can also be factory owners via stock purchases. Co-op "management fixes the piece rates at which they work; the management can expel them for substandard work or for failure to obey the regulations. The management, in other words, can hire or fire the homeworkers,"[74] meaning they are employees.

Whittaker dissented, joined by Brennan and Stewart. First, Whittaker argued that the Supreme Court was bound by lower court findings that Whitaker House was a true co-operative and not a sham to evade the minimum wage law. Justice Whittaker said the Supreme Court could not revisit that factual determination and find otherwise. Here he was arguing that procedure had to take precedence over facts, the classic stance of a litigator who wants to direct attention away from uncomfortable facts. Whittaker then argued that co-op members were working for themselves and not for the co-op, selling their work to the co-op less deductions made by management to reimburse the co-op for its expenses and depreciation. "I fail to see in this any element of employment by the cooperative of its members."[75] Such comment perhaps indicates the vision with which Whittaker perceived labor relations cases that helped build his reputation back in Kansas City.

Arbitration Issues

Litigation can be tiring and expensive for all parties. One way to hold down those costs is to use arbitration rather than litigation. An arbitrator is an individual chosen by the employer and the workers to hear facts of a dispute and impose a binding settlement on both parties. Arbitration is a way of settling hotly contested matters without using a court.

Questions may arise, however, about the scope of arbitrators' power in labor disputes. During Whittaker's years in Washington the Supreme Court helped define that power when an arbitrator ordered that dismissed employees be rehired with back pay.[76] The decision came after expiration of the collective bargaining agreement under which the arbitration had been done. Given that expiration, the company argued it should not have to rehire nor provide back pay for the period that elapsed after the agreement expired.

Speaking for the Court, Douglas supported the arbitrator's power to make such an award and ruled that the arbitrator's decision was binding on the company.

Whittaker offered a strong dissent. Setting the factual foundation, he agreed that the dismissals were arbitratable, and that the arbitrator had power to order the workers rehired with back pay. The issue, as defined by Whittaker, was whether the workers must be rehired after expiration of the collective bargaining agreement under which the arbitration was made, and whether they must receive back pay covering time that passed after the expiration date.

Whittaker conceded that retroactive arbitration could occur about an expired collective bargaining agreement, but was adamant that an arbitrator's jurisdiction ended with expiration of an agreement. After expiration he could not force the company to rehire workers, nor could an arbitrator's order for back pay cover any date subsequent to the date on which an agreement ended.

Whittaker's argument did not, however, address a situation in which a worker is wrongfully dismissed as a collective bargaining agreement terminates. The former worker certainly continues to suffer harm. The company did something that hurt the worker, and the harm continued regardless of the agreement's cut-off date. How is the worker to be made whole? Whittaker's analysis of the case did not address harm caused by a company's conduct but was concerned instead with limiting the liability of an employer who caused harm.

The permissible scope of arbitration was also questioned when the United Steelworkers and Warrior & Gulf Navigation had a collective bargaining agreement prohibiting strikes and lockouts.[77] It also provided a grievance procedure including arbitration. The contract said that strictly managerial decisions were excluded from arbitration, but disagreement about the contract's meaning could be grieved.

The employer was laying off workers while simultaneously contracting-out work. Some laid-off workers were rehired by the contractor to do work at Warrior but at a lower wage. The union sought to grieve, alleging a partial lock out. Warrior refused to submit to arbitration, and the union sued to compel arbitration.

Justice Douglas delivered the Court's decision. "Apart from matters that the parties specifically exclude, all of the questions on which the parties disagree must . . . come within the scope of the grievance and arbitration provisions of the collective agreement." Douglas added, "When . . . an absolute no-strike clause is included in the agreement, then . . . everything that management does is subject to the agreement. . . . 'Strictly a function of management' must be interpreted as referring only to that over which the contract gives management complete control and unfettered discretion. Respondent [Warrior] claims that the contracting out of work falls within this category. Contracting out work is the basis of many grievances; and that type of claim is grist in the mills of the arbitrators. A specific collective bargaining agreement may exclude contracting out from the grievance procedure. . . . Here, however, there is no such provision." The Court held this dispute was over the collective bargaining agreement's meaning and was therefore subject to arbitration. Douglas said it was desirable "to bring into operation an arbitral process which substitutes a regime of peaceful settlement for the older regime of industrial conflict."[78]

In vigorous dissent, Whittaker complained that the Court had not found the law but changed it.[79] In one passage he said the district court had noted that for nineteen years the union had unsuccessfully sought to negotiate limits to contracting-out. He then added, "Although acquiescing for 19 years in the employer's interpretation that contracting out work was 'strictly a function of management,' and having repeatedly tried—particularly in the negotiation of the agreement involved here—but unsuccessfully, to induce the employer to agree to a covenant that would prohibit it from contracting out work, the union, after having agreed to and signed the contract involved, presented a 'grievance' on the ground that the employer's contracting out work, at a time when some employees in the unit were laid-off for lack of work, constituted a partial 'lockout' of employees in violation of the antilockout provision of the agreement."[80]

Whittaker describes nineteen years of effort to change management policy as nineteen years of acceptance. That was surely news to the union. Whittaker's rhetoric that the union accepted and signed the collective bargaining agreement implies that the union was violating its word by attempting to grieve an issue that management contended was its prerogative. Whittaker's rhetoric implies that the union was untrustworthy. In contrast, his rhetoric lacks even a hint of suspicion about management motives in finding a way to force laid off union members to work for less pay by using a contractor as go-between. Whittaker's rhetoric sees nothing questionable about terminating employees and taking back those who would work for less, sees no element of lockout in that. In addition, the term "grievance" is repeatedly used within quotation marks by Whittaker. This is typical of his rhetorical technique. If challenged, he could allege that the quotation marks simply indicate he feels it improper to define the union's objection as a grievance, because he believes grieving is not allowed on this issue. The rhetorical impact, however, is to question the legitimacy of the issue being grieved, to ridicule what is upsetting the union. Nonetheless, if challenged, Whittaker could deny saying any such thing. This is a powerful technique for evading accountability, and illustrates how formidable Whittaker must have been as a courtroom litigator.

The rhetorical intention of Whittaker's quotation marks is even more apparent if the lower court opinions are examined. The district court ruled against the union but did not put "grievance" within quotation marks. Although the appeals judges split on whether a union grievance should be allowed, none of the judges—pro or con—used quotation marks around "grievance." Whittaker's use of quotation marks was not standard.

Whittaker's dissent claimed, "The District Court, holding that the contracting out of work was, and over a long course of dealings had been interpreted and understood by the parties to be, 'strictly a function of management,' and was therefore specifically excluded from arbitration . . . denied the relief prayed."[81] Support for Whittaker's assertion about the district court decision is elusive. It does not seem to say both parties have long accepted contracting-out as management prerogative. Nor does the appeals court decision[82] contain such acceptance by both parties. Those decisions show the union had long failed to achieve a collective bargaining agreement limiting contracting-out, but not that union had ever agreed that a contract silent on the point meant that the union forswore any right to grieve.

After failing to get contracting-out covered by the labor agreement, and thereupon signing an agreement saying that strictly managerial functions were not subject to arbitration, according to Whittaker the union thereby "agreed to exclude at least that matter [contracting-out] from arbitration." In effect Whittaker argued that silence (in the agreement) was consent (by the union). He directly asserted that the Supreme Court's decision forced the employer to arbitrate an issue excluded from the labor agreement's arbitration provision.[83] Whittaker declared, "The District Court found, and the Court of Appeals approved its finding, that by the terms of the contract, as interpreted by the parties over 19 years, the contracting out of work was 'strictly a function of management' and 'not subject to arbitration.' "[84] Other persons who have examined those lower court opinions have failed to find any passage indicating the union accepted that contracting-out was none of its business.

In conclusion Whittaker inveighed against the alleged tyranny of arbitrators: "Courts must exercise their jurisdiction, when properly invoked, to protect the citizen against the attempted use by arbitrators of pretended powers actually never conferred."[85]

A consistent theme of Whittaker's decisions in labor cases is that the employer's stance is correct. This is seen whether the issue is collective bargaining, compensation for injuries, or suspected communist leanings of a worker. The theme is so consistent, despite varying issues and facts, as to suggest Whittaker had a predisposition to favor employers.

Chapter 7

Retirement

Whittaker's first Supreme Court law clerk noted, "There were four rock-ribbed conservatives and four rock-ribbed liberals." Whittaker viewed his vote, though just one of nine, as continually deciding cases. "He felt like he was the whole Supreme Court," the clerk said. "It was just too much of a burden on him."[1]

COLLAPSE

During his first term on the court in 1957 he had trouble focusing on matters demanding his attention and was noticeably jittery. Justice Burton's diary said at this time, "Justice Whittaker has been on the edge of a nervous breakdown but hopes to finish the term and then recuperate."[2] His depression and anxiety worsened during the spring term of 1957. Exasperated on one hot afternoon, he combined imagery of American slavery and a Bible story about treating something of great value as a mere trifle, telling one of his clerks "that he had 'sold himself down the river for a pot of porridge.' He should, he said, never have left the trial court bench where he could interact with the real people of the world. He seemed ready to quit right then and there. Just a bad day at the office, I thought at the time. But it was more than that. He was not just unhappy. He was distraught and in serious emotional distress."[3] That autumn his attempts to cope included a regimen of drug taking that would have been a doper's paradise in a later era. His prescriptions included Neurosene, Thorazine, Ultran, and Desbutol—drugs used to combat manic behavior, attention deficit, and poor sleep.[4] A fellow justice recalled that Whittaker "used to come out of our conference literally crying."[5] His precarious health may have contributed to inconsistencies in his opinions that still baffle students of his work.

An old Kansas City acquaintance saw Whittaker in 1957 without recognition. His frame lacked the comfortable pounds he had taken to Washington, and only his voice permitted positive identification of the sickly appearing man.[6] On another occasion Whittaker complained about the unrelenting strain of his responsibility.[7] Even court customs caused anxiety. Whittaker commented about his uneasiness at having to speak last at judicial conferences but vote first; he complained that this "put the monkey on the junior's back."[8] A former law partner added that the justice appreciated visits from his old friend but gave an impression that such social calls interfered with pressing work.[9]

Cigarettes were his constant companions. Without them "I just can't concentrate," he said. This was true throughout his adult life. One of his sons retained a childhood memory when "he was really working on something . . . in the middle of a trial or something in the middle of the night you could see the glowing end of his cigarette walking through the house. It would be totally dark and he would be up in the middle of the night wandering around with this glow." When he suffered a collapsed lung late in life, he switched to filter-tips as a gesture for good health.[10]

Midway in his Supreme Court service his spirits briefly improved, an improvement coinciding with a burst of procedural cases in which he did not have to ponder constitutional issues but could instead concentrate on technical issues. Justice Harlan noted Whittaker's pleasure in dealing with such cases: "He made no secret, that he found the non-constitutional aspects of the Court's work more congenial than its constitutional cases." Harlan added that Whittaker "was a prodigious worker who was satisfied with nothing less than full mastery of every record and brief. When circumstances made it impossible to realize that goal, he regarded it as a matter for self-reproach."[11] Grappling with *Baker* v. *Carr* he became particularly troubled, especially as Frankfurter and other justices sought his support. At one point he was prepared to join a majority if he did not have to be the swing vote; at another point he was ready to join Frankfurter in dissent. This case was perhaps the most important ever brought to the Warren court, a case which asked whether the principle of "one man, one vote" was mandated by the Constitution, thereby invalidating traditional ways in which state legislatures were selected. The stress Whittaker felt with this case has been blamed for his health's catastrophic breakdown.[12]

More than once Whittaker described service on the Supreme Court as "the most solemn quest for light that can proceed from the broodings of a human soul."[13] In 1961, however, he used the same phraseology in a different context: "Before man knows either his origin or his destiny, he knows that he is to die. Then comes the most solemn quest for light that can proceed from the broodings of the human soul."[14] His language linked Supreme Court service to death.

Early in 1962 Whittaker collapsed. A family member found him ready to commit suicide,[15] and the justice admitted himself to Walter Reed Hospital. In addition to his mental disability, he was found to be in a state of physical exhaustion. Through a haze of cigarette smoke he frankly told a reporter, "I was burning the candle at both ends."[16] Chief Justice Warren insisted on having Whittaker evaluated by a group of doctors. Medical opinion declared that continued service on the court would be fatal.[17] According to what one of Whittaker's clerks heard from Justice Clark, Warren virtually forced Whittaker to retire. In a state of agitation Whittaker departed from the Supreme Court. "I hate to leave the court," Whittaker said publicly. "This is a distressing experience for me."[18] Warren did, however, urge Whittaker to keep his judicial commission, thereby allowing him to receive a lifetime annuity of $17,500 (an amount subject to increase).

AFTERLIFE

Unlike many retired Washington notables, Whittaker chose to leave the seat of government and returned home to Kansas City. The summer after his retirement he tried to spend several weeks relaxing in Colorado. A friend who saw him there remembered that nothing held his attention more than a few minutes. He continually flitted from one diversion to another without seeming to enjoy them, never finding any rest.[19] In some ways he acted as a person suffering from "shell shock," later called post-traumatic stress disorder.

Whittaker said he hoped to resume some judicial duties, as most retired judges do. His help was solicited by more than one federal appeals court, and he expected to begin presiding over appeals cases in his old Eighth Circuit in September of 1962. Under federal judiciary rules, all he needed was permission from Chief Justice Warren. That permission never came. The reason is unclear. Allegedly Warren was exasperated with Whittaker's agonizing about decision-making. "I never could get him to make up his mind," Warren reportedly complained when he heard that Whittaker wanted to resume judicial work, "and I'll be damned if I will let him do that to me again trying cases. So the answer is no."[20] Warren was also concerned that Whittaker's health would not permit him to withstand judicial duties. Due to Whittaker's interest in resuming a judicial position, Warren compelled him to undergo examination by a medical board, and following that examination Warren never approved resumption of judicial responsibilities by Whittaker.

Even before retiring from the Supreme Court Whittaker began accepting invitations to make speeches. Income from such activity was meager, but he enjoyed opportunities to present his views to the public. His speeches often expressed disdain for emotion in public debate while paradoxically inflaming feelings about the Supreme Court and about social justice.

These addresses showed inspiration from prominent Republicans of his era who were considered spokesmen for the party's conservative branch. In 1961 Whittaker told the graduating class of Juniata College, "The strength, or weakness, of America lies not in its farms and forests, its factories and fortresses, nor in the glorious achievements of its past, but it lies in the character, strength, determination and faith of its people."[21] Compare those sentiments to Herbert Hoover's 1937 address before the Massachusetts State Republican Club: "A nation is great not through dams in its rivers or its ships on the sea or the deposits in its banks. It is great by the moral fiber and character of its citizens."[22] Whittaker publicly rated Calvin Coolidge as "a great President,"[23] and in speeches quoted him along with military men such as Admiral Hyman Rickover, Admiral Burke, Admiral William Halsey, and General and Republican Douglas MacArthur.[24]

Like many orators who pursue a vigorous speaking schedule, Whittaker not only repeated themes but even repeated entire speeches from one audience to the next, and specific passages from one speech to the next. "Cliches or Fundamentals?" was delivered at Southeast Missouri State College on February 16, 1964, and again at the Kansas City Rotary Club on February 27. The latter half of that speech was repeated in "Immutable Moral Values" delivered to the Judicial Section of the State Bar of Texas on July 3.[25] The opening of "Immutable Moral Values," referring to the musical *My Fair Lady*, was duplicated in "Law and Order." Whittaker might also revise a speech from one delivery to the next, for example "Faith of the Free" given at a college commencement and at a bar association meeting.[26]

Rules governing his judicial retirement status prohibited him from resuming a law practice, but he found other ways to practice his profession. He soon became legal consultant to the American Medical Association and served on commissions examining how the medical field and science in general were influenced by federal research grants[27] and examining postgraduate medical education.[28] The "research grant" commission headed by Whittaker interviewed witnesses for about two years and produced results typical of the committee genre: "The report of the commission includes a series of 21 conclusions and 15 recommendations. Among the recommendations are the following: (1) AMA should support in general the federal biomedical research program but has an obligation to the profession and the public to question any facet of the program which it considers ill-advised or in need of constructive counsel; (2) the AMA Council on Medical Education should be asked, in cooperation with other interested organizations, to make additional studies."[29]

In 1966 Whittaker served as counsel to the U.S. Senate Select Committee on

Standards and Conduct investigating Sen. Thomas Dodd's (D–CT) campaign financing, an investigation culminating in a formal censure of Dodd by the Senate. This was not an investigation relished by any senator, and concern was felt that the effort would be perceived as an "old boy" whitewash or—at the other extreme—as a partisan inquisition. At the committee's first meeting chairman John Stennis (D–MS) announced, "From the beginning, the Committee planned to obtained [*sic*] an able and eminent lawyer to serve as Consultant Counsel for the Committee. Most fortunately we were able to obtain the services of the Hon. Charles E. Whittaker, formerly a Justice of the Supreme Court of the United States. Mr. Whittaker is a man of rare judgment, an able jurist and practitioner of vast experience." This announcement added instant credibility to the committee's work, but Stennis instantly qualified the extent of Whittaker's participation: "His services as Consultant Counsel will be of great value to the Committee and will be available in all deliberations of the Committee, including these hearings, that is as a Consultant only, gentlemen."[30] His presence at any public hearing was unapparent in committee and staff rosters, and his health problems would seem to preclude active participation in a highly publicized controversy.

In 1965, however, General Motors contacted Whittaker about helping to resolve disputes between the corporation and its dealers. Such a job would require Whittaker to give up his judicial commission. As he had been unable to receive Chief Justice Warren's permission to serve on federal benches that had been offered to him, the main question posed by GM's offer was whether Whittaker could afford to give up his federal disability pension of $19,750 a year. To accept employment by GM, Whittaker would have to relinquish his judicial commission, which meant losing the retirement income and health insurance it guaranteed to both him and his wife. Whittaker explained privately at the time, "While I did not want to appear greedy, or avaricious for money, I would really like to have, and would be made happy by, a retainer of $100,000.00 per year, plus office, secretary and the use of a new Cadillac car, under such a 10-year contract."[31] Whittaker also wanted complete freedom to take on other law clients along with public speaking engagements not inconsistent with his responsibilities to GM. The company persuaded him to accept a $75,000 retainer with all the perks he had specified. The deal more than doubled his gross annual income, and even after a higher tax bite his net income increased by over $25,000.[32] At the age of sixty-four Whittaker resigned his judicial commission to re-enter the business law field that was so familiar to him.

The General Motors Dealer Relations Umpire Plan was developed by the corporation as a way of settling disputes without a lawsuit. If dealers felt themselves unfairly treated by the corporation they could submit their grievance to the umpire. Unlike an arbitrator, whose decision is binding on both parties, the

GM umpire's decision was binding only upon the corporation. A dealer dissatisfied with the decision could take the matter to court. Thus taking advantage of Whittaker's services was a no-lose proposition for GM dealers.[33]

At first Whittaker convened umpire hearings in his Kansas City office but eventually decided to travel to the dealer's home town and conduct hearings there. Although Whittaker strove to follow legal principles, he recognized that he was not conducting a trial and therefore was more liberal in consideration of evidence than a judge might be. For example, he would consider hearsay. Also, the burden of proof did not rest on one party; both the dealer and the corporation were expected to prove their assertions. Although Whittaker had broad power to revise any corporation decision that he deemed unfair to dealers, he did not have authority to award monetary damages.

He observed that dealers initiated umpire proceedings for a wide variety of causes, from small to large, and that many disputes were resolved before a hearing was held. Whittaker felt the umpire plan's most important function was psychological, promoting good dealer–corporation relations by assuring both parties that disputes could be put to an objective umpire. Whittaker felt this assurance made the corporation more cautious in its actions, and allowed dealers to worry less about a chance of being victimized. He estimated that he decided in the corporation's favor about eighty percent of the time, but was unaware of any dealer going to court afterward. His reputation as an arbitrator and judge grew prominent enough to help earn him appointment to the International Court of Arbitration in 1967. That organization was founded in the 1920s by the International Chamber of Commerce as a way of settling business disputes without resort to national or international judicial systems. Proceedings are confidential, and no records available to the public indicate the extent of Whittaker's involvement. Given his health and the lack of activity that visitors noted at his office, we have no reason to believe he performed many duties for the international arbitration body.[34]

Whittaker's GM workload was light. He said he umpired ten or fewer controversies in a year. Indeed, he took the job on the understanding that umpire cases would average one per year.[35] Contractually he was free from performing any other duties for GM. A visitor found Whittaker's spacious Kansas City office in this era to be luxurious and undisturbed by evidence of activity—no reading matter for waiting visitors, no papers on the secretary's desk, not one phone call during an entire hour.[36]

Whittaker may have done additional legal consulting. A Kansas City attorney remembered Whittaker doing probate and mortgage work,[37] but that had to be mere puttering.

Influenza slowed his pace in the summer of 1973, and he began fretting more and more that he could not keep up with tasks needing his attention.[38] Once again physical and psychic weariness incapacitated Whittaker, and once again he checked into a hospital. While there, the drug regimen prescribed to combat his depression caused kidney failure, and after starting dialysis he died from a burst aneurysm on November 26. He had receded so far from public view that even the *Kansas City Star*, the newspaper of his old friend Roy Roberts, had forgotten how to spell his name correctly in its editorial memorializing "Justice Charles E. Whitaker."[39]

"Religion," said Whittaker, "teaches every man that he is to live again; that the duties of this life have reference to, and are only in preparation for, the life that is to come."[40] If Whittaker found such a new life, we can only hope it was more satisfying and serene than the one he left.

Notes

CHAPTER 1

1. James R. Ashlock, "Justice Whittaker Credits Troy, Kas., Background," *Kansas City Times*, April 4, 1960, p. 4.

2. Whittaker, "Faith" (Juniata), 3.

3. Quoted in *Kansas City Times*, Sept. 25, 1953, p. 3 and in Joe Henderson, "Charles Whittaker's Call to a Career," *Kansas City Star*, Sept. 20, 1964, p. E1.

4. U.S. Senate, *Nomination*, 32.

5. Dorothy Kiehnhoff in Smith, "Charles," 6.

6. Arthur Huey story in *Kansas City Times*, March 4, 1957.

7. Ibid.

8. Copious contemporary accounts can be found in the late November and early December files of the *Kansas City Post*. The *Kansas City Journal*, *Kansas City Star*, and *Kansas City Times* also had coverage.

9. Quoted in Henderson, "Charles," *Kansas City Star*, Sept. 20, 1964, p. E1. Ironically, Whittaker's own law practice was far removed from this kind of case.

10. Cole, "Mr.," 13.

11. Kent Whittaker in Cole, "Mr.," 14.

12. Whittaker, "Lawyers," 335. Although Whittaker does not say explicitly that he is describing justice of the peace courts where he practiced, it is difficult to imagine where else he would have observed such details of atmosphere. Working cuspidors, for example, were not routine courtroom furnishings in the 1960s.

13. Quoted in John R. Cauley, *Kansas City Star*, March 9[?], 1957, p. 1 (envelope file of Missouri Valley Room, Kansas City, Missouri, Public Library).

14. William M. McAdams, quoted in Cole, "Mr.," 15–16.

15. Whittaker, "Advocacy," 235.

16. Quoted in Schwartz, *History*, 272.

17. Frankfurter, *Of Law*, 166–67.

18. Kent Whittaker, quoted in Tom Jackman, "Whittaker Courthouse a Tribute to'Great Lawyer'," *Kansas City Star*, Aug. 2, 1994.

19. Smith, "Charles," 9.

CHAPTER 2

1. Compiled from legal directories, this representative list of clients illustrates the kind of law practice that Whittaker pursued.

1928 Watson, Gage & Ess

Specializing in bankruptcy, corporation, insurance, probate, and railway. Clients included:

Constitution Indemnity Company
Kansas City Live Stock Exchange
Kansas City Star
Postal Telegraph Cable Company
Produce Exchange Bank
Traders National Bank
Union Pacific Railroad Company
Wilson & Company
Witte Engine Works

1932 Watson, Gage, Ess, Groner & Barnett

General practice. Emphasis on bankruptcy, corporation, insurance, probate, railway. Clients included:

Barrick Publishing Company
Chicago Northwestern Railway Company
Columbian Electric Company
Constitution Indemnity Company
Interstate Transit Lines, Inc.
Jensen–Salsbery Laboratories, Inc.
Kansas City Hay Dealers Association
Kansas City Live Stock Exchange
Kansas City Public Service Company
Kansas City Star
Kansas City Testing Laboratories, Inc.
Mid-Continent Air Transport Company
Postal Life & Casualty Insurance Company
Postal Telegraph–Cable Company
Produce Exchange Bank
Public Indemnity Company
R. V. Aycock Company
Seidlitz Paint & Varnish Company
Silica Products Company
Southern Pacific Company
Traders National Bank
Union Pacific Railroad Company
Wilson & Company

Witte Engine Works
Yellow Cab Company

1942 Watson, Ess, Groner, Barnett & Whittaker
General practice, corporation. Clients included:
American Surety Company
Burroughs Adding Machine Company
Chicago Northwestern Railway Company
City National Bank & Trust Company
Dierks Lumber & Coal Company
Eagle Indemnity Company
George Muehlebach Brewing Company
Interstate Transit Lines
Jensen–Salsbery Laboratories, Inc.
Joyce & Company
Kansas City Public Service Company
Kansas City Star
London Guarantee & Accident Company, Ltd.
Manufacturers Casualty Company
Minneapolis–Moline Power Implement Company
Montgomery Ward & Company
New York Casualty Company
Pickering Lumber Corporation
Phoenix Indemnity Company
Postal Telegraph–Cable Company
Royal Indemnity Company
Southern Pacific Company
Standard Surety and Casualty Company
Sun Indemnity Company
Sutherland Lumber Company
Toplis & Harding
Traders & General Insurance Company
Union Pacific Railroad Company

1953 Watson, Ess, Whittaker, Marshall & Enggas
General practice, corporation law. Clients included:
American Surety Company
Armour & Company
Bordon Company
Burroughs Adding Machine Company
Central Surety & Insurance Corporation
City National Bank & Trust Company
Cook Chemical Company
Corn Products Corporation
Dierks Lumber & Coal Company

Eagle Indemnity Company
Falls Spring Corporation
George Muehlebach Brewing Company
Globe Indemnity Company
Interstate Transit Lines
Jensen–Salsbery Laboratories, Inc.
J. I. Case Company
Joyce & Company
Kansas City Star
Minneapolis Moline Power Implement Company
Montgomery Ward & Company
New York Casualty Company
Overland Greyhound Lines
Phoenix Indemnity Company
Pickering Lumber Corporation
Robinson Shoe Stores, Inc.
Royal Indemnity Company
Safeway Stores, Inc.
Southern Pacific Company
Sun Indemnity Company
Sutherland Lumber Company
Union Pacific Railroad Company

2. "Fur Trapping as a Farm Youth Started Whittaker on Law Path," *Kansas City Star*, Feb. 19, 1954.
3. Lowell L. Knipmeyer, quoted in "Charles" (*Missouri Bar*), 61.
4. Lowell L. Knipmeyer, quoted in ibid., 61.
5. Volz, "Mr.," 164.
6. Abe Margolin interview with Cynthia Dodge, spring 1998.
7. William M. McAdams in Cole, "Mr.," 16.
8. Jesse Childers interview with Cynthia Dodge, May 14, 1998, p. 3.
9. Cole, "Mr.," 16–17; Abe Margolin interview with Cynthia Dodge, spring 1998.
10. Jesse Childers interview with Cynthia Dodge, May 14, 1998, p. 3.
11. Lowell L. Knipmeyer, quoted in "Charles" (*Missouri Bar*), 61.
12. Tom Clark in "Charles" (*Texas Law*), 747.
13. Whittaker, "Cliches," 2.
14. Whittaker, "Immutable," 3–4.
15. Lowell L. Knipmeyer, quoted in "Charles" (*Missouri Bar*), 61.
16. Walter A. Raymond to Marlin M. Volz, Dec. 20, 1957, quoted in Volz, "Mr.," 165.
17. Whittaker, "Some" (Nebraska), 358.
18. *Payne* v. *Arkansas*, 356 U.S. 560 (1958).
19. Kohn, "Supreme," 47–48.
20. Whittaker in Whittaker and Coffin, *Law*, 7.
21. Coffin in ibid., 48.
22. Whittaker in ibid., 52.
23. Whittaker in ibid.

24. Whittaker in ibid.
25. Whittaker in ibid.
26. Whittaker in ibid.
27. Whittaker in ibid.
28. Coffin in ibid., 98.
29. Coffin in ibid., 154.
30. Whittaker in ibid., 155.
31. Ibid., 74–78.
32. Whittaker, "Faith" (Juniata), 9.
33. Whittaker, "Faith," (Kansas), 10.
34. Newman, *Hugo*, 517.
35. Quoted in *Kansas City Star*, Sept. 20, 1964, p. E1.
36. Quoted in ibid.
37. Charles E. Whittaker to Samuel E. Whitaker, Oct. 29, 1964, in Smith, "Charles," 161.
38. 317 U.S. 111 (1942).
39. Charles E. Whittaker to Samuel E. Whitaker, Oct. 29, 1964, in Smith, "Charles," 161.
40. Whittaker in Whittaker and Coffin, *Law*, 66.
41. "Ex-Jurist Appeals for Order in U.S." *Kansas City Times*, Nov. 12, 1968. These criticisms of "lesser men" who refused opportunity to serve in military combat came from an apparently able-bodied man who spent World War II at home in Kansas City earning a handsome income as a lawyer. Plenty of attorneys obtained military commissions allowing them to contribute their professional talents to the war effort, and men entering their forties were even known to risk combat service. As a teenager Whittaker could have enlisted in World War I but stayed on the farm. Regardless of inherent merit in his choices, they bring a whiff of hypocrisy to his complaints about men who declined military service during the Vietnam War.
42. Whittaker, "Cliches," 5.
43. Whittaker, "Immutable," 4–5.
44. Whittaker, "Cliches," 6–7 and "Immutable," 4–5.
45. Quoted in *Kansas City Star*, Sept. 20, 1964, p. E2.
46. Smith, "Charles," 15; *Kansas City Star*, March 1957, p. A2 (envelope file of Missouri Valley Room, Kansas City, Missouri, Public Library).
47. Jesse Childers interview with Cynthia Dodge, May 14, 1998, p. 8.
48. *Miller* v. *Union Pacific*, 63 F.2d 574 (8th Cir. 1933).
49. *Rhodes* v. *Dierks Lumber & Coal Co.*, 108 F.2d 846 (8th Cir. 1940).
50. *Dierks Lumber & Coal Co.* v. *Mabry*, 128 F.2d 1005 (8th Cir. 1942).
51. *Elastic Stop Nut Corporation* v. *National Labor Relations Board*, 142 F.2d 371 (8th Cir. 1944).
52. Ibid., 376.
53. Ibid., 377.
54. For analysis of Whittaker's consistent stance against labor unions in his Supreme Court opinions, see Barbara Christensen, "Mr. Justice Whittaker: The Man on the Right," *Santa Clara Law Review* 19 (1979): 1043–49.

55. *United States* v. *Union Pacific*, 32 F. Supp. 917 (W.D. Mo. 1940); *United States* v. *Union Pacific*, 34 F. Supp. 4 (W.D. Mo. 1940); *Union Pacific* v. *United States*, 313 U.S. 450 (1941).

56. 32 Stat. 847 (1903); 34 Stat. 584 (1906).

57. *Kansas City Star*, March 1957, p. A2 (envelope file of Missouri Valley Room, Kansas City, Missouri, Public Library).

58. Kent Whittaker interview with Cynthia Dodge, May 13, 1998, p. 14.

59. U.S. Senate, *Nomination*, 32.

60. Lowell L. Knipmeyer, quoted in "Charles" (*Missouri Bar*), 61.

61. Cole, "Mr.," 23–24.

62. "Burglary Loss by Whittakers," *Kansas City Star* or *Kansas City Times*, Feb. 1966 (Missouri Valley Room envelope file, Kansas City, Missouri, Public Library).

63. Russell Baker in Smith, "Charles," 17.

64. Darrell L. Havener in Smith, "Charles," 25.

65. Quoted in *Kansas City Star*, June 12, 1955.

66. Smith, "Charles," 17 says 240A; Kent Whittaker (interview with Cynthia Dodge, May 18, 1998, p. 6) says about 360A at first, increasing to 500A.

67. Jesse Childers interview with Cynthia Dodge, May 14, 1998, pp. 2–3.

68. *Washington Evening Star*, March 2, 1957.

69. Kent Whittaker interview with Cynthia Dodge, May 18, 1998, p. 5.

70. Kent Whittaker interview with Cynthia Dodge, May 13, 1998, p. 12.

71. Kent Whittaker interview with Cynthia Dodge, May 18, 1998, pp. 10–12, 29.

72. Whittaker, "Advocacy," 245.

73. Quoted in *Kansas City Star*, July 19, 1954.

74. Quoted in *Kansas City Star*, June 22, 1956.

75. Cole, "Mr.," 172.

76. Clyde Rayburn, Jr., in Smith, "Charles," 65; Tom C. Clark to John D. Randall, June 3, 1965, Tom Clark Papers, Box 127, Folder 3, Tarlton Law Library, Austin, Texas, as given in Smith, "Charles," 96 n. 51.

77. Whittaker, "Judicial," 8.

78. John R. Cauley, "Supreme Court Isolation Is a Problem to Whittaker," *Kansas City Star*, March 20, 1960, p. F1.

79. Quoted in Cole, "Mr.," 159.

80. Russell W. Gunn, "Remarks of Russell W. Gunn," in *In Memoriam*, 27.

81. Quoted in ibid., 29.

82. Harry F. Rosenthal, "As Whittaker Views Court Balance," *Kansas City Star*, Jan. 29, 1970, p. 34.

83. Celia J. Barrett in Smith, "Charles," 23.

84. William M. McAdams in Cole, "Mr.," 18.

85. Kent Whittaker interview with Cynthia Dodge, May 13, 1998, p. 10.

86. Kent Whittaker interview with Cynthia Dodge, May 18, 1998, p. 10.

87. Clyde Rayburn, Jr., in Smith, "Charles," 65.

88. *Kansas City Times*, June 1, 1957 (Missouri Valley Room envelope file, Kansas City (Missouri) Public Library.

89. Harry F. Rosenthal, "As Whittaker Views Court Balance," *Kansas City Star*, Jan. 29, 1970, p. 34.

90. "Inventory and Description of Stocks Issued in the Name of and Owned by Winifred R. Whittaker, Feb. 26, 1962," in "Stocks—Lists as of 9-1-62 and Subsequent Sales and Acquisitions" folder, Charles Evans Whittaker Papers.

91. Earl Warren in "Charles" (*Texas Law*), 744.

92. Tom Clark in "Charles" (*Texas Law*), 747.

93. Ada Elliott in Cole, "Mr.," 17.

94. Russell Baker in Smith, "Charles," 23.

95. Bruce M. Forrester, "Remarks of Judge Forrester" in *In Memoriam*, 19.

96. Floyd Gibson, quoted in Tom Jackman, "Whittaker Courthouse a Tribute to 'Great Lawyer'," *Kansas City Star*, Aug. 2, 1994.

97. Smith, "Charles," 80; Kohn, "Supreme," 47.

98. Keith Whittaker in Smith, "Charles," 26.

99. Kent Whittaker, quoted in Cole, "Mr.," 21.

100. Celia J. Barrett in Smith, "Charles," 24.

101. U.S. Senate, *Nomination*, 32.

102. Smith, "Charles," 8.

103. Whittaker, "Some" (ABA), 1089.

104. Ibid.

105. Kent Whittaker in Smith, "Charles," 21.

106. Smith, "Charles," 58.

107. Kent Whittaker in Smith, "Charles," 29; interview with C. Keith Whittaker, Aug. 27, 1996, cited in Atkinson, *Leaving*, 130. See also Kent Whittaker, quoted in Tom Jackman, "Whittaker Courthouse a Tribute to 'Great Lawyer'," *Kansas City Star*, Aug. 2, 1994.

108. Walter A. Raymond to Marlin M. Volz, Dec. 20, 1957, quoted in Volz, "Mr.," 166.

109. Lowell L. Knipmeyer, quoted in "Charles" (*Missouri Bar*), 62.

110. Jesse Childers interview with Cynthia Dodge, May 14, 1998, p. 12.

111. Bob Donnellan interview with Cynthia Dodge, April 20, 1998, p. 8.

112. Tom Jackman, "Whittaker Courthouse a Tribute to 'Great Lawyer'," *Kansas City Star*, Aug. 2, 1994.

113. Russell W. Gunn, "Remarks of Russell W. Gunn," in *In Memoriam*, 28.

CHAPTER 3

1. Jack W. Peltason, *Federal Courts in the Political Process* (New York: Random House, 1955), 15; Henry M. Hart, Jr., "The Time Chart of the Justices" in Robert Scigliano, *The Courts: A Reader in the Judicial Process* (Boston: Little, Brown and Company, 1962), 287.

2. Quoted in *Time*, March 11, 1957, p 16.

3. Whittaker, "Some" (ABA), 1090.

4. Cole, "Mr.," 29. See also 164, 166.

5. Eisenhower, *Mandate*, 227.

6. Rogers, "Judicial," 39–40.

7. *Public Papers of the Presidents of the United States: Dwight D. Eisenhower, 1956*, Sept. 11, 1956, p. 762. See also Sept. 27, 1956, p. 819.

8. Frankfurter, *Of Law*, 55.

9. Carl Enggas and Anonymous, in Cole, "Mr.," 47 n. 38.

10. Quoted in *New York Times*, March 3, 1957, p. 58.

11. Bernard G. Segal to James O. Eastland, March 8, 1957, printed in U.S. Senate, *Nomination*, 2.

12. Charles C. Rhyne, quoted in *Kansas City Times*, May 30, 1957, p. 3.

13. Quoted in *Kansas City Times*, May 30, 1957, p. 3.

14. Chase, *Federal*, 98. See also 215 n. 3 about Brownell.

15. Whittaker, "Judicial," 2.

16. Quoted in Volz, "Mr.," 167.

17. Jesse Childers interview with Cynthia Dodge, May 14, 1998, p. 6.

18. Kohn, "Supreme," 46.

19. Douglas, *Court*, 250.

20. Cole, "Mr.," 37.

21. Chase, *Federal*, 94.

22. *Congressional Record*, 85th Cong., 1st sess., March 19, 1957, p. 3929.

23. Duke Shoop, "Whittaker to Be Judge," *Kansas City Star*, Feb. 19, 1954, p. 1.

24. Ibid.

25. Cole, "Mr.," 25 n. 40, 172.

26. Clyde J. Rayburn, Jr., in Smith, "Charles," 55.

27. Clyde J. Rayburn, Jr., in ibid.

28. Quoted in Cole, "Mr.," 52–53.

29. Albert A. Ridge in "Charles" (*Texas Law*), 750.

30. In "Charles" (*Texas Law*), 746.

31. Kent Whittaker in Cole, "Mr.," 54.

32. Quoted in Henderson, "Charles," *Kansas City Star*, Sept. 20, 1964, p. E2.

33. Smith, "Charles," 60. See also Larsen, *Federal*, 231.

34. Clyde J. Rayburn, Jr., in Smith, "Charles," 58.

35. Vincent E. Rawson memorandum, Sept. 16, 1991, Author's files.

36. Whittaker, "Some" (ABA), 1090.

37. *Farm Bureau Cooperative Mill and Supply* v. *Blue Star Foods*, 137 F. Supp. 486 (W.D. Mo. 1956).

38. Ibid., 489.

39. Ibid., 488–89.

40. *Miller* v. *Connell*, 141 F. Supp. 361 (W.D. Mo. 1956)

41. William O. Douglas to Charles E. Whittaker, May 29, 1958, as given in Douglas, *Douglas*, 129.

42. *Flora* v. *United States*, 362 U.S. 145, 178 (1961).

43. *New York Times*, Jan. 28, 1956, pp. 1, 35.

44. Cole, "Mr.," 68.

45. Duke Shoop, "Whittaker up in Courts," *Kansas City Times*, March 5, 1956, p. 3.

46. Whittaker, "Some" (Nebraska), 358–59.

47. Quoted in *Kansas City Star*, March 2, 1957, p. 3.
48. Clyde Rayburn, Jr., in Smith, "Charles," 64.
49. Quoted in Cole, "Mr.," 73.
50. Albert A. Ridge, quoted in *Kansas City Times*, March 3, 1967, p. 2.
51. Charles E. Wyzanski, Jr., "The Importance of the Trial Judge" in Murphy and Pritchett, *Courts*, 109.
52. Smith, "Charles," 64.
53. Clyde Rayburn, Jr., in Smith, "Charles," 65.
54. Whittaker, "Some" (ABA), 1090.

CHAPTER 4

1. Douglas, *Court*, 250.
2. Cole, "Mr.," 81.
3. Chase, *Federal*, 92–93; Eisenhower, *Mandate*, 230.
4. Berman, "Mr.," 10.
5. Douglas, *Court*, 250.
6. Abraham, *Justices*, 396 n. 55. Abraham also credits Arthur Eisenhower with having great influence in Whittaker's first appointment as a district judge (270).
7. Whittaker, "Some" (ABA), 1090.
8. Cole, "Mr.," 102.
9. John R. Cauley, "Supreme Court Isolation Is a Problem to Whittaker," *Kansas City Star*, March 20, 1960, p. F1.
10. Alan Kohn in Smith, "Charles," 44.
11. Quoted in John R. Cauley, *Kansas City Star*, March 9[?], 1957, p. 1 (envelope file of Missouri Valley Room, Kansas City, Missouri, Public Library).
12. Smith, "Charles," 102.
13. Quoted in James E. Clayton, "Whittaker, on Bench, Stuck to Biblical Goal," *Washington Post*, March 30, 1962, p. A4.
14. Cole, "Mr.," 131.
15. Harlan in "Charles" (*Texas Law*), 748.
16. Berman, "Mr.," 14.
17. Leon Friedman, "Charles Whittaker," in Friedman and Israel, *Justices*, 2903.
18. Charles E. Whittaker to A. Scott Mandelup, April 20, 1973, Whittaker Papers, quoted in Smith, "Charles," 83–84.
19. Douglas, *Court*, 4. Also 175.
20. Woodward and Armstrong, *Brethren*, 241.
21. Douglas, *Court*, 172, 174.
22. Privately he was known to complain that he lacked resources to do all that was necessary, and berated a clerk for not providing enough help (Douglas, *Douglas*, 52).
23. Kent Whittaker, quoted in Tom Jackman, "Whittaker Courthouse a Tribute to 'Great Lawyer'," *Kansas City Star*, Aug. 2, 1994.
24. Quoted in Douglas, *Court*, 8.
25. Douglas, *Court*, 171.

26. Quoted in John R. Cauley, "Supreme Court Isolation Is a Problem to Whitaker," *Kansas City Star*, March 20, 1960, p. F1.

27. Quoted in *Kansas City Times*, June 1, 1957.

28. *Kansas City Times*, June 28[?], 1957 (envelope file of Missouri Valley Room, Kansas City, Missouri, Public Library).

29. John R. Cauley, "Accepted the Call to Tribunal Because of a Sense of Duty," *Kansas City Star*, March 29, 1962.

30. Darrell L. Havener in Smith, "Charles," 55.

31. Cole, "Mr.," 7–8.

32. John R. Cauley, "Supreme Court Isolation Is a Problem to Whittaker," *Kansas City Star*, March 20, 1960, p. F1.

33. Quoted in ibid.

34. Cole, "Mr.," 149, 151.

35. Quoted in *Kansas City Times*, Sept. 25, 1953, p. 3.

36. Frankfurter, *Of Law*, 82–83.

37. Ibid., 55.

38. Ibid., 97.

39. William O. Douglas in "Charles," 746.

40. Whittaker, "Some" (ABA), 1090.

41. Alan C. Kohn in Smith, "Charles," 132.

42. Volz, "Mr.," 163, 166.

43. Whittaker, "Tribute," 198–99.

44. William O. Douglas in "Charles," 745.

45. Whittaker, "Advocacy," 234.

46. John R. Cauley, "Supreme Court Isolation Is a Problem to Whittaker," *Kansas City Star*, March 20, 1960, p. F1.

47. *Kansas City Star*, June 2, 1957, p. 1.

48. Joe Lastelic, "Whittaker Off Court," *Kansas City Star*, March 29, 1962.

49. *Washington Evening Star*, March 29, 1962, p. A2.

50. James E. Clayton, "Whittaker, on Bench, Stuck to Biblical Goal," *Washington Post*, March 30, 1962, p. A4.

51. Whittaker, "Advocacy," 243.

52. Elmo Hunter, quoted in Tom Jackman, "Whittaker Courthouse a Tribute to 'Great Lawyer'," *Kansas City Star*, Aug. 2, 1994. Hunter was a federal judge when he made these remarks, but had observed Whittaker in an earlier era.

53. Whittaker, "Obligations," 6.

54. Quoted in Cole, "Mr.," 128–29.

55. Kohn, "Supreme," 42.

56. Kenneth Dam in Smith, "Charles," 103.

57. Quoted in Cole, "Mr.," 151.

58. Likely this article was in *U.S. News and World Report*, July 12, 1957, 45–48 (see Cole, "Mr.," 120 n. 11 and Kohn, "Supreme," 43). Justice Douglas concurred that clerks were doing opinions (Douglas, *Court*, 172–73).

59. Heywood H. Davis in Smith, "Charles," 85; Cole, "Mr.," 130–31.

60. 356 U.S. 525 (1958).

61. Smith, "Charles," 87–88; Kohn, "Supreme," 52.

62. Cole, "Mr.," 121, 123, 173.

63. James N. Adler and Charles E. Whittaker in Smith, "Charles," 85–86.

64. Whittaker in Whittaker and Coffin, *Law*, 6.

65. Whittaker, "Some" (ABA), 1090. Same "quest" language is in Whittaker, "Judicial," 8.

66. Rice, *Warren*, 249.

67. Quoted in Cole, "Mr.," 115.

68. Smith, "Charles," 76; Tom Jackman, "Whittaker Courthouse a Tribute to 'Great Lawyer'," *Kansas City Star*, Aug. 2, 1994.

69. Schwartz, *History*, 272.

70. Ibid., 85.

71. *Boynton* v. *Virginia*, 364 U.S. 454, 464, 468, 470 (1960) (dissent).

72. *Staub* v. *City of Baxley*, 355 U.S. 313 (1958).

73. *Boynton* v. *Virginia*, 364 U.S. 454 (1960) (dissent).

74. *Goldberg* v. *Whitaker House*, 366 U.S. 28, 34–35 (1961) (dissent).

75. *United Steelworkers of America* v. *Warrior & Gulf Navigation Co.*, 363 U.S. 574, 585–87, 589, 592 (1960) (dissent).

76. Quoted by Russell Baker in Smith, "Charles," 27.

77. Quoted in *Time*, March 11, 1957, p. 16.

78. Whittaker, "Role," 13.

79. Quoted in *Kansas City Star*, Aug 5, 1971, p. 12. Almost the same phraseology is used in Whittaker, "Judicial," 9, showing that the intervening decade had not changed Whittaker's view.

80. Quoted in John R. Cauley, "Supreme Court Isolation Is a Problem to Whittaker," *Kansas City Star*, March 20, 1960, p. F1.

81. Michael T. Ghiselin, *Intellectual Compromise: The Bottom Line* (New York: Paragon House, 1989), p. 172.

82. For some of these observations on formalism, realism, evolution, and primary versus secondary sources, I am indebted to Ghiselin's *Intellectual Compromise*, p. 3, and discussion with Jeffery Thomas.

83. James N. Adler in Smith, "Charles," 86.

84. 369 U.S. 186 (1962).

85. Quoted in Newman, *Hugo*, 517.

86. 361 U.S. 138 (1959).

87. Quoted in *New York Times*, Dec. 15, 1959, p. 25. See also *Kansas City Times*, Dec. 15, 1959, p. 1; "Supreme Court Justices Disagree on What's Funny," *U.S. News and World Report* (Dec. 28, 1959), 16–17.

88. Quoted in *New York Times*, Dec. 15, 1959, p. 25.

89. Joseph E. Stevens, Jr., quoted in Tom Jackman, "Whittaker Courthouse a Tribute to 'Great Lawyer'," *Kansas City Star*, Aug. 2, 1994.

90. Douglas, *Court*, 173.

91. Quoted in Tom C. Clark to John D. Randall, June 3, 1965, Tom Clark Papers, Box

127, Folder 3, Tarlton Law Library, as given in Smith, "Charles," 95.

92. John M. Harlan in "Charles" (*Texas Law*), 748.

93. Tom C. Clark in "Charles" (*Texas Law*), 747.

94. 362 U.S. 73 (1960).

95. Smith, "Charles," 125; Cole, "Mr.," 133–34.

96. 363 U.S. 166 (1960).

97. Smith, "Charles," 125.

98. John M. Harlan in "Charles" (*Texas Law*), 748.

99. Quoted in Cole, "Mr.," 106, 108–14; quoted in *Kansas City Star*, Sept. 18, 1971, p. A2; Charles E. Whittaker to Felix Frankfurter, Aug. 30, 1962, Whittaker Papers, quoted in Smith, "Charles," 98.

100. Cole, "Mr.," 109–10.

101. Douglas, *Court*, 173.

102. Quoted in Schwartz, *Super*, 428.

103. William O. Douglas to Charles E. Whittaker, Oct. 30, 1964, as given in Douglas, *Douglas*, 129. When Douglas wrote the second volume of his autobiography he was still irked by Whittaker's speech (Douglas, *Court*, 51).

104. Charles E. Whittaker to A. Scott Mandelup, April 20, 1973, Whittaker Papers, quoted in Smith, "Charles," 161.

105. Whittaker, "Confusion," 27.

106. Ibid., 28.

107. Ibid.

108. Cole, "Mr.," 156.

109. Whittaker, "Confusion," 29.

110. Art. I, sect. 8, clause 3.

111. 295 U.S. 495 (1935).

112. 301 U.S. 1 (1937).

113. Whittaker, "Confusion," 31.

114. Quoted in Patricia Jansen Doyle, "Respite From Duties of High Court," *Kansas City Times*, Dec 24[?], 1960 (envelope file of Missouri Valley Room, Kansas City, Missouri, Public Library.

115. Whittaker in Whittaker and Coffin, *Law*, 72–73.

116. 317 U.S. 111 (1942).

117. Whittaker, "Confusion," 32.

118. Ibid.

119. Quoted in Harry F. Rosenthal, "As Whittaker Views Court Balance," *Kansas City Star*, Jan. 29, 1970, p. 34.

120. Walter A. Raymond to Marlin M. Volz, Dec. 20, 1957, quoted in Volz, "Mr.," 165.

121. Volz, "Mr.," 166.

122. Whittaker, "Judicial," 4–6.

123. Walter A. Raymond to Marlin M. Volz, Dec. 20, 1957, quoted in Volz, "Mr.," 165.

124. *Meredith* v. *Krauthoff* (*In re* Krauthoff), 177 S.W. 1112, 1113 (Mo. Ct. App. 1915).

125. Whittaker, "Reflections," 6–7.

126. William C. Canby in Smith, "Charles," 118–20.

127. Abraham, *Justices*, 271.

128. Lewis, *Gideon's*, 83.

129. Quoted in John R. Cauley, "Supreme Court Isolation Is a Problem to Whittaker," *Kansas City Star*, March 20, 1960, p. F1.

130. Quoted in Cole, "Mr.," 130.

131. Coffin in Whittaker and Coffin, *Law*, 45.

132. Kenneth W. Dam and James N. Adler in Smith, "Charles," 85–86.

133. Volz, "Mr.," 170.

134. Whittaker, "Tribute," 198.

135. *Lehmann* v. *United States ex rel. Carson*, 353 U.S. 685, 689–90 (1957).

136. Ibid., 691 (dissent).

137. 365 U.S. 109 (1961).

138. Tom C. Clark in "Charles" (*Texas Law*), 747.

139. *Perez* v. *Brownell*, 356 U.S. 44 (1958).

140. Ibid., 85.

141. Douglas, *Court*, 173–74; Woodward and Armstrong, *Brethren*, 63. The opinion in question was for *Meyer* v. *United States*, 364 U.S. 410 (1960).

142. Cole, "Mr.," 146. See also Smith, "Charles," 127–28 and Kohn, "Supreme," 47.

143. Carl E. Enggas, "Remarks of Mr. Enggas" in *In Memoriam*, 13.

144. *Miller* v. *United States*, 124 F. Supp. 203, 204–205 (W.D. Mo. 1954).

145. *Davis* v. *University of Kansas City*, 129 F. Supp. 716, 718 (W.D. Mo. 1955).

146. *Davis* v. *University of Kansas City*, U.S. District Court—Western District of Missouri, Western Division, Kansas City, Missouri, Civil Case Files, #9667. Box 971, R-51, U7, S8.

CHAPTER 5

1. Quoted in *Kansas City Star*, March 8[?], 1957, p. A1 (envelope file of Missouri Valley Room, Kansas City, Missouri, Public Library).

2. Whittaker, "Some," 1090. Nearly the same phraseology is in Whittaker, "Judicial," 7–8.

3. William O. Douglas in "Charles" (*Texas Law*), 746.

4. John M. Harlan in "Charles" (*Texas Law*), 748.

5. *Miller* v. *United States*, 124 F. Supp. 203, 205 (W.D. Mo. 1954).

6. *Southern Kansas Greyhound Lines, Inc.*, v. *United States*, 134 F.Supp. 502, 506 (W.D. Mo. 1955).

7. J. B. Matthews, "Relief for America's Reds," *American Legion Magazine* (Oct. 1957), 14.

8. Whittaker, "Faith" (Kansas), 2.

9. Whittaker, "Law," 400 (emphasis in original).

10. Whittaker, "Cliches," 9–12; Whittaker, "Immutable," 7–8.

11. *University of Kansas City Bulletin The Catalogue Number 1947–1948.*

12. *University of Kansas City Bulletin The Catalogue Number 1948–1949.*

13. *University of Kansas City Bulletin The Catalogue Number 1953–1954.*

14. "University," 193.

15. Ibid.

16. Ibid., 183–84.

17. Clyde Rayburn, Jr., in Smith, "Charles," 61. This report came long after Rayburn's student days.

18. *Chicago Tribune*, June 8, 1953, p. 7.

19. June 10, 1953, p. 7.

20. *Time*, March 7, 1949, 44.

21. Quotations in *New York Times*, Jan. 24, 1949, p. 12.

22. *Time*, March 7, 1949, 44.

23. Linus Pauling, "Spitzer Case" (letter to editor), *Chemical and Engineering News* 27 (1949): 935.

24. "Strand and Spitzer Issue Statements on Spitzer's Dismissal," *Chemical and Engineering News* 27 (1949): 906.

25. "State Science" (editorial), *Chemical and Engineering News* 26 (1948): 3815; Ralph Spitzer, "Source of Controversy" (letter to editor), *Chemical and Engineering News* 27 (1949): 306–307; "Strand and Spitzer Issue Statements on Spitzer's Dismissal," *Chemical and Engineering News* 27 (1949): 906–909; Linus Pauling, "Spitzer Case" (letter to editor), *Chemical and Engineering News* 27 (1949): 935–936; *Time* (March 7, 1949), 44; A. H. Sturtevant, letter to editor, *Chemical and Engineering News* 27 (1949): 935–936, 955; Sydney Hook, letter to editor, *New York Times*, March 7, 1949, p. 20.

26. "University," 191.

27. June 11, 1953, p. 36.

28. Sept. 24, 1953, p. 36.

29. U.S. Senate, Hearings, 1121–26.

30. Ibid., 1114–21.

31. Ibid., 1117.

32. Fyke Farmer, quoted in U.S. Senate, *Nomination*, 15.

33. *Deutch* v. *United States*, 367 U.S. 456 (1961).

34. June 12, 1953. Other *Tribune* coverage can be found June 9, pp. 1–2 and June 11, p. 13. The *Chicago Daily News* coverage was low-key in comparison: June 9, p. 4; and June 11, p. 10.

35. U.S. Senate, "Subversive Influence in the Educational Process."

36. Ibid., 11–14.

37. Ibid., 25.

38. Ibid., 26–27.

39. Ibid., 28.

40. Davis contended this was not an official board meeting but rather was an occasion allowing certain trustees to confront him; the AAUP found the proceedings to be regular ("University," 187–88).

41. Quoted in U.S. Senate, *Nomination*, 9.

42. *Killian* v. *United States*, 368 U.S. 231, 247, 251 (1961).

43. Quoted in U.S. Senate, *Nomination*, 10.

44. 18 U.S.C. §241 (1952 ed.).

45. Fyke Farmer in U.S. Senate, *Nomination*, 19. More than one attorney represented Davis in various proceedings.

46. Fyke Farmer in ibid., 13–15.

47. Fyke Farmer in ibid., 22.

48. *Davis* v. *University of Kansas City*, U.S. District Court—Western District of Missouri, Western Division, Kansas City, Missouri, Civil Case Files, #9667. Box 971, R-51, U7, S8.

49. *Slochower* v. *Board of Higher Education of New York City*, 350 U.S. 551, 557–58 (1956).

50. *Shelton* v. *Tucker*, 364 U.S. 479, 485–86 (1960).

51. *Wieman* v. *Updegraff*, 344 U.S. 183, 195 (1952) (concurring opinion).

52. *Sweezy* v. *New Hampshire*, 354 U.S. 234, 250 (1957).

53. *Shelton* v. *Tucker*, 364 U.S. 479, 496, 499 (1960) (dissent).

54. "University," 482–83.

55. Affidavit in Support of Plaintiff's Motion for a New Trial, Etc. filed Apr 25, 1955, *Davis* v. *University of Kansas City*, U.S. District Court—Western District of Missouri, Western Division, Kansas City Missouri, Civil Case Files, #9667. Box 971, R-51, U7, S8.

56. Davis believed the conspiracy extended to the *Kansas City Star*. Roy Roberts, Whittaker's close friend and chief of the *Star*, was on the UKC trustees executive committee. On September 23 the *Star* printed a front page article about Davis's June appearance before the U.S. Senate subcommittee. He believed this article was timed to promote public support for the university's dismissal proceedings. The next day the *Star*'s morning edition (called the *Times*) printed an editorial saying "the public" believed Davis had the responsibility to prove himself innocent of charges. "About two weeks after the publication of the editorial," Davis's court complaint said, "a member of the editorial staff of the Star was made a member of the Board of Trustees of the university." The newspaper's treatment of Spitzer was no more friendly. September 23 coverage included this version of comments from Oregon State president Strand: "Dr. Spitzer has chosen to espouse dialectical materialism. A better name would be dialectical murder." Such attacks on Spitzer helped run him out of town. The *Kansas City Times* editorial (Sept. 24, 1953, p. 36) noted, "Dr. Ralph Spitzer has sold his home and gone to the West coast." The *Star* cited its quotation of Strand to the March 7, 1949, issue of *Time*. Here is the quotation as it appeared in *Time*: "Many men in Soviet Russia . . . have died in concentration camps, or by other means, because they would not accept the untruths that Dr. Spitzer has chosen to espouse. . . . Dialectical materialism! A better name would be dialectical murder" (ellipses in *Time*). Here is the closing of Strand's remarks about Spitzer as appearing in *Chemical and Engineering News* 27 (1949): 909: "Many men in Soviet Russia besides Vavilov have died in concentration camps, or by other means, because they would not accept the untruths which Ralph Spitzer has chosen to espouse. Hundreds of other men, as Goldschmidt points out, who know better, are suffering mental torture in order to escape a similar fate. Dialectical materialism! A better name would be dialectical murder. The case is closed so far as I am concerned." Strand's reference to dialectical materialism may have been inspired by the close of Spitzer's fateful letter in *Chemical and Engineering News*: "The value of controversy in the development of Soviet thought, as well as the use made of dialectical materialism as a guide in research and practice, is thoroughly discussed by John Somerville in *Soviet Philosophy* (Philosophical Library, 1946)."

57. *Davis* v. *University of Kansas City*, 129 F. Supp. 716, 718 (W.D. Mo. 1955).

58. Smith, "Charles," 64.

59. Quoted in *Kansas City Star*, June 2, 1957, p. 3.

60. *Slochower* v. *Board of Higher Education of New York City*, 350 U.S. 551 (1956).

61. "University," 191–92, 195. At the time of this investigation the UKC administration was still under AAUP censure invoked in 1941 as a result of assorted faculty–administration battles ("Censured," 796; "University," 478–93).

62. Douglas, *Court*, 79.

63. *Beilan* v. *Board of Education*, 357 U.S. 399 (1958).

64. Ibid., 405-406.

65. Ibid., 411 (dissent).

66. Ibid., 424 (dissent).

67. Ibid., 425 (dissent).

68. *Board of Public Education School District of Philadelphia* v. *Herman A. Beilan*, 125 A.2d 327 (Pa. S. Ct. 1956).

69. Ibid., 336–37 (dissent).

70. *Beilan* v. *Board of Education*, 357 U.S. 399, 411 (1958) (dissent).

71. Ibid. (dissent).

72. Ibid., 414 (dissent).

73. Ibid., 415 (dissent).

74. *Deutch* v. *United States*, 367 U.S. 456 (1961).

75. 357 U.S. 468 (1958).

76. *Slagle et al.* v. *Ohio*, 366 U.S. 259 (1961).

77. Ibid., 265.

78. Ibid., 267.

79. *Uphaus* v. *Wyman*, 360 U.S. 72 (1959).

80. Ibid., 79.

81. Ibid., 80.

82. Ibid., 82 (dissent).

83. Ibid., 84 (dissent).

84. 357 U.S. 449, 462 (1958).

85. *Uphaus* v. *Wyman*, 360 U.S. 72, 85 (1959) (dissent).

86. Ibid., 86–87 (dissent).

87. Ibid., 90–91 (dissent).

88. Ibid., 91 (dissent).

89. Ibid., 91–92 (dissent).

90. Ibid., 92 (dissent).

91. Quoted in ibid., 92 n. 5–93 n. 5 (dissent).

92. Ibid., 108 (dissent). *United States* v. *Lovett*, 328 U.S. 303 (1946) examines bills of attainder in the context of anti-communist investigations.

93. *Uphaus* v. *Wyman*, 360 U.S. 72, 93 (1959) (dissent).

94. Ibid., 94 (dissent).

95. Ibid., 99 (dissent).

96. Ibid., 101 (dissent).

97. *Flemming* v. *Nestor*, 363 U.S. 603 (1960).

98. *Rowoldt* v. *Perfetto*, 355 U.S. 115 (1957).
99. *Flemming* v. *Nestor*, 363 U.S. 603, 617 (1960).
100. Ibid., 622 (dissent).
101. Ibid., 626 (dissent).
102. *United States* v. *Lovett*, 328 U.S. 303, 315 (1946), quoted in *Flemming* v. *Nestor*, 363 U.S. 603, 627 (1960) (dissent).
103. *Flemming* v. *Nestor*, 363 U.S. 603, 629 (1960) (dissent).
104. Ibid., 631 (dissent).
105. Ibid., 635 (dissent).
106. Ibid., 635, 638, 640 (dissent).
107. Quoted in *Rowoldt* v. *Perfetto*, 355 U.S. 115, 130 (1957) (dissent).
108. *Rowoldt* v. *Perfetto*, 355 U.S. 115, 120 (1957).
109. *Bonetti* v. *Rogers*, 356 U.S. 691 (1958).
110. *Heikkinen* v. *United States*, 355 U.S. 273 (1958).
111. 64 Stat. 1006, 1008.
112. *Heikkinen* v. *United States*, 240 F.2d 94 (7th Cir. 1957); *Heikkinen* v. *United States*, 355 U.S. 273 (1958).
113. 364 U.S. 454 (1960).
114. Ibid., 455.
115. Ibid., 466–67 (dissent).
116. 364 U.S. 206, 234 (1960) (dissent).
117. Whittaker, "Former," 59.
118. *Gomillion* v. *Lightfoot*, 364 U.S. 339 (1960).
119. *Kansas City Star*, Sept. 20, 1964, p. E2.
120. Whittaker, "Cliches," 4–7.
121. Whittaker, "Immutable," 4–5.
122. Ibid., 2.
123. Ibid.
124. Ibid.
125. Some examples from 1966 and 1967 can be seen in *Congressional Record*, 89th Cong., 2d sess. and 90th Cong., 1st sess. On April 20, 1966 (p. 8608), Sen. Herman Talmadge of Georgia said, "I wholeheartedly join Justice Whittaker," and adding, "There also appeared in yesterday's Washington Evening Star a fine editorial which addresses itself to some of the very same points made by Justice Whittaker" (p. 8608). That editorial referred to "the Watts riots and other so-called demonstrations" (p. 8610). See also April 28 insertion of Whittaker remarks by Sen. John Sparkman of Alabama (pp. 9332–35), Aug. 15 insertion of Whittaker remarks by Sen. Harry Byrd of West Virginia (pp. 19400–02) and Sept. 26 insertion (pp. 23828–29). On Feb. 16, 1967, Rep. John R. Rarick of Louisiana declared, "Since many of our people have short memories, I am asking that the article covering a speech by the Honorable Charles E. Whittaker . . . be inserted at this point." Following the article about Whittaker, Rarick declared, "Government should let the dedicated jurists and lawmen alone and, under the eye of society in their own backyard, if permitted to proceed unhampered I am convinced they will restore law and order, and deter crime" (pp. 3739–40). Introducing Whittaker remarks on Feb. 20, Rep. McMillan stated, "I think Justice Whittaker has placed proper emphasis on certain areas of crime and law

enforcement" (p. 3841). These examples of exploitation of Whittaker's remarks by congressional opponents of civil rights activism are not exhaustive.

126. Whittaker, "Law," 398 (emphasis in original), 402.
127. Whittaker, "Mass."
128. Whittaker, "Law," 398 (emphasis in original).
129. Ibid., 399 (emphasis in original).
130. Ibid. (emphasis in original).
131. Ibid., 402 (original paragraphs run together here).
132. Ibid., 403–4.
133. Whittaker, "Former," 59.
134. Quoted in "Disorder Eyed by Ex-Justice," *Kansas City Times*, Nov. 13, 1968.
135. Bob Donnellan interview with Cynthia Dodge, April 20, 1998, p. 15.
136. Whittaker in Whittaker and Coffin, *Law*, 6.
137. Whittaker in ibid., 7.
138. Whittaker in ibid., 11–12.
139. Whittaker in ibid., 17. See also Kathleen Farmann's review of that book in *Notre Dame Lawyer* 43 (1968): 1028. Whittaker's charges against high Johnson administration officials received news media coverage (for example, *Washington Evening Star*, Feb. 15, 1967 and John R. Cauley, "Negro Misled in Race Cause," *Kansas City Times*, Feb. 15, 1967).
140. Whittaker in Whittaker and Coffin, *Law*, 18–20, 54.
141. Ibid., 84.
142. 367 U.S. 497 (1961).

CHAPTER 6

1. Quoted in Cole, "Mr.," 108.
2. Whittaker and Coffin, *Law*, 89–90.
3. *Staub* v. *City of Baxley*, 355 U.S. 313 (1958).
4. *Times Film Corp.* v. *Chicago*, 365 U.S. 43 (1961).
5. Ibid., 69, 72–73 (dissent).
6. *Chapman* v. *United States*, 365 U.S. 610 (1961).
7. *Draper* v. *United States*, 358 U.S. 307 (1959).
8. Ibid., 313.
9. Ibid., 315, 324 (dissent).
10. *Frank* v. *Maryland*, 359 U.S. 360 (1959).
11. *Oliver* v. *United States*, 239 F.2d 818 (8th Cir. 1957).
12. *Bartkus* v. *Illinois*, 359 U.S. 121 (1959).
13. *United States* v. *Vasen*, 222 F.2d 3, 9–10 (7th Cir. 1955) (dissent).
14. *Bartkus* v. *Illinois*, 359 U.S. 121, 137 (1959).
15. Ibid., 163 (dissent).
16. Ibid., 156 (dissent).
17. Ibid., 158 (dissent).
18. Ibid., 168 (dissent).
19. Newman, *Hugo*, 481–82.

20. *Wilson* v. *Schnettler, et al.*, 365 U.S. 381 (1961).
21. Leon Friedman, "Charles Whittaker" in Friedman and Israel, *Justices*, 2901.
22. *Wilson* v. *Schnettler, et al.*, 365 U.S. 381 (1961).
23. Ibid., 388 (concurring).
24. Ibid., 385.
25. Ibid., 391 (dissent).
26. John P. Frank, *Lincoln as a Lawyer* (Urbana, University of Illinois Press, 1961), 56.
27. *Wilson* v. *Schnettler, et al.*, 365 U.S. 381, 393 (1961) (dissent).
28. Ibid., 398 (dissent).
29. *Gore* v. *United States*, 357 U.S. 386 (1958).
30. 284 U.S. 299, 304.
31. *Gore* v. *United States*, 357 U.S. 386, 397–98 (1958) (dissent).
32. *Green* v. *United States*, 355 U.S. 184 (1957). For an excellent discussion of this case consult Barrett Prettyman, Jr., *Death and the Supreme Court* (New York: Harcourt, Brace & World, Inc., 1961), 68–89.
33. Kohn, "Supreme," 45.
34. 199 U.S. 521 (1905).
35. Quoted in *Kansas City Star*, Sept. 20, 1964, p. E2.
36. Whittaker, "Judicial," 4.
37. *Payne* v. *Arkansas*, 356 U.S. 560 (1958).
38. *Payne* v. *State of Arkansas*, 332 S.W.2d 233 (Ark. S. Ct. 1960). Still more litigation followed that second trial.
39. Chapter 2 notes Whittaker's valiant effort to satisfy the Court's rules in a way that would allow consideration of *Payne*. Having satisfied those rules, he did not have to face the question of whether to defy them.
40. *Reck* v. *Pate*, 367 U.S. 433 (1961).
41. Ibid., 449 (dissent).
42. Ibid., 455 (dissent).
43. *Thomas* v. *Arizona*, 356 U.S. 390 (1958).
44. Ibid., 399.
45. Ibid., 396.
46. Ibid., 401.
47. Whittaker, "Judicial," 5.
48. Whittaker, "Advocacy," 233 n. 2.
49. *Crooker* v. *California*, 357 U.S. 433 (1958).
50. *McNeal* v. *Culver*, 365 U.S. 109 (1961).
51. *Escobedo* v. *Illinois*, 378 U.S. 478 (1964) and *Miranda* v. *Arizona*, 384 U.S. 436 (1966).
52. *McNeal* v. *Culver*, 113 So.2d 381, 382 (Fla. S. Ct. 1959).
53. *McNeal* v. *Culver*, 132 So.2d 151 (Fla. S. Ct. 1961).
54. *McNeal* v. *Culver*, 365 U.S. 109, 117–19 (1961) (concurring).
55. *Moore* v. *Michigan*, 355 U.S. 155 (1957).
56. *Moore* v. *Buchko*, 144 N.W.2d 670 (Mich. App. Ct. 1966).

57. Whittaker, "Faith" (Kansas), 2 (emphasis in original).

58. Ibid., 2–3.

59. Ibid., 5–6.

60. Whittaker, "Faith" (Juniata), 6–7.

61. Whittaker, "Law," 398 (emphasis in original). He expressed the same sentiments to the Missouri Bankers Association ("Demonstration as Mockery of Laws," *Kansas City Star* or *Kansas City Times*, May[?] 5, 1965[?] (envelope file of Missouri Valley Room, Kansas City, Missouri, Public Library).

62. 361 U.S. 138 (1959).

63. Kent Whittaker interview with Cynthia Dodge, May 13, 1998, p. 5.

64. *Inman* v. *Baltimore and Ohio Railroad*, 361 U.S. 138, 142 (1959).

65. *Moore* v. *Terminal Railroad Association of St. Louis*, 358 U.S. 31 (1958).

66. *Still* v. *Norfolk & Western Railway Co.*, 368 U.S. 35 (1961).

67. Ibid., 49 (1961) (dissent).

68. Smith, "Charles," 132–33.

69. *Arnold* v. *Ben Kanowsky, Inc.*, 361 U.S. 388 (1960).

70. Ibid., 397 (dissent).

71. *Goldberg* v. *Whitaker House Cooperative*, 366 U.S. 28 (1961).

72. Ibid., 30–31.

73. Ibid., 32.

74. Ibid., 33.

75. Ibid., 33–34 (dissent).

76. *United Steelworkers of America* v. *Enterprise Wheel & Car Corp.*, 363 U.S. 593 (1960).

77. *United Steelworkers of America* v. *Warrior & Gulf Navigation Co.*, 363 U.S. 574 (1960).

78. Ibid., 581, 583–85.

79. Ibid., 585–86 (dissent).

80. Ibid., 588 (dissent).

81. Ibid., (dissent).

82. *United Steelworkers of America* v. *Warrior & Gulf Navigation Co.*, 269 F.2d 633 (5th Cir. 1959).

83. *United Steelworkers of America* v. *Warrior & Gulf Navigation Co.*, 363 U.S. 574, 591 (1960) (dissent).

84. Ibid., 591–92 (dissent).

85. Ibid., 592 (dissent).

CHAPTER 7

1. Alan Kohn, quoted in Tom Jackman, "Whittaker Courthouse a Tribute to 'Great Lawyer'," *Kansas City Star*, Aug. 2, 1994.

2. Quoted in Atkinson, "Retirement," 17.

3. Kohn, "Supreme," 47. The Biblical reference is to Gen. 25:29–34.

4. Smith, "Charles," 103 n. 68. Whittaker would not be the last justice taking drugs that would be expected to impair performance. In 1981 William Rehnquist had become so

physically dependent on a prescription pharmaceutical that his mind was affected while undergoing a withdrawal syndrome in a hospital, prompting public speculation about his ability to continue holding office. See Eliot Marshall, "Rehnquist's Drug Dependence Poses Dilemma," *Science* 215 (January 22, 1982), 379–80.

5. Quoted in Schwartz, *History*, 272.

6. Clyde J. Rayburn, Jr., in Smith, "Charles," 103.

7. Cole, "Mr.," 103.

8. Charles E. Whittaker, quoted in Atkinson, *Leaving*, 128.

9. Carl E. Enggas, in Cole, "Mr.," 105.

10. Kent Whittaker interview with Cynthia Dodge, May 13, 1998, pp. 8–9.

11. John M. Harlan in "Charles" (*Texas Law*), 748.

12. Atkinson, *Leaving*, 130; Schwartz, *Super*, 427–28; Woodward and Armstrong, *Brethren*, 176.

13. Whittaker, "Some"(ABA), 1090. Same "quest" language is in Whittaker, "Some" (Nebraska), 360 and Whittaker, "Judicial," 8.

14. Whittaker, "Faith" (Juniata), 4.

15. Atkinson, *Leaving*, 130; Smith, "Charles," 105–106.

16. Quoted in John R. Cauley, "Accepted the Call to Tribunal Because of a Sense of Duty," *Kansas City Star*, March 29, 1962.

17. Cole, "Mr.," 156.

18. Quoted in John R. Cauley, "Accepted the Call to Tribunal Because of a Sense of Duty," *Kansas City Star*, March 29, 1962.

19. Darrell Havener in Smith, "Charles," 149.

20. Quoted by William H. Becker in Lawrence Larsen, "Observations on One Hundred Years of Federal Judging in Western Missouri District Court" in Wunder, *Law*, 146.

21. Whittaker, "Faith" (Juniata), 4. Compare to page 6 of the Kansas version: "The strength, or weakness, of America lies not in its farms and forests, its factories and fortresses, nor in the glorious achievements of its past generations, but it lies in the patriotic character, strength, determination and faith of its present people." Compare to the conclusion in "A Confusion of Tongues": "The strength or weakness of our nation lies not in its farms and forests, its factories and fortresses, but in the patriotic character, united strength, determination, faith and honor of its citizens, who, after all, are empowered to control our government, and who, in final analysis, must be responsible for its destiny" (Whittaker, "Confusion," 32).

22. Herbert Hoover, *Addresses Upon the American Road, 1933–1938* (New York: Charles Scribner's Sons, 1938), 269.

23. Whittaker, "Some" (Nebraska), 362.

24. Whittaker, "Faith" (Kansas), 7, 9, 11; "Try to Please No One," *Kansas City Times*, Feb. 11, 1961.

25. Charles Evans Whittaker to Helen Newman, March 5, 1964, in U.S. Supreme Court Library vertical file.

26. Whittaker, "Faith" (Juniata College and Kansas Bar Association versions).

27. Leon Friedman, "Charles Whittaker" in Friedman and Israel, *Justices*, 2904; *Kansas City Times*, Oct. 19, 1965, pp. 1–2.

28. *Kansas City Star*, Sept. 20, 1964, p. E2; Edward Levi, *In Memoriam*, 37.

29. Council on Medical Education, "Medical Education in the United States," *Journal of the American Medical Association* 202 (Nov. 20, 1967): 728.

30. U.S. Senate. Select Committee on Standards and Conduct. Hearings. Part 1. 89:2. P. 2. (SuDocs Y4.St 2/2:D66/pt. 1.)

31. Memo, Aug. 6, 1965, p. 1, "General Motors—Contractual Relationship" folder, Charles Evans Whittaker Papers.

32. Page toward end of hasp-clipped packet, "General Motors—Contractual Relationship" folder, Charles Evans Whittaker Papers.

33. Description of the plan's operation is taken from Whittaker, "General"; Whittaker, "Plan"; *Kansas City Times*, Oct. 23, 1965, p. 35.

34. Sylvie Picard Renaut, Special Counsel, Documentation & Research, International Court of Arbitration, to Author, May 11, 2000, e-mail, Author's files.

35. Memo, Aug. 6, 1965, p. 1, "General Motors—Contractual Relationship" folder, Charles Evans Whittaker Papers.

36. Cole, "Mr.," 26–27 n. 44.

37. Bob Donnellan interview with Cynthia Davis, April 20, 1998, pp. 3–4.

38. Kent Whittaker in Smith, "Charles," 169

39. "Justice Charles E. Whitaker" editorial, *Kansas City Star*, Nov. 28, 1973, p. B18 (envelope file of Missouri Valley Room, Kansas City, Missouri, Public Library. The error was noticed in time to correct later editions.

40. Whittaker, "Faith" (Juniata), 5.

Selected Bibliography

If notes give full citations and information on location of sources, that data is not repeated here. Notes referring to the *Kansas City Star* and *Kansas City Times* occasionally cite copies of articles in the microfilmed envelope file of the Missouri Valley Room Special Collections at the Kansas City, Missouri, Public Library. Date stamps and handwritten source notations on those articles are not always legible, nor can the articles always be found in standard microfilm versions of those two newspapers, which went through several editions each day.

MANUSCRIPTS

Whittaker, Charles Evans. Papers in custody of Kent Whittaker.

INTERVIEWS

Childers, Jesse. Interview with Cynthia Dodge. May 14, 1998. Author's files.
Donnellan, Bob. Interview with Cynthia Dodge. April 20, 1998. Author's files.
Margolin, Abe. Interview with Cynthia Dodge. Spring 1998. Author's files.
Whittaker, Kent. Interview with Cynthia Dodge. May 13 and 18, 1998. Author's files.

SPEECHES

Speeches printed in books or articles are listed below in those sections.

Whittaker, Charles Evans. "Cliches or Fundamentals?" Southeast Missouri State College, Feb. 16, 1964 and Kansas City Rotary Club, Feb. 27, 1964. Version from U.S. Supreme Court Library.
———. "The Faith of the Free." Commencement address, Juniata College, June 4, 1961.

Printed version from U.S. Supreme Court Library.
———. "The Faith of the Free." Convocation of Kansas Bar Association, Olathe, Kansas. Printed version from U.S. Supreme Court Library.
———. "Judicial Discretion." Sept. 17, 1960, Federal Bar Association, Chicago, Illinois. Printed version from U.S. Supreme Court Library.
———. "Obligations of Lawyers and Judges, *Inter Se*, and to the People." May 9, 1959, University of Minnesota Law School. Typed version from U.S. Supreme Court Library.
———. "The Role of the Supreme Court." Arkansas State Bar Association, April 16, 1963. Printed version from U.S. Supreme Court Library.

BOOKS

Abraham, Henry J. *Justices and Presidents: A Political History of Appointments to the Supreme Court.* 3rd ed. New York: Oxford University Press, 1992.
Atkinson, David N. *Leaving the Bench: Supreme Court Justices at the End.* Lawrence: University Press of Kansas, 1999.
Chase, Harold W. *Federal Judges: The Appointing Process.* Minneapolis: University of Minnesota Press, 1972.
Douglas, William O. *The Court Years, 1939–1975.* New York: Random House, 1980.
———. *The Douglas Letters: Selections from the Private Papers of Justice William O. Douglas.* Edited by Melvin I. Urofsky. Bethesda, MD: Adler & Adler, 1987.
Eisenhower, Dwight D. *Mandate for Change: 1953–1956.* Garden City, New York: Doubleday & Company, Inc., 1963.
Frankfurter, Felix. *Of Law and Life & Other Things That Matter: Papers and Addresses of Felix Frankfurter, 1956–1963.* Edited by Philip B. Kurland. Cambridge: The Belknap Press of Harvard University Press, 1965.
Friedman, Leon, and Fred L. Israel. *The Justices of the United Sates Supreme Court 1789–1969: Their Lives and Major Opinions.* Vol. 4. New York: Chelsea House Publishers in association with R. R. Bowker Company, 1969.
Larsen, Lawrence. *Federal Justice in Western Missouri: The Judges, the Cases, The Times.* Columbia, MO: University of Missouri Press, 1994.
Lewis, Anthony. *Gideon's Trumpet.* 1964. Reprint. New York: Vintage Books, 1989.
Murphy, Walter F., and C. Herman Pritchett, eds. *Courts, Judges, & Politics: An Introduction to the Judicial Process.* 4th ed. New York: McGraw-Hill, Inc., 1986.
Newman, Roger K. *Hugo Black: A Biography.* New York: Pantheon Books, 1994.
Rice, Arnold S. *The Warren Court 1954–1969.* The United States Supreme Court, vol. 8. Danbury, CT: Grolier Educational Corporation, 1995.
Schwartz, Bernard. *A History of the Supreme Court.* New York: Oxford University Press, 1993.
———. *Super Chief: Earl Warren and His Supreme Court—A Judicial Biography.* New York: New York University Press, 1983.
Whittaker, Charles Evans, and William Sloane Coffin, Jr. *Law, Order and Civil Disobedience.* Rational Debate Seminars. Washington, DC: American Enterprise Institute for Public Policy Research, 1967.

Woodward, Bob, and Scott Armstrong. *The Brethren: Inside the Supreme Court.* New York: Simon and Schuster, 1979.
Wunder, John R., ed. *Law and the Great Plains.* Westport, CT: Greenwood Press, 1996.

THESES

Cole, Judith. "Mr. Justice Charles Evans Whittaker: A Case in Judicial Recruitment and Behavior." Master's thesis, University of Missouri—Kansas City, 1972.
Smith, Craig Alan. "Charles Evans Whittaker, Associate Justice of the Supreme Court." Master's thesis, University of Missouri—Kansas City, 1997.

GOVERNMENT DOCUMENTS

U.S. Senate. Committee on the Judiciary. Hearing. *Nomination of Charles E. Whittaker.* 85 Cong., 1 sess., 1957.
U.S. Senate. Committee on the Judiciary. Subcommittee to Investigate the Administration of the Internal Security Act and Other Internal Security Laws. Hearings. Part 12. 83 Cong., 1 sess., pp. 1114–26. (SuDocs Y4.J89/2:Su 1/10/pt 12.)
U.S. Senate. Committee on the Judiciary. Subcommittee to Investigate the Administration of the Internal Security Act and Other Internal Security Laws. "Subversive Influence in the Educational Process." 83 Cong., 1 sess. (SuDocs Y4.J89/2:Su 1/11/953.)
U.S. Supreme Court. *In Memoriam, Honorable Charles Evans Whittaker: Proceedings of the Bar and Officers of the Supreme Court of the United States.* 1975.

ARTICLES

Atkinson, David N. "Retirement and Death on the United States Supreme Court: From Van Devanter to Douglas." *UMKC Law Review* 45 (1976): 1–15.
Berman, Daniel M. "Mr. Justice Whittaker: A Preliminary Appraisal." *Missouri Law Review* 24 (Jan. 1959): 1–15.
"Censured Administrations." *American Association University Professors Bulletin* 41 (1955): 796.
"Charles E. Whittaker." *Missouri Bar Journal* (Jan.–Feb. 1974): 61–62.
"Charles Evans Whittaker—The Supreme Court Years." *Texas Law Review* 40 (1962): 744–50.
Kohn, Alan C. "Supreme Court Law Clerk, 1957–1958: A Reminiscence," *Journal of Supreme Court History* 2 (1998): 40–52.
Rogers, William P. "Judicial Appointments in the Eisenhower Administration." *Journal of the American Judicature Society* 41 (Aug. 1957): 39–40.
"University of Kansas City." *Bulletin of the American Association of University Professors* 27 (1941): 478–93.
"The University of Kansas City." *AAUP Bulletin* 43 (1957): 177–95.
Volz, Marlin M. "Mr. Justice Whittaker." *Notre Dame Lawyer* 33 (1958): 159–77.

Whittaker, Charles Evans. "Advocacy—Advance or Adieu?" *Kansas Law Review* 13 (1964): 233–45.

———. "The Causes, and the Effects upon Public Order, of Planned, Mass Violations of the Law." Printed in Whittaker and Coffin, *Law*.

———. "A Former Justice Warns: Return to Law, or Face Anarchy." *U.S. News and World Report* (April 25, 1966): 58–62.

———. "A Confusion of Tongues." *American Bar Association Journal* 51 (1965): 27–32.

———. "The General Motors Dealer Relations Umpire Plan." *Business Lawyer* 28 (January 1973): 623–26.

———. "Immutable Moral Values." *Texas Bar Journal* 27 (1964): Supplement, 1–8.

———. "Law and Order." *New York Bar Journal* 37 (1965): 397–404. This speech given to the Tennessee Bar Association in June is preliminary to his 1967 speech "The Causes, and the Effects upon Public Order, of Planned, Mass Violations of the Law" printed in Whittaker and Coffin. A revised version of "Law and Order" was published as "Mass Disobedience Endangers Nation" (*see below*).

———. "Lawyers, Laymen and Traffic Courts: Concerted Effort Needed for Improvement." *American Bar Association Journal* 49 (1963): 333–36.

———. "Mass Disobedience Endangers Nation," *Kansas City Star*, July 25, 1965, p. E-11.

———. "A Plan, of Experience–Tested Merit, of a Large and Geographically Widespread Franchisor, to Assure, as Nearly as Can Be Done, That None of Its Decisions Affecting the Franchise Relationship Shall Be 'Unfair' to the Franchisee." Aug. 16, 1972, address to the Arbitration Committee, Section of Corporation, Banking and Business Law, American Bar Association. These remarks (available from the American Arbitration Association Library) have details omitted from "The General Motors Dealer Relations Umpire Plan" in *Business Lawyer*.

———. "Reflections on Mr. Justice Brandeis." *Saint Louis University Law Journal* 11 (1966): 6–8.

———. "Some Reminiscences." *American Bar Association Journal*. 47 (1961): 1087–91.

———. "Some Reminiscences." *Nebraska Law Review* 43 (Feb. 1964): 352–63.

———. "A Tribute to Judge John B. Sanborn." *Minnesota Law Review* 44 (1959): 197–99.

Index

About the Author

RICHARD LAWRENCE MILLER is an independent scholar. His pioneering biography of Harry Truman's rise to power generated controversy. He challenged assumptions of America's foreign policy establishment in *Heritage of Fear: Illusion and Reality in the Cold War.* His books *The Case for Legalizing Drugs* and *Drug Warriors and Their Prey* became classics among drug war skeptics. *Nazi Justiz* probed the question of why people decide to destroy their neighbors.

Recent Titles in
Contributions in Legal Studies

Contract Law and Morality
Henry Mather

The Appearance of Equality: Racial Gerrymandering, Redistricting, and the Supreme Court
Christopher M. Burke

Religion, Law, and the Land
Brian Edward Brown

The Supreme Court's Retreat from Reconstruction: A Distortion of Constitutional Jurisprudence
Frank J. Scaturro

Respecting State Courts: The Inevitability of Judicial Federalism
Michael E. Solimine and James L. Walker

Basic Principles of Property Law: A Comparative Legal and Economic Introduction
Ugo Mattei

Inherent Rights, the Written Constitution, and Popular Sovereignty: The Founders' Understanding
Thomas B. McAffee

Constitutional Structure and Purposes: Critical Commentary
Michael Conant

Constitutional Interpretation: Illusion and Reality
Jeffrey M. Shaman

Prisoners' Rights: The Supreme Court and Evolving Standards of Decency
John A. Fliter

The Four Faces of Affirmative Action: Fundamental Answers and Actions
W. Robert Gray

Choice of Law for American Courts: A Multilateralist Method
Edwin Scott Fruehwald

www.ingramcontent.com/pod-product-compliance
Ingram Content Group UK Ltd.
Pitfield, Milton Keynes, MK11 3LW, UK
UKHW020818290926
15470UKWH00003B/1234

9 780313 312502